Praise for
RETURN ON AMBITION

"Your ambitions are often the biggest investment that you make in life. Yet managing the return in a deliberate and conscious manner can be challenging. This book will show you the way."

—RASMUS HOUGAARD, Founder and managing director of Potential Project and best-selling author of *One Second Ahead* and *The Mind of the Leader*

"Leaders everywhere are facing increasingly uncertain and volatile operating environments and must continue to evolve at a commensurate pace. *Return on Ambition* provides a practical toolbox to help leaders better understand their motivations, uncover mindsets that do not serve them, and embark on a continuous development journey to stay ahead of the curve."

—CLAUDIO FESER, Former McKinsey & Company senior partner, founding member of McKinsey's Leadership Development Practice, and author of *Serial Innovators, When Execution Isn't Enough,* and *Leadership at Scale*

"Finally! *Return on Ambition* kills one of the unhealthiest 'truths' and self-fulfilling prophecies in the professional world—that people with bold professional ambitions simply need to sacrifice most other important areas in their lives to become successful. The authors not only kill this long-lived myth, but they also explain how it leads to diminishing returns of the efforts you put into pursuing your ambition. They convincingly explain how decisive it is for you to instead integrate your professional ambition with areas such as learning, personal growth, well-being, and a rich social life to drive true success. But most importantly, they give you well-proven and simple tools to succeed at this unfortunately rare achievement among the vast majority of professionals. This is what awaits you in *Return on Ambition*. What are you waiting for? Is it not time you get more bang for your buck?"

—STEFAN FALK, Human performance expert, coach, and author of *PSYCHED: How to be Healthier, Happier, and More Productive in the High-Pressure Workplace of the Future*

"*Return on Ambition* helps readers answer three fundamental questions about their life: What is my ambition, what gets in the way of my ambition, and how can I improve my return on ambition? Each question has rich the-oretical underpinnings and is brought to life through stories and anecdotes. This book shows how too much ambition can actually trip you up, and helps readers shift mindsets and behaviors that may be holding them back. A must-read if you have pedal to the metal in life!"

—DR. CHÉRIE CARTER-SCOTT, MCC, #1 *New York Times* best-selling author of *If Life Is a Game, These Are the Rules, Transformational Life Coaching, Negaholics: Stop Being Negative . . . Reclaim Your Happiness,* and 18 other titles

"The concept of a 'return' on ambition was eye-opening for me. In the same way that we manage the return on assets or return on investments, it is critical to optimise the outputs of the colossal efforts we put into our ambitions. *Return on Ambition* shows you how to do this, in fun, inspiring, and often surprising ways."

—**PHIL CHAMBERS,** CEO and cofounder of Peakon

"In a world of increasing complexity and change, simply running faster is no longer enough. *Return on Ambition* helps readers to think more holistically about their ambitions and make conscious choices about what is right for them. It includes a unique 'self-coaching' approach, which helps readers bring the theory into practice in a sustainable way."

—**DR. NICK VAN DAM,** Chief of the IE University Center for Corporate Learning Innovation, internationally recognized thought leader on learning innovations and leadership development, and author or co-author of more than 25 books and articles

"As all of us are faced with a now urgent need to create new maps for our lives and refine our own sense of purpose, what is needed is wise guidance on decision criteria, frameworks for powerful introspection, and potent coaching. *Return on Ambition* offers just such practical insight, and will help you understand the meaning available from, and the pitfalls to avoid in, pursing ambition and devoting oneself to excellence."

—**AMY ELIZABETH FOX,** CEO, Mobius Executive Leadership

"The concept of ambition is evolving as are most human mindsets and structures. This book dives deeper into the concept of the more conscious approach to ambition and how you can design a more elegant, deliberate, and patient form of it."

—**JOHN SANEI,** Keynote speaker, foresight strategist, and author of the bestsellers *What's Your Moonshot?*, *Magnetiize*, and *FOREsight*

"*Return on Ambition* reveals a truth about leadership—ambition can actually make it more difficult to succeed and, even as we do succeed, it can rob much of the joy from the effort. This book helps us to become aware of how our ambitions can manage us. It instructs us how to start managing our ambitions more consciously. Among many actionable suggestions, it encourages all of us to carefully reflect on our philosophy of success: Do we strive to prove ourselves worthy or to serve something larger than ourselves? *Return on Ambition* can help anyone with big dreams to achieve them and do so while enjoying the ride."

—BOB ANDERSON, Founder of The Leadership Circle and co-author of *Mastering Leadership* and *Scaling Leadership*

"Too often we speed towards our goals without thinking sufficiently about the direction and speed we are driving. *Return on Ambition* gives you a framework to reflect deeply on what's really important to you—and pro-vides practical 'self-coaching' tools that anyone can apply. Read this book!"

—LARS TVEDE, Cofounder of venture capital fund Nordic Eye and the prediction company Supertrends Institute, and best-selling author of 17 books including *Entrepreneur, Supertrends, The Creative Society,* and *The Psychology of Finance and Business Cycles*

"Some ambitious people are fortunate enough to have a mentor or relative who can help them escape the nightmare side effects of seeking out their dreams. Most, unfortunately, learn the hard way after sacrificing the wrong things on the altar of their ambitions. Nielsen and Tillisch, as it turns out, are the kind uncles we have all been missing, who take us aside after din-ner to show us a better path. Backed by their experience and cutting-edge research, these two Nicolais help us make better choices as we integrate all of our dreams into one full life. Ambition can be a corrosive power that ulti-mately ruins our joys, or, with the help of this wise and practical guide, can be the fuel for forging beautiful lives of accomplishment and connection."

—JENNIFER GARVEY BERGER, Cofounder of Cultivating Leadership and author of *Unlocking Leadership Mindtraps* and *Changing on the Job*

"*In Return on Ambition*, the two Nicolais provide a hands-on approach to how all of us ambitious people can ensure that we actually get enough bang for our buck and not only succeed professionally, but also achieve personal growth, well-being, and, ultimately, a better life. Dive in and let the authors guide you through a journey towards your own unique return on ambition."

—KRIS ØSTERGAARD, Cofounder of SingularityU Nordic and best-selling author of *Transforming Legacy Organizations*

"We are often told that elements such as perseverance, boldness, competitiveness, and desire are unanimously positive, and that we should strive to cultivate more of each one. However, *Return on Ambition* gives you the space to reflect on and question your true motivations and guides you towards a more deliberate and creative manifestation of your dreams. The core principles it outlines are relevant for everyone, regardless of the size and nature of their ambition. I wholeheartedly recommend this book."

—WADIA AIT HAMZA, Head of the Global Shapers Community, World Economic Forum

"The world desperately needs a new breed of self-aware and authentic leaders who stay true to an elevating, virtuous calling, especially when in the face of adversity. This refreshing book provides a powerful approach to reconsider what 'success' means to you, to grapple with what can get in the way of achieving it, and a novel method to 'self-coach' yourself forward and up, even in the toughest weather. Read this book, and keep climbing!"

—DR. PAUL G. STOLTZ, Founder and CEO of PEAK Learning, Inc, creator of the globally acclaimed AQ® (Adversity Quotient®) theory and methods, and author of five best-selling books including *Adversity Quotient*, *The Adversity Advantage*, **and** *GRIT*

"*Return on Ambition* counsels ambitious people to live a full and hopefully harmonious life and achieve success. The book argues convincingly, based on extensive research, that well-being and personal growth are powerful factors in achieving results over time. My professional work has meant and continues to mean a lot to me, and yet I would never be who I am or do what I do without living a full life with my family, friends, and activities and interests detached from work. The two Nicolais offer helpful ways to think of ourselves and provide highly practical tools to apply in daily life."

—SUSANNE MØRCH KOCH, CEO of Tivoli

"*Return on Ambition* will guide you through some of the most important questions in life: Is ambition all you are about? Who are you truly? Are you living life as fully as you can? The deep paradox about this book is that it cautions you about blind ambition, while also asking you to be supremely ambitious in thinking more deeply about what drive and a multidimensional life truly mean to you. With a beautiful combination of research, storytelling, and practical tools, this book is a must-read for anyone open to a fresh recalibration of their lives."

—DR. SRINI PILLAY, CEO of NeuroBusiness Group,
CMO and cofounder of Reulay, former Assistant Professor
of Psychiatry at Harvard Medical School, and author of
Tinker, Dabble, Doodle, Try: Unlock the Power of an Unfocused Mind

"I have been in close contact with thousands of highly ambitious people, from young graduates to middle managers to executives. Most of them would have had an easier life without sacrificing their ambitions, had they only applied two or three of the principles outlined in this book."

—KENT JONASEN, CEO, Leadership Pipeline Institute

"*Return on Ambition* helps any ambitious adult to take their life into perspective and excel at what means most for them. The book elegantly combines powerful questioning techniques and tools that the readers can apply daily. It draws insights and asks questions that are typically accessible otherwise only in sophisticated leadership development programs or through top-notch coaches."

—**TOR MESOY,** Founder and Managing Director, Agnus Consulting, author of *Musings on Leadership*, and lecturer at The University of Hong Kong

"I have met countless fantastic and ambitious people with phenomenal drive and passion who have a hard time finding the right balance in their life and sometimes live with regrets. However, when leaders use their ambition and drive combined with a sense of purpose, it changes their life and the lives of those they interact with. *Return on Ambition* will show you how to achieve this balance and be a better you. Isn't that what we are all aiming for?"

—**MURIELLE PEREIRA,** Head of Leadership Development, Majid Al Futtai

"What a brilliant principle articulated with such simplicity that this book should be in everybody's life curriculum. You crack it right at the very beginning with your excellent definition of ambition—achievement, growth and well-being! Well-being comes from within and it is when your ambition is driven intrinsically that it delivers the real return; the return of deep satisfaction, contentment and self-worth. I see so many people distracted by false ambition, and ambition driven by the external forces of societal expectation. The return always disappoints. The Nicolais have captured the essence of true ambition in an accessible style. Brilliant—read, enjoy, and reap the benefits."

—**MANLEY HOPKINSON,** FRSA FRGS, explorer, speaker, business leader and performance catalyst. Founder of the Compassionate Leadership Academy and author of the highly acclaimed book, *Compassionate Leadership*

A Radical Approach to Your
Achievement, Growth, and Well-Being

RETURN ON
AMBITION

Nicolai Chen Nielsen
& Nicolai Tillisch

**FAST
COMPANY**
Press

Fast Company Press
New York, New York
www.fastcompanypress.com

Distributed by Greenleaf Book Group

For ordering information or special discounts for bulk purchases, please contact Greenleaf Book Group at PO Box 91869, Austin, TX 78709, 512.891.6100.

Design and composition by Greenleaf Book Group
Cover design by Greenleaf Book Group

Publisher's Cataloging-in-Publication data is available.

Print ISBN: 978-1-7343248-6-0

eBook ISBN: 978-1-7343248-7-7

Part of the Tree Neutral® program, which offsets the number of trees consumed in the production and printing of this book by taking proactive steps, such as planting trees in direct proportion to the number of trees used: www.treeneutral.com

Printed in the United States of America on acid-free paper

20 21 22 23 24 25   10 9 8 7 6 5 4 3 2 1

First Edition

Nicolai Chen Nielsen:

To Mama, Baba, and Natasja—our family has been the bedrock of everything I do. Thank you for your unconditional love, support, and encouragement.

Nicolai Tillisch:

To Margaux and Axel—follow your dreams and be ambitious without compromising your beautiful souls. We all learn our own lessons, and yet I hope that this book, at some point, can help you on your way.

Contents

INTRODUCTION

Bang for Your Buck

Most ambitious people struggle to achieve their aspirations while also maintaining their personal growth and well-being, and they question whether the large investment they are making to reach their goals is worth it.

DO YOU HAVE grand achievements you hope to accomplish? Do you constantly try to develop yourself? Are you striving to live a more balanced life? If you answered an emphatic "yes" to even one of these questions, this book is for you.

We have worked with some of the most ambitious people in the world, and we've seen firsthand how ambition can drive people to great heights and bring tremendous fulfillment. But we've also seen how ambition can result in painful setbacks. Why is this? The reality is that most people could get a higher return on their efforts if they understood the underlying drivers of ambition—and also how to get the most out of those drivers. You can get more bang for your buck if you know how to do it.

The efforts sparked by your ambition may be the biggest investments you make in your lifetime, consuming great swathes of your time, energy, and money. It compels people to make things happen, to become better at something, and to take on new challenges. Your ambitions shape the way you work and the way you treat your loved ones and yourself.

Ambition can be driven by a hunger for power, fame, and fortune, or it can be motivated by a more altruistic aspiration to make the world a better place. Often it is a combination of both. Yet while ambition can foster dreams, it also can lead to punishing sacrifices, regrets, and desolation. If left unchecked, ambition can run wild and take control, leading to impulsive and even harmful decisions. We have seen countless stories of ambitious people focusing on the wrong goal—the wrong mountain to climb, so to speak—only to regret the destination once they reach the summit. Others climb the right mountain, but do it the wrong way, and end up feeling exhausted and unfulfilled. While research shows that ambitious people generally become more educated, secure higher-status jobs, and make more money than their less ambitious peers, this often comes at the expense of close relationships and personal well-being.[1]

So ask yourself: How can I make sure I get the most positive Return on Ambition? What can I do to manage this investment better? Are the efforts I'm putting into my ambitions worth the time I'm spending, or could I accomplish my goals differently or with a more efficient use of my energy?

This book is for readers of all ages; ambition doesn't have an age limit. Maybe you're young, at university, and brimming with confidence. Perhaps you're 10 or 15 or more years into your career and wondering what's next. Maybe you're looking back on decades of experience and thinking about your legacy. The purpose of this book is threefold: to help you understand your ambition, to show you how to measure it, and to give you the tools—backed by research and practice—to improve your returns.

A More Holistic Approach to Ambition

We find in our research and practice that the vast majority of professionals across industries consider themselves to be ambitious.[2] However, ambitious people are often unaware of how much their ambition governs them and of the potential they have to take charge and master it, to unleash it more fully. The difference can be substantial, and is often untapped. To our astonishment, in our survey of professionals working across different industries globally, approximately 60% said they were struggling to achieve their aspirations while also maintaining their personal growth and well-being. We didn't expect the majority of people to answer this way. Similarly, about half of the respondents told us that they doubted whether their ambitions would serve them well in the long run, and they wondered whether all their hard work would actually pay off in the future.

The pervasiveness of ambition coupled with the widespread challenge in managing it surprised us. When we looked into it further, we discovered four main reasons ambitious people seem to struggle so much.

First, while numerous books set out to help people pursue their goals and aspirations, none of them focus specifically on the nature of ambition, its strengths and pitfalls, and how to manage it better. Ambitious people face unique opportunities and challenges that derive from the very fact that they have relentless drive and grand visions for themselves and for the world. Generic personal development approaches—such as those described in many books and websites on personal development—don't cut it for them, because these sources fail to describe the essential nuances of ambition and how it impacts people's behaviors and mindsets.

Second, despite the market's overload of self-development strategies, we found a gap in the applied coaching practice when dealing with ambitious people. Yes, there are various tools to assess your personality, measure your leadership competencies, and connect with your inner voice. But ambitious people differ in that they won't be satisfied with success in just one arena; they want to succeed in everything they do. To do this, we took a holistic approach and developed a way for our clients to measure and manage precisely how well they were realizing their ambitions—in their personal *and* professional lives.

Third, there is extensive and expanding evidence that people in general—ambitious or not—struggle to change, even when they deeply desire to do so. Our beliefs and assumptions about ourselves and each other limit us, and we are much more prone to biases and instinctive reactions than we realize. The domain within psychology called "stages of adult development" describes, for example, the difficulty and discomfort people have in breaking down old paradigms and transcending to higher and more intentional stages of development.[3]

Ambitious people are particularly prone to these struggles as they move from unconsciously following social norms to carving out their own paths in life. This shift entails creating their own unique identity and making conscious choices that might be informed by, but are not formed by, external influences. Ambitious people may experience friction as they question previously held beliefs and assumptions and experiment with new ways of living and being.

Fourth, we realized that all the great books and coaches in the world can't help people achieve their ambitions if they don't take time for self-reflection. That's right—good old-fashioned quiet time for introspection. Self-reflection is a key component of personal development, yet people often neglect it. We found that a vast majority (87%) of ambitious people claim that reflecting on their goals, growth, and well-being helps them fulfill their ambitions—yet of this majority, only 65% actually take the time for it. In other words, almost 4 out of 10 people who believe that self-reflection matters don't bother to make time for it.[4]

Why not? For starters, ambitious people are busy and often feel "underwater," to use a term we heard frequently in our interviews. Even when ambitious people *do* carve out time for reflection, many don't know how to go about it.

That's where we come in: This book will help you create the space to get to know yourself better and stretch your "ambition" muscles further. Through our research and in our coaching practices, we have cracked the code of ambition and present it here to help the reader manage it, rather than be managed by it.

Our approach is grounded in science and experience. In addition to extensive research, a global survey, and a wide range of interviews with people who have consciously managed the return they get on their ambition, we authors have battle-tested this approach in the field. We have designed and facilitated development programs involving thousands of professionals and have coached many hundreds of individuals across four continents—including highly successful CEOs, athletes, artists, entrepreneurs, and even new graduates. We've applied our approach in our professional practices, and we continue to evaluate what works for our clients and the circumstances under which it succeeds.

But because we can't be there to work with you in person, this book offers an innovative process of "self-coaching." It will help you learn how to reflect, which will help you understand yourself better and allow you to make any necessary adjustments in your life.

Throughout the book we pose three overarching questions: What is your Return on Ambition? What gets in the way of your Return on Ambition? How do you increase your Return on Ambition?

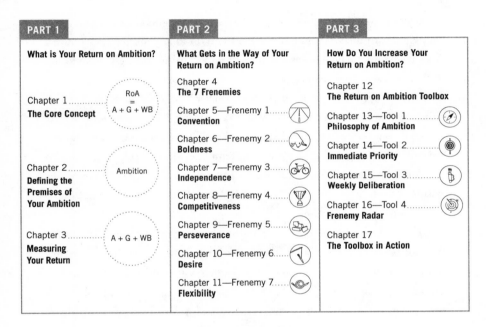

Figure 1—Book Structure

The Journey Ahead

We are inviting you to undertake a deeply personal endeavor: to see your professional and personal ambition from new and different perspectives, and to answer questions that can expand your awareness and help you make vital choices. While you may have an intellectual understanding of the importance of thinking holistically about your ambition and the factors that may be holding you back, that insight merely scratches the surface of the challenge. You must dig deeper to increase your Return on Ambition.

As you read this book, we have three requests. First, because we use dialogue to address you directly, we encourage you to respond, and to respond aloud if you feel so inclined. We want our direct approach to inspire debate—with yourself and, possibly, with us. We believe speaking directly to you allows us to put the ball in your court so you feel the need to make the next play.

Second, we recommend slowing down as you read and making sure you take time for reflection. Take the time to go on long walks or do whatever frees your mind. Make notes when reading. We bring these chapters to life with numerous insightful stories. Everyone can learn from these stories, and they may inspire you; but the personal reflection, the application of this information to your life and your way forward, must ultimately be your own. We want to help you understand yourself better as a human being, but we can't do that for you. You must contemplate what is truly important to you and how you will move toward it. To this end, each chapter concludes with a section called "Over to You" comprised of questions and suggestions for personal contemplation.

Third, don't put the book down after the last page and let it disappear on your bookshelf or e-reader. This book is about reflecting differently and living differently. So make something happen. Consult it frequently as you go out and change your world in a positive way. Your new companions are wider awareness, well-considered choices, and a deliberate effort to think things through.

We hope our ideas will foster enlightening "aha" moments to help you increase your awareness, attain clarity, and make more conscious choices about how to live, ultimately leading you to a higher return on your ambition and greater fulfillment. At an aggregate level, we believe this also can contribute to bettering the future of all humanity. Our intention is that the fuel of ambition should propel us all forward in a more collaborative, loving, and peaceful manner.

PART 1

What Is Your Return on Ambition?

PART 1 HELPS you answer the first key question of the book: What is your Return on Ambition? Here we introduce the core concept of Return on Ambition, which is made up of two elements: your ambition itself and the holistic returns you are getting in terms of achievement, growth, and well-being. We then break down these two elements. We review the premises of your ambition, which serve as a point of departure for assessing your returns. Then we present a quantitative assessment to measure your returns and review the underlying areas that have an impact on your Return on Ambition.

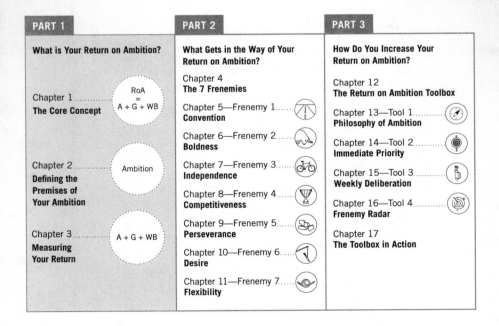

ONE

The Core Concept

Invest your ambition wisely. It can fuel your future and drive society forward, but left unchecked, it can lead to bankruptcy and despair.

WE DEFINE AMBITION as "a powerful yearning and drive to attain a future state that is different from today and challenging to reach."

This definition is a slight stretch compared to the dictionary's version, but if any word should have a grander definition, this is the one. "Future states" can be anything from buying a villa with a garage sheltering a nice sports car to raising a flourishing family to making the world a better place—or, indeed, a combination of all the above. "Yearning" is attached to "drive" to signify that you are determined to realize your ambition and not purely dreaming, while "different" and "challenging" emphasize that reaching your ambition requires a real effort.

To further elaborate on the concept of ambition, let's use money as a metaphor. Money is neither inherently good nor bad. It is a medium for making things happen, rather like the fuel that powers a car. Our society is built on people's eagerness to invest their money and earn more. For some people, having a lot is important. For others, it is secondary. Everyone can benefit from maximizing their money's return (measured broadly and not just in financial terms). However, handled wrongly or irresponsibly, money can lead to ruin.

Much in the same way as money, ambition in itself is neither inherently good nor bad; rather, it is a fuel for attaining a future state that is meaningful and different from today. Your specific purpose and degree of ambition is personal, and more is not necessarily better. However, all ambitious people invest time, energy, and resources in their ambitions, and they expect a return from all their efforts.

The Return on Ambition Equation

You can consider your ambition and your return in many ways. Some people like quiet contemplation. Others think with a piece of paper in front of them. Some talk with their friends, relatives, and mentors. Others formalize the process with a coach. In any case, reflection helps. We've found that ambitious people who can carve out the time for personal reflection are more than four times as likely to reach their aspirations—while maintaining a high degree of growth and well-being—as those who don't make time for this. On the other hand, people who do not take the time for personal reflection are 62% more likely to struggle to prioritize competing commitments and 2.1 times more likely to be stressed than those who do make time for personal reflection. They're also more likely to doubt whether the effort they are putting into realizing their ambitions is really worth it.[1]

While simply paying more attention to your current Return on Ambition is helpful, it is not the full answer. You also need to know where to look for inspiration, what drives your return, and how you could do things better.

Let's start by defining Return on Ambition holistically, with an equation outlined in Figure 1.1. We measure your Return on Ambition as the sum of your achievement, growth, and well-being.

RETURN ON AMBITION = ACHIEVEMENT + GROWTH + WELL-BEING

Figure 1.1—The Return on Ambition Equation

This holistic view of ambition includes the degree to which you achieve meaningful personal and professional goals, your degree of learning and development, and your level of personal happiness, purpose, health, and connection.

It stems from a complete picture of what it means to be a fulfilled human being, and is consistent with ancient wisdom traditions, more modern research, and indeed in our own research and practice.

You should not focus only on your returns, however. Your degree of achievement, growth, and well-being are all functions of your specific ambition. For instance, if you want to become a top tennis player, you would evaluate how you're doing compared to other tennis players; you wouldn't compare yourself to a judo wrestler. It is critical to have clarity on what is important to you and how you characterize your ambition before you evaluate your returns. If you compare your returns to those of other people who are pursuing different ambitions, you risk misjudging your outcomes, either valuing them too low or too high. Similarly, if your ambitions change significantly, you would likely also evaluate your returns across achievement, growth, and well-being differently.

Three Truisms of Return on Ambition

In practice, we find that there are three main ways that the nature of your ambition impacts your returns. First, *as your ambitions increase, the bar for fulfillment becomes higher*. A bigger ambition requires a higher return, and it becomes more difficult to be satisfied with less.

For example, entrepreneurs who want to build the "next Facebook"—social media platform—will inevitably be disappointed if they are able to sign up only a few million users at launch. For others with a less bold ambition, a few million users might be a very satisfying achievement. We are not suggesting you should lower your aspired Return on Ambition. Rather, we're cautioning you to be aware that a higher degree of ambition places increased requirements on you to attain certain outcomes.

Also be aware of your unique context. Different individuals will have to expend different levels of effort to reach a given type of ambition, based on their starting point, skills, and work ethic. While we believe everyone has the capacity to stretch greatly, people also need to be realistic. To avoid unnecessary and perpetual frustration, you need to understand the size and type of your ambition relative to your current context. As your ambitions grow, continue to consider the relationship between the size of your ambition and your resulting need to manage the returns even more vigilantly.

Second, *as your ambitions grow and you stretch yourself further, it increases the risk of falling short.* The more you aim to get out of a given amount of effort, the more stretched your investments in time, energy, and money become. At one extreme, you will have almost no margin for error. If you seek a higher return on your ambition relative to what you are able and willing to put in, you must be sure you can handle a higher risk of falling short.

Third, *as you increase your ambition, it becomes increasingly challenging to balance all three elements of your return.* The greater the size of your ambition and corresponding expectations across achievement, growth, and well-being, the greater the investment you will need to reach your aspired outcomes. The more you want, the more you need to sacrifice. Ambition can saddle you not only with work commitments but also with personal and social obligations that draw on your resources. Your anticipation of, and fixation on, a greater future can lead to an unsustainably high velocity of commitments and costs. Realistically catalogue the investments you will be required to make in order to realize your ambition and make sure you're willing and able to put in the necessary resources and effort.

Bringing the Concepts to Life

Here and throughout the book, we will illustrate the key concepts and varieties of ambition with the stories of Bella, Jitesh, and Nora and Alexander.

Take **Bella** as an example of the first truism—*as your ambitions increase, the bar for fulfillment becomes higher.*

Bella is not just studying art—she is living it. Her ambition is to use her creations to change people's perceptions about how humans affect nature. The playfulness with which she once entertained her aspirations turned immediately more serious when a leading art school accepted her as a student. Overnight, the stakes became higher, and with them so did Bella's ambitions.

Although her bubble of self-confidence burst when she first met all of the school's other incredibly talented students, she remains determined to stand out among them in her own way. Due to her steadfast focus on her ambition, her world revolves around school. She thinks about art during almost all her waking hours—as if she were breathing it.

She wakes up at night to write down new ideas, so handwritten notes pile up on her bedside table. The time around exams and assignment deadlines leaves her in a state of insomnia. Her high grades comfort her, but only until the next time she is tested. As her ambitions grow, so does her yearning to become better technically and to produce true masterpieces.

How does Bella's story evolve from here? A person like her could become the next new sensation at an Art Basel exhibition, creating a name that's known for generations to come. Or she could push herself too hard, to the point where her progress plateaus and some of her blossoming fellow students move past her and into the spotlight. When are her ambitions helping her focus on and pursue her dream of changing people's perceptions about the natural world through her art? And when are they strangling her fascinating but fragile spirit? Bella is battling with the first of the three truisms regarding ambition: The bigger her ambitions become, the higher she sets the bar for becoming fulfilled.

To illustrate the second truism—*as your ambitions grow and you stretch yourself further, it increases the risk of falling short*—consider **Jitesh**.

A well-dressed young urban professional who favors bespoke shirts and suits, Jitesh sparks smiles and laughs from most people when he is fully present and relaxed. His friends look forward to spending time with him, and they admire his accomplishments. He knew from a young age that he wanted to become a businessman. He completed his MBA with distinction and then landed a great job—complete with a desk in an impressive skyscraper.

Jitesh moved quickly up the ranks by delivering thorough work on time. He seemed unstoppable at first—until he was promoted to be the manager of his team after 18 months.

For him, the move is, in principle, just checking off another box on his way to the very top. But for the first time, Jitesh has become shaky in his professional role. He now has increased visibility in the company, which opens up opportunities for further promotions if all goes well. However, this new role also brings with it higher expectations from his superiors and from Jitesh himself. The stakes are raised, and the ways in which things can go wrong are multiplying.

He was never impressed with his colleagues, and now as his subordinates they seem downright disappointing. Jitesh could live with their lackluster commitment to work if that was the only problem, but it isn't. They're incompetent; it's painfully hard to get them to perform in exactly the way they need to. If he leaves them on their own, the quality of their work comes in below Jitesh's expectations. His team members make mistakes all the time, and they're defensive about it. Everything seems unintentional from their side, but Jitesh increasingly feels they have no respect for him—or for how important it is for him to succeed. His efforts to gather his team members and talk through these problems are unfruitful. The team uses the sessions to complain about other departments and to air new excuses—always without taking ownership for fixing things.

Due to his great expectations, Jitesh ends up working even harder than ever before to compensate for his underperforming team members. Often, after a long day's work, he sits up much of the night to redo work for which one of his subordinates was responsible. Keeping his sleeves rolled up merely to ensure the delivery of expected weekly work has left Jitesh overworked and tired and has reduced the overall effectiveness of the team, instead of enhancing it. He feels challenged and caught up in a whirlwind of expectations, but he does not dare do anything different for fear of failing.

To what extent are Jitesh's ambitions helping him during these late nights? He might very well think he is doing everything he can to succeed, but does his focus on avoiding any deviations from his high standards risk overshadowing his need to motivate and develop his team? And how is doing all the work himself actually training his team to improve? Is Jitesh playing to win or to avoid losing?

Nora and **Alexander** appear highly successful, but they face substantial personal concerns. They illustrate the third truism: *As you increase your ambition, it becomes increasingly challenging to balance all three elements of your return.* They are much further into their impressive careers than most people their age, and they balance

continued

high degrees of achievement, growth, and well-being. Everyone wants to spend time with them. They are happily married, witty, energetic, and rich with stories from lives spent traveling and living abroad. Other parents envy Nora and Alexander's three children and their good manners, outstanding grades, and well-rounded activities—from sports to volunteer work. From the outside, everything about Nora and Alexander is perfect. They are role models in the "work hard, play hard" category.

However, their personal reality is different. Maintaining their balance as they juggle careers, family, and friends demands higher and higher degrees of effort. Their burn rate is exceptionally high and, with it, their challenges. Nora is proud of everything she has accomplished and loves her children and husband, but she battles a guilty conscience over not being there for her children as much as she would like. Their childhood is passing by while she stays late at the office or travels on business trips. She is never really off the clock—even when she's home—since emails keep her smartphone buzzing, crying out for rapid replies.

Her private life, which is filled with guests and prestigious social events, distances her from her children as much as her work does. Regardless, Nora still manages to give her children more attention than her own parents gave her, though much of her time with the kids is focused on homework and involves a lot of nagging. The children are tired by the time Nora is ready to sit down with them each evening. They would rather play while she stresses about not doing as much with them as the other mothers from their school. Everyone has such great expectations of her, and her ambitious nature allows these expectations to drag her down. She would like to do many things differently, but she doesn't know where to start.

Alexander loves Nora and the children, and he's grateful for where they are in life, but he has recurring feelings of incredible loneliness. He frequently feels that he is at the bottom of Nora's pyramid of needs—after their kids, her work, her extended family, and all of their many friends. Alexander is better than Nora at spending whole days or, at least, half days of quality time with one, two, or all three children, but he is more overworked and often has weekend meltdowns of exhaustion.

Alexander reports directly to the CEO of a large international corporation. The CEO is new to the company, doesn't understand the business intimately, and frequently sets unrealistic expectations. If Alexander were not so well compensated, or if his family's mortgage were not so big, he would grab his briefcase and leave without ever coming back. Alexander is an obvious candidate for a midlife crisis, like the ones that many of his closest friends have been going through, but he doesn't have the energy to consider other options seriously.

Why can't Nora and Alexander, who have accomplished so much, adjust their priorities to thrive more than they strive? Will they ever reach a point when they feel fulfilled? Are they waiting to achieve complete economic independence—or is that just something they keep telling themselves? And when they one day get more leisure time, as they hope to, will they be able to truly enjoy it, given that they can barely appreciate all they have now? Their ambitious aspirations in all areas of their lives have led Nora and Alexander to spread themselves too thin, yet they have to make a constant effort to keep up with their high burn rate composed of fixed monthly costs, expensive add-ons, and all their explicit and implicit time commitments.

OVER TO YOU

Bigger ambitions are exciting, but they can lead you to feel unfulfilled even if you achieve impressive results on the surface, just like Bella, Jitesh, and Nora and Alexander. Your ambitions might be so big that you are constantly frustrated, or constantly exhausted, or both. Or you might be among those who neither succeed nor fail, but organize their lives to maintain an external image so they appear to be much closer to success than they really are. That can become an almost all-consuming lie. Most ambitious people can't imagine going to a dinner party and answering the question about whether they are busy with a big smile and the words, "No, not at all."

Before you move on to the next chapter, reflect on these questions:

- *How do you think about what you are getting out of your ambitions today?*

- *Do you recognize the struggles of Bella, Jitesh, and Nora and Alexander?*

Clearly ambition is complex and often misunderstood and mismanaged. Many people struggle with their ambitions and end up unfulfilled despite putting in great effort. The Return on Ambition Equation serves as a starting point and challenges you to think about the type and degree of your ambitions, and the growth, well-being, and achievement return you are getting from them.

Let's move on to the next chapter and discuss your ambitions in more detail.

TWO

Defining the Premises of Your Ambition

The degree and nuances of your ambitions are highly personal, and getting clear about the premises of what you aspire to accomplish is the first step toward fulfillment.

IN AN ENDEARING passage in the Lewis Carroll novel *Alice's Adventures in Wonderland*, Alice is wandering through a forest, wondering which way to go. She encounters the Cheshire Cat and has this exchange:

"Would you tell me, please, which way I ought to go from here?"

"That depends a good deal on where you want to get to," said the Cat.

"I don't much care where—" said Alice.

"Then it doesn't matter which way you go," said the Cat.[1]

Defining the premises of your ambition is the first step toward increasing your Return on Ambition. The premises are the basis of your ambition, the determinants or factors that shape the return that you expect to get. Recall that ambition is "a powerful yearning and drive to attain a future state that is different from today and challenging to reach." You can't be fulfilled if you don't have a sense of perspective about what would be more valuable to you in the future compared to the present.

Some ambitious people run fast, but they remain unfulfilled because they never quite know when they have gotten to where they want to go. Other ambitious people set an unrealistically high bar without analyzing their actual starting point and current capabilities, and, as a result, they are unsatisfied with their returns. Others lack the devotion and perseverance to succeed, though they expect quick successes from their efforts. To avoid falling into these traps, clarify your ambition by defining its premises.

The Four Premises of Ambition

Consider the four premises of ambition—specificity, uniqueness, size, and priority—as the foundation for beginning to define where you want to go in life, the magnitude of your aspirations, and the speed and intensity at which you wish to reach your goals.

1. SPECIFICITY

First, the granularity with which you define your ambition can vary greatly. Some people prefer to have detailed goals, with carefully laid plans and milestones, leaving as little as possible to chance. For example, New Zealand's prime minister Jacinda Ardern—the world's youngest female head of state at the time of her election—developed an interest in politics early on. "I always wanted to help people and I realized that politics was the way to do that," she says. She joined the Labour Party at age 17. Upon college graduation at age 21, she started working in then prime minister Helen Clark's office as a researcher, and, at age 28, she became the youngest member of New Zealand's Parliament.[2]

Other people do not believe in specific goals. For example, South African stand-up comedian Trevor Noah, who stunned the world in 2014 by taking over *The Daily Show* from iconic host Jon Stewart, believes, "Dreams will limit you."[3] Noah never intended to be a comedian and, in fact, aspired to fix computers. Instead, one opportunity after another opened up for him in entertainment through a combination of chance and his continuous efforts to grow personally. As he demonstrates, ambition can also be an energy simmering beneath the surface as opposed to a laser beam aiming for a specific future state.

2. UNIQUENESS

Second, you can follow a tried-and-tested path, or you can orient yourself very differently than anyone else in terms of your ambitions and what you aspire to accomplish. British maverick chef Jamie Oliver rose to impressive heights at a young age through his TV show and cookbooks, under the title *The Naked Chef*. From there, he started to deviate from the common pattern. In 2002, Oliver gave himself the challenge of training a group of young people from disadvantaged backgrounds, creating both the TV documentary series *Jamie's Kitchen* and the high-end restaurant in London that he staffed with his apprentices. Viewers learned new recipes and enjoyed extraordinary entertainment thanks to this social experiment and Oliver's expressive temperament. And Oliver was able to live out his dream of contributing to society.

He pursued a new path again in the series *Jamie's School Dinners* and *Jamie's Ministry of Food*, as well as several variations afterward, taking on unhealthy school meals and neighborhoods with poor eating habits. In reality, the focus of a person's ambitions is often a combination of many things, all at once. Oliver originally became famous by sharing his gastronomical creativity—as so many TV chefs have done before him—but afterward, he created his own niche, combining public service with entertainment in the food show category, and he excelled.

No particular "type" of ambition is more or less desirable than another, as long as you do no harm to others. Excelling at your career, being the best parent you can be, creating a new art genre, or setting obscure world records are all equally valid—provided that the ambition represents your desire for a future state that is different from today's state and demands a better you.

3. SIZE

Third, you can have various magnitudes of ambition compared to where you are today. Angling back to our definition of ambition, the future state you wish to attain may be slightly—or radically—different from your current state. Beyond a doubt, *The Naked Chef* is highly ambitious. That said, Oliver's wife, Juliette, and their five children do more than just play supporting roles in some of his TV shows. Oliver has arranged a career with dedicated space for family time.[4] His equal focus on family tempers his professional ambition, enabled by a business model that generates income from a steady stream of new shows, books, and restaurants, rather than an abrupt flush of activity.

Stars like Rihanna are at the extreme end of the spectrum of ambition. She was only 16 when she signed with Def Jam Recordings, a major American label, and soon afterward she released her debut album, *Music of the Sun*. She constantly breaks new boundaries that seem impossible for anyone else, and the results speak for themselves: Rihanna has released 7 more studio albums, which have sold more than 60 million copies. She's also sold more than 215 million digital tracks worldwide, making her the top-selling digital artist of all time. This includes putting out 14 number one singles and winning 9 Grammy Awards.[5]

However, Rihanna has not limited herself to music. She released the fragrance Reb'l Fleur in 2011, co-founded the music streaming service TIDAL in 2015, launched the highly anticipated cosmetic company Fenty Beauty under LVMH's Kendo Brands in 2017, and in 2018 introduced the lingerie brand Savage X Fenty, which caters to all body types and sizes. She is also engaged in a wealth of philanthropic endeavors, including the Believe Foundation, which supports terminally ill children, and the Clara Lionel Foundation, which supports people across the globe by investing in advocacy and innovative local projects.[6]

All this is impressive, but the time frame of her accomplishments is even more so. Rihanna turned 30 in 2018. To put this into perspective, she has, on average, released a record or launched a major business or philanthropic venture every year for the past 14 years, had an annual number one single, and won a Grammy Award approximately every 18 months.

As you think about the magnitude of your ambitions, remember that everyone has a unique set of capacities and skills. A given ambition may seem like a stretch that is too far away for some people, but a mark that's easy to reach for others. To understand the relative magnitude of what you are trying to attain, defining your current reality is just as important as defining your desired future state.

4. PRIORITY

Fourth, the intensity of focus you devote to your ambition determines what you can accomplish. This premise of ambition involves how much your goals fill your daily life and how you pursue them.

In line with the saying "the early bird gets the worm," the internet is peppered with articles about the early-morning routines of ambitious people. For example, Tim Cook, Apple's CEO, is known to get up at 3:45 a.m. and send out emails from 4:30 a.m. onward. He admits he gets 700–800 emails per day, most of which he reads, and he likes to get an early start. Cook usually sleeps seven hours, so he must be in bed by 8:45 p.m. to maintain his early-morning schedule.[7] Media mogul Oprah Winfrey gets up between 5:30 a.m. and 6:00 a.m. and immediately spends an hour in the gym. When she had her talk show, she was in the makeup chair by 7:30 every morning. This allowed her to film two shows by 11:30 a.m.[8]

It is tempting to believe that you must follow a certain routine to achieve your ambitions. However, not all ambitions or ambitious people are alike. The key is to design your daily routine and tailor the intensity of your focus to your ambitions so they work for you and support your broader aspirations.

Take Pharrell Williams in his roles as a 13-time Grammy-winning singer-songwriter and record producer, entrepreneur, and designer—with creations from glasses for Louis Vuitton, furniture and a bike for Domeau & Pérès, and a sculpture for the prestigious Art Basel fair. Williams has also produced films and started a charitable foundation.

His resume further includes being voted the best-dressed man in the world and nurturing a long-time relationship with model Helen Lasichanh, now his wife and the mother of their four children. Williams has gotten through much of his adult life without using an alarm clock. He generally gets up at 9:00 a.m., and his preference is to structure his work into a rhythm: His days start with personal time for reflection, followed by conference calls, work in the studio, more conference calls, returning to the studio, and ending with private time in the evening.[9]

Being ambitious centers on what your desires are and how you support them. Some people keep a journal; some do not. Some people prefer structure and to-do lists; others shun them. Some people prefer group brainstorming;

others like quiet contemplation. Some people work 16 hours a day; others limit it to 8. While certain behaviors may help, the strategies that work best to help you attain your ambitions are highly personal. The main thing is to align what you want with the degree of your devotion to reaching it.

OVER TO YOU

The stories of Jacinda Ardern, Trevor Noah, Jamie Oliver, Rihanna, Tim Cook, Oprah Winfrey, and Pharrell Williams illustrate the different premises of ambition. Their ways of being ambitious are examples from an infinite spectrum of variations across each premise: specificity, uniqueness, size, and priority.

You can be ambitious whether or not you have a dream or a clearly articulated goal, whether you follow a well-trodden path or invent your own definition of fulfillment, whether you have a grandiose or modest aspiration compared to where you are today, and whether that aspiration is your center of gravity for most of your waking hours or something you work toward among all the other things you do.

The clearer a picture you have about how your ambitions fall along the four premises, the better a foundation you have for pursuing them and assessing whether—and when—you can consider yourself successful and fulfilled. Any of these impressive people may inspire you, but their dreams and their paths to success are unique to them. You can't follow another person's path. If you try, you'll find plenty of reasons to judge yourself as inadequate or unfulfilled. You have to drive down your own road to fulfill your ambition.

We invite you to reflect on your ambitions along each of the four premises as a starting point for defining your Return on Ambition:

- *How specific is your ambition? To what extent is your ambition a broad direction versus a clearly articulated destination?*

- *How unique is your ambition? Do you wish to follow a well-trodden path or carve out your own niche?*

- *How big are your ambitions relative to where you are today? How far will you have to reach to get there?*

- *Are your ambitions one of your many priorities, or does your life revolve around your ambitions?*

These questions will help you measure your returns according to the Return on Ambition Equation. However, these calibrations are dynamic in nature. If you change your premises, the returns you expect—and attain—will change also. Knowing the premises behind your ambitions will help you align them with your reality and may also help you see them in a new perspective.

In the next chapter, taking the premises you have just defined as your point of departure, we will look at the returns you are getting—and the untapped potential—from your ambitions.

THREE

Measuring Your Return

Every journey has to start somewhere, and understanding this point of departure is every bit as important as defining the direction or destination.

WE STARTED DELVING into the Return on Ambition Equation by defining your ambition along four premises so that you ultimately measure your returns against *your* unique ambition. Now we come to measuring the returns.

Before you review the underpinnings of your returns, please complete the Return on Ambition Assessment below. For each of the 30 statements, please answer whether you largely agree or largely disagree by marking the letter in the corresponding right-hand column:

#	Statement	Largely agree	Largely disagree
1	I regularly feel that I am performing at the peak of my abilities and at my best	C	F
2	I believe that intelligence is largely innate and that I either have the ability to do something or I don't	E	B
3	I generally eat healthily, exercise regularly, and get sufficient sleep	A	F

continued

#	Statement	Largely agree	Largely disagree
4	I am progressing at the rate I would like on accomplishing my professional goals or aspirations	C	E
5	My development at work has largely stagnated	F	B
6	I often find that I have too many things going on and that I am not able to handle them all	F	A
7	My job provides adequate financial security, and I rarely think about financial issues	A	D
8	I am generally in my comfort zone, and I rarely stretch myself in new ways	E	B
9	I feel strong ownership of the goals that I am pursuing	C	D
10	I regularly spend time on introspection and deepening my self-awareness	B	F
11	I do not feel enough love from my family and friends	D	A
12	I am not achieving the quality of output that I would like on my goals or aspirations	D	C
13	I sometimes feel I lack the right support or tools to accomplish my goals or aspirations	F	C
14	I feel that I am happier than my friends and other people with whom I compare myself	A	E
15	I have a flexible approach to life and adapt quickly to new situations	B	F

#	Statement	Largely agree	Largely disagree
16	I am often "in the zone" or "in flow," where I am completely absorbed by the task at hand	C	F
17	I am often bored at work and bored with life in general	D	B
18	I use my strengths daily	C	E
19	I often doubt my abilities or who I truly am as a person	F	A
20	I have the required support (e.g., mentors, colleagues, training) to meet challenges that are outside of my comfort zone	B	E
21	I sometimes wish I had more close friends and people I could rely on	D	A
22	I generally have fun in my life and am able to pursue the leisure activities I enjoy	A	D
23	I often feel that I am focusing on short-term issues or objectives at the expense of longer-term success	E	C
24	I do not have the required skills or ability to influence others in order to accomplish my goals	F	C
25	I am greatly motivated by financial rewards, and less by the actual task at hand	E	A
26	I am frequently asked to overcome challenges that are unrealistic given my current skills or training	E	B

continued

#	Statement	Largely agree	Largely disagree
27	I am living my purpose on a daily basis and know that what I am currently doing is right for me	A	D
28	I have a diverse network of people who help me learn and see new perspectives	B	D
29	I am keenly aware of the areas where I need personal development, and I am working on improving them	B	E
30	I sometimes feel that my work-related goals are impeding my ability to accomplish my personal goals	D	C

Before we explain the motivations for these 30 statements, we would like you to count your scores:

Total number of A's (Well-being)	
Total number of B's (Growth)	
Total number of C's (Achievement)	
Total (A + B + C)	

A's represent your "well-being" score, B's represent your "growth" score, and C's represent your "achievement" score—explained in more detail in the next section. The maximum number you can tally in each category is 10, and you should now have a total for each factor. You can ignore the other letters, which have no meaning by themselves and exist only to create testing alternatives.

By taking your ambition, which you reflected on in the last chapter, as the point of departure, your Return on Ambition is the total score across the three components (A + B + C). The maximum score is 30, and it is important to look at your overall score, the balance of the scores within each area (well-being, growth, and achievement), and whether the scores are surprising to you, given your context and priorities. Over time, were you to redo the assessment, you would be able to plot your returns on a chart with three separate points representing the scores for each area on a given date, and see the evolution and broader trends in your returns.

In the remainder of this chapter, we break down why it is important to understand your returns across these three areas, and how you can identify areas where you have potential to further improve your Return on Ambition.

Breaking Down Your Returns

As with ambition itself, your returns are multifaceted, so your evaluation will be highly subjective. We are not asking you to think about whether you have reached a certain monetary goal or accumulated a certain number of close friends; we're asking whether you feel that you scored high or low, based on your own evaluation of each extreme.

To uncover the factors that lead to a "high" Return on Ambition, we looked at elements that ambitious people believe made the biggest difference in achieving a high return. In our research, we defined a high Return on Ambition as "being fulfilled and satisfied with life, relative to your ambition." Similarly, we studied people who didn't feel they have realized a high Return on Ambition. We noted two primary differences between those with high versus low rates of return.

First, people who reported feeling satisfied generally scored high over time across three core areas in their lives: well-being, growth, and achievement. Although dips sometimes occurred in each of these areas, they were usually short-lived. On the other hand, people who reported feeling less satisfied and who scored low on Return on Ambition fell short in one or two of these three areas for extended periods of time.

Second, people who've realized a high Return on Ambition have the sense that their assessment scores were in line with or exceeded their expectations, based on their level of ambition. They did not find any major surprises; instead, they clearly knew where they were investing their time and what they were getting from that investment.

This self-awareness requires developing a clear, realistic view of what success looks like for you in terms of well-being, growth, and achievement and then making deliberate choices to attain it. For example, those whose professional aspirations fill the vast majority of their waking lives were realistic about how that affects their well-being. Similarly, those who chose to focus more on well-being or growth, for example by pursuing higher education, were realistic about what that meant for their achievements.

Clearly when one is ambitious, feeling satisfied and fulfilled requires more than pursuing merely professional achievements. You wouldn't have a high Return on Ambition if you reached your achievement-oriented professional aspirations but still felt miserable or sensed that you were missing "something" in terms of your personal goals, well-being, or growth. Balance is essential. Ambitious people need strong scores in these three interrelated factors to increase their Return on Ambition over time. If just one is missing, it has a disproportionately negative impact on the total return, while when the three are combined they reinforce one another. Much like a tripod, you can carry many times more than your own weight when all three legs are properly in place.

In fact, the concept of a tripod tells a more complete story than the term "work-life balance," which focuses on only two dimensions—your career and your personal life—positioned as either-or opposites. Our tripod covers a holistic range of human needs—where achievements go beyond success at work, where growth encompasses meaningful learning and personal development, and where well-being builds on personal happiness, purpose, health, and connection.

The three dimensions—well-being, growth, and achievement—are highly interdependent. If one factor plummets, it will drag you down over time. Your achievement will decrease if you stop growing or can't maintain your well-being. Be aware, in such cases, that either you're not expanding your capabilities sufficiently or you're not maintaining your focus and sensitivity. These findings are consistent with spiritual and philosophical wisdom, which teaches that a life focused solely on achievement does not satisfy one's soul. Every spiritual tradition outlines a path of growth that includes making a difference for others. To be compassionate toward other people, you must know and love yourself, cherish your well-being, and relish your personal growth.

This does not mean that people who fulfill their aspirations score high in all three dimensions all the time. You will bounce through ups and downs and sway back and forth. This might result from a deliberate choice to focus on one or two of the three dimensions for a time, if that's what you need to do, for example, to complete exhaustingly long hours of medical residency for the benefit of your long-term aspiration to become a physician, or to take a break to recharge your batteries after exiting your first start-up. Over time, however, make sure any short-term imbalances are the result of your conscious choices. In the medium and long run, you must nurture an equilibrium among the three pillars to maximize your Return on Ambition.

Two of our friends gained great insights into this necessity at painfully low points in their lives when one of the three components of their Return on Ambition collapsed. Their stories illustrate the ways these three components form a closely linked, mutually reinforcing tripod, and how recovering a healthy equilibrium across all three elements will enable you to reach even higher.

Michael Rennie, a retired senior partner at the management consulting firm McKinsey & Company, was diagnosed with late-stage terminal cancer when he was a high-flying associate partner. Rennie was doing well in terms of achievement, but—for reasons beyond his control—he found himself moving quickly toward zero on well-being. Doctors found cancerous tumors throughout his body, including a large one in his stomach. When life seems to be progressing smoothly, you don't always notice what is happening in your body. Extreme situations invite extraordinary choices, and Rennie needed to make a choice.[1]

Rennie was determined to cure himself and to use alternative practices.

The doctors had practically given up hope and could offer only intense che-motherapy to prolong his life, but without any serious prospects of saving it. Rennie turned down that offer. He de-prioritized his achievement drive to focus on well-being and stopped working completely for half a year. Among other things, he sought spiritual advice and started an intense meditation and visualization regimen. If miracles are possible, then he experienced one: Six months later—to everyone's disbelief—the physicians found Rennie free of cancer. Not only had he survived against any scientifically based odds, but he had received the gift of understanding the power of his mind and spirit.

Rennie regained his well-being, and he also made a giant leap in personal growth. Today, more than two decades later, his personal develop-ment has been pivotal in how he has helped clients create transformations beyond their imagination. As a managing partner, he also turned around one of the firm's local offices, making it the single highest-performing unit in the company. In his spare time, he helps people with cancer survive, just as he did. From a distance, on a busy day, you could mistake Rennie for just another management consultant, but he is now living a rich personal life, and he takes pleasure in helping others, clients or not, with his hard-earned wisdom.

The other profile is a great success story that led to personal failure.[2] Sadaffe Abid was among the founders of the Kashf Foundation, which she helped start in 1996 as a philanthropic action and research program. It pro-vides micro-financing in poor rural areas of Pakistan, with a special focus on women. The Kashf Foundation has helped hundreds of thousands of households earn extra income through small-scale entrepreneurship. Abid worked in various roles in the booming operation before being appointed CEO in 2006. Being the top executive was never part of her plan; instead, her drive came from passion for the greater cause.

In hindsight, Abid admits that her former self had a classic case of imposter syndrome. This is the sensation that some people, typically very high achievers, feel when they fear they are a fraud in their important role and could be exposed as unqualified. She doubted herself and did not dare own the success in which she clearly had a big stake.

You could say that Abid was rocking on the achievement dimension when she took the top job at the foundation, but her well-being suffered, and she struggled to push her growth to match her achievement. Meanwhile, she was increasingly challenged by the effort to drive the change needed in the rapidly expanding organization, and she shied away from being assertive when she needed to be. Her heavy focus on achievement created a clear disequilibrium in her life as she fell behind in growth and well-being. This ultimately caused her to hit a wall.

Today, Abid speaks openly about her difficulties as CEO. She stepped down from that role after not much more than a year and decided to go to Harvard's John F. Kennedy School of Government to study entrepreneurship and leadership. She elevated her focus, in terms of the Return on Ambition Equation, on growth and well-being after having not paid much attention to them. One reason she shifted was to make sense of her "scares," as she refers to the anxieties she experienced. This is the complete opposite of being an imposter, and Abid is now working confidently and with renewed purpose. Throwing herself into a new, ambitious nonprofit initiative, she co-founded CIRCLE, a social enterprise promoting leadership, entrepreneurship, and employment for women in the Middle East and North Africa.

We have the utmost respect for what Sadaffe Abid and Michael Rennie have gone through and for how each is contributing to a better world. Together, they illustrate how closely the highs and lows of well-being, growth, and achievement are connected. Next, let's review more detailed insights about each of these three elements of ambition and their underlying drivers.

The Potential of Well-Being: Your A's

Take a look at A's, which represent well-being. Anything below a score of 10 could indicate that you have untapped potential.

Consider this: You can probably recall times when you worked at nearly your maximum capacity and disregarded otherwise valuable aspects of your life. You may have accomplished more than you thought you could, or perhaps you did something you look back on with pride. You may have thought that if you continued like that, nothing could stop you. You may have found such great joy in the experience of intensity that you desired more. Your body's release of adrenaline and dopamine can make such an experience addictive, even without any external substances, such as sugar, caffeine, nicotine, or whatever else can lead to the perception of enhanced achievement.

But—and this is a big but—suppressing your well-being for extended periods of time limits how high you can fly and how much time you can spend at the higher altitude. The questions in the self-assessment that relate to well-being cover the physical, emotional, social, and spiritual aspects of your life. These areas govern how individuals survive and thrive. Each area is important, and you can't ignore any of them. The physical, emotional, social, and spiritual aspects of your well-being are closely connected.

A simple yet remarkable illustration of the significant impact physical well-being has on achievement unfolded when four researchers from Rhode Island College in the United States invited 60 students to do a half-hour workout.[3] The group had an equal number of males and females. All were reasonably fit. They had to do different types of exercise, including jogging, swimming, fast walking, riding stationary bikes, and climbing stairs. They filled out creativity tests before exercising and immediately after exercising or when two hours had passed. The researchers mixed up the various possibilities systematically to keep any single combination of exercise and test timing from influencing the outcomes.

A clear result emerged through these carefully designed activities: The participants were more creative after half an hour of exercise, and they stayed more creative for two hours afterward. The workout had a sustained impact, not just a blip of extra brilliance. Your relative fitness is important, and the widespread advice to do at least thirty minutes of exercise three to four times per week continues to hold true, for even more good reasons than we knew previously.

Are you training intentionally on the days when you need to make your most important decisions?

Even if you work out, you may be caught in another common trap among ambitious people: compromising on your sleep. You may have a lot of work to do, short deadlines, dependencies on people in different time zones, and a need to travel extensively and cope with jet lag. While your body allows you some flexibility in regard to sleep, an accumulated sleep deficit is serious.

Do you frequently have days where you wake up exhausted?

In Australia, 39 people took part in an unusual experiment in which they had to stay awake for 28 hours after having slept properly during the previous days.[4] Researchers selected them from the army or the transportation industry, where the days can be extra long. On another occasion, the subjects had to consume alcohol according to a meticulously measured process. The researchers wanted to learn whether sleep deprivation would affect the participants' response speeds and accuracy in the same way as drinking alcohol.

That certainly turned out to be the case. Individuals with a blood alcohol concentration of 0.05% had the same response speed as when they had been awake for 18 hours (equal to 6 hours of sleep a day). A 0.05% blood alcohol concentration is about what you'd have immediately after drinking two glasses of wine in quick succession if you weighed 175 pounds (close to 80 kilograms) and started out completely sober. A single glass brings a person weighing 130 pounds (about 60 kilograms) close to 0.05%.

Another way to put this is that if you were to wake up at 6:00 a.m. and stay up until midnight, then you would reach a state that is similar to having drunk the legal limit that 136 countries set for driving a vehicle.[5] At this point, the response speed of the people participating in the experiment was reduced by more than 50% in some tests.

This experiment studied only the consequences of a single night of insufficient sleep. Many ambitious people sleep less than six hours per night frequently, and some even feel a bit of pride in their supposed ability to do that. But a shortage of sleep can have serious consequences. Other studies show that sleep deprivation over time harms your attention span, concentration, problem-solving ability, learning, memory, decision-making, emotional reactions, and relationships with other people.[6]

Working with top international athletes, Dr. Nicholas Hall, a neuroimmunologist, found another example of the primacy of well-being.[7] These experts study the linkages among the brain, nervous system, and immune system, which are tightly connected in your body. They discovered something valuable about winning and losing. The way tennis players, for instance, carry their bodies tends to reflect their unconscious mental state. They are more upright when they're playing well, but their bodies bend slightly when they aren't sharp and self-doubt sneaks in.[8]

Your brain and your body are so closely wired that your body gives away what's on your mind. The groundbreaking finding is that this relationship also works the other way around: If you force yourself to stand upright when you feel challenged, you can actually boost your self-confidence and determination.[9] That is, your level of achievement affects your well-being, and your posture reflects that impact.

A performance setback or a difficulty in understanding something you need to know can weigh your body down with troubled thoughts and feelings. When you carry your body in the downtrodden posture that feels natural at such moments—slumped and shuffling—you are allowing your emotional and mental unrest to affect you more severely. You risk starting a vicious circle where your lowered well-being burdens your achievement, which dilutes your well-being further, which then undermines your achievement even more.

Other factors to consider related to well-being: You have a strong understanding of who you are as a person, the extent to which you are pursuing your purpose on a daily basis, the strengths of your relationships with friends and family, and whether you are able to balance the many commitments that your have.

Did information in this section uncover any new insights about your well-being?

Think forward into the next 6–12 months. With your current trajectory, what trends do you see in your well-being?

Are there aspects of your well-being that you could enhance in order to have a positive impact on your Return on Ambition?

Growth Potential: Your B's

Of all the mythic punishments a person could receive, one stands out as particularly awful: The Greek god Zeus forced King Sisyphus to roll a big boulder endlessly up a steep hill. Sisyphus was guilty of believing that he was smarter than Zeus, who showed his supremacy by making the boulder slip and roll down the hill just as Sisyphus approached the top, thus forcing Sisyphus to start again, after every attempt, for all eternity. You can imagine how frustrating it would feel to be so close to the peak over and over and then miss it—repeatedly. Oh so close, but never making it!

Recent research provides a new perspective on the Sisyphus myth. Overwork is not the only cause of burnout. An equally significant force is the feeling of not developing, or even stagnating.[10] A real-life Sisyphus would be at least as irritated about their inability to outsmart Zeus as they would be at the continuous hard work. Every single day, Sisyphus goes through the same activity without ever becoming smarter about it. Similarly, ambitious people can find themselves doing something they are really good at, over and over. This is sustainable only for a little while, after which boredom and apathy set in.

Furthermore, if you fail to develop while others around you grow, you will quickly get left behind in terms of achievement. A research study on doctors provides an example. It found that some doctors achieve better outcomes than their colleagues with similar groups of patients, and it asked why.[11] What made the performance of a small group of doctors stand out?

While any doctor should be able to cure an otherwise healthy person suffering from a simple infection, some excel in more difficult treatment situations. Medicine has a history of honoring experience, as do other academic fields, which is clearly reflected in the stiff hierarchies within the closed worlds of many hospitals and institutes of medicine. This is based on an implicit assumption that the more experience doctors have, the more capable they are. This correlation has some truth—such as when newly graduated doctors go from having no practical experience to getting much more within a few years, but beyond that, the assumption is completely wrong.

This research echoes similar studies in other areas, including careful empirical studies of chess players and violinists, among others. A small group of people in a given field perform significantly better than others. Having sharp eyesight and precise fine-motor skills boosts a doctor's performance. A lot of firsthand experience is also a prerequisite. Having good teachers and mentors helps. As appealing as these explanations may be, these factors are also common among doctors without outstanding performance who peak well before the aging of their bodies would dictate.

The ultimate difference lies in each individual's mindset about personal development and growth. Those who perform in a league above the rest simply think completely differently about what they are doing. They do not rest on their laurels. Instead, they continuously push their competencies beyond what is comfortable. They speculate about, study, and practice skills at which they are not yet good enough, and they purposely give themselves more complex challenges in areas where they are already adept. They think carefully about their own development and how they will act in new and unknown situations. They continually take inventory of the skills they need, assess how well they are doing at each skill, and practice stretching themselves further within some selected abilities. This mindset means that they not only perform better than most of their peers, but that they also keep enhancing their performance throughout their careers.

Neurology adds substance to this point. Brain scans show that when people perform the same task repeatedly, the extent of the active areas in the brain drops. The activity becomes a habit, and the brain chooses the easy path when it comes to habits. It optimizes and strengthens its most relevant neural paths. This is highly practical in situations when you have to do the same thing over and over again in a static environment. When Sisyphus realized that he had no way around Zeus's shrewd spell, he most likely allowed habit to take over: He thought very little about what he was doing and just got on with the mindless routine. Roll upward. Walk down. Roll upward. Walk down.

We are circling around the core of the difference between outstanding performers—those who systematically and continuously undertake deliberate practice to stretch themselves—and other people. The others may be as ambitious and hardworking, but they get stuck in arrested development and make many unnecessary mistakes when they encounter something unfamiliar.[12] Meanwhile, people who frequently stretch themselves keep shaping and strengthening new neural paths. If you don't remain conscious of your context, you risk exposing yourself to errors when you face new, unexpected circumstances. If you are not trying to become better all the time, then you will get relatively worse.

The bottom line is that a shortcoming in growth has a negative impact on achievement and well-being over time. The number of B's that you checked in your self-assessment earlier in the chapter indicates how effective you are in deliberately growing and in finding ways to grow.

To what extent do you pinpoint the areas of your life where you can grow and adapt, and work on these areas in a deliberate way?

How much are you likely to develop over the next 6–12 months if you keep going at your current pace?

Are there aspects of your growth that you could enhance to have a positive impact on your Return on Ambition?

How can you gain a better understanding of your development opportunities by asking others or establishing new feedback mechanisms?

Achievement Potential: Your C's

The two previous sections have explored potential explanations for why your achievement might not be where it could be. Over time, either low well-being or low growth can ruin your otherwise sound achievement. However, you could have selected many A's and B's in the self-assessment while giving yourself fewer C's, which represent achievement. That means you have the right conditions for high performance, but you are not fully utilizing them. Here are four possible reasons for this.

First, attention. Perhaps you are simply not paying adequate attention to your achievement-related priorities. Results don't materialize just because you are capable and in good spirits. One study shows that 78% of people who exercise and play sports enhance their performance moderately or strongly just by setting goals.[13] Unless you have some idea about where you want to go and by when, you won't know when you get there. In addition, you must be prepared to put in the necessary effort and to be critical in assessing whether you're doing what it takes to deliver the required quality of output at the right time.

Second, expectations. Maybe your expectations about future achievements are misplaced. Even the most brilliant people can overestimate or underestimate their own capabilities, and that mistake has consequences. The desired results could be too difficult to reach, leading to capitulation or an unsatisfying outcome. When people do not develop quickly enough and constantly feel stretched too far outside their comfort zone, they can experience anxiety, lower self-esteem, and reduced self-confidence. This has a negative impact on achievement and well-being. The reverse is also true, especially for ambitious people—the results you're seeking could be too easy to reach, so they don't force you to stay on your toes. As a result, you can become so comfortable with what you're doing that boredom and apathy begin to creep in.

Extensive studies confirm this need to balance between being in your comfort zone and being challenged too much. In one study, researchers randomly prompted thousands of people to answer a set of questions approximately every two hours during their waking hours over a two-week period.[14] The results gave rich insights into what people spend their time on and what they experience.

The researchers found that work is one of the activities where people experience the highest degree of full engagement. People report peak engagement when they are highly challenged in an activity at which they are very skilled, yet not stretched so far that they flounder. Other more immediately attractive activities, such as eating, watching TV, and reading, are high in motivation but not in engagement. This pattern can explain why retirement and, to some extent, holidays are hard for many people, even though they looked forward to them.

Third, ownership. Do you feel psychological ownership of your goals when you set them? When you have a stake in an idea, achieving it tends to appear more realistic and appealing than pursuing ideas that other people force on you. In corporate settings, boards and managers must strike a fine balance between setting stretch goals and setting unrealistic goals that are discouraging, and between ensuring that employees co-develop their own goals while keeping their targets in line with overall organizational objectives.

Fourth, assessment. It's possible you assess your past performance too harshly. Ambitious people often focus too heavily on the negative aspects of their efforts and associated outcomes, rather than viewing negative and positive aspects in equal measure. In addition, many harbor a degree of self-doubt and insecurity, leading them to focus even more heavily on minor, often understandable mistakes, instead of feeling proud of what they have accomplished.[15]

There are yet other factors to consider: the degree to which you use your strengths regularly so you are consistently at your best, whether you have the right tools and people helping you achieve your goals, how well you balance your short-term and long-term goals so that urgent priorities do not sabotage you and derail you from the bigger picture, and whether you are adequately balancing your professional and personal goals.

How satisfied are you with your current levels of achievement?

When you look ahead to the next 6–12 months, what trends do you see?

Are there aspects of your achievement that you could enhance to have a more positive impact on your Return on Ambition?

Red Flags

Before we move on, we want to make an important detour. We sometimes encounter clients or acquaintances who are experiencing personal or professional difficulties that are much deeper than they originally perceived. Please review these six statements, answering "Yes" (Y) or "No" (N) for each one.[16]

| 1 | I often experience low energy or feel tired or exhausted for no good reason | Y | N |

2	I often feel bad about myself or experience a sense of worthlessness or hopelessness	Y	N
3	I often have difficulty concentrating or maintaining focus	Y	N
4	I have recently experienced significant changes in my sleep (e.g., trouble falling asleep, sleeping more or less) or eating (e.g., no appetite or overeating)	Y	N
5	I often feel sad or depressed or find it difficult to enjoy hobbies or other activities	Y	N
6	I often feel worried, nervous, or anxious	Y	N

A medical doctor formulated these six questions to serve as red flags indicating a high risk of burnout or other possible negative consequences of having pushed yourself too hard. They also serve as indications that you might suffer from a clinical condition, such as depression, anxiety, psychological distress, or untreated trauma. The questions are carefully defined so that if you largely agree with just one of them—and circle just a single "Yes"—that is a strong reason to get a checkup from a doctor or psychologist. This book is not intended to address any of these red flag symptoms.

A range of scientific studies has explored the possible flip side of being highly ambitious and possessing related traits, such as competitiveness, drive, impatience, and perfectionism. The more ambitious you are, the greater your risk can be of suffering from negative stress, anxiety, burnout, depression, physical health issues, and various mild forms of mania including but not limited to being a workaholic.[17, 18, 19]

Ambitious people often play with fire, and they can get badly burned. You may believe that only one path is available to you in your current situation and that you have to make hard sacrifices, including your health. We have seen too many ambitious people with that kind of tunnel vision, which can lead to severe pain both for them and for the loving, caring people around them. Burnout is all too common, and so is undiagnosed depression. If you answered "Yes" to one or more of the red flag questions, we urge you to take the matter seriously and seek professional help. Before you can fulfill your Return on Ambition, prioritize your return to good health.

OVER TO YOU

We hope you have gained insights about your untapped potential and reflected on where you need further harmony among the tripod of factors—well-being, growth, and achievement. They are so interrelated that an improvement in one is likely to transplant itself to the others after a while.

After you read the questions that follow, we invite you to put down the book and carve out time to contemplate them. Perhaps you could take a walk for a change of scenery in order to block out distractions. Give yourself the luxury of just thinking.

- *Do your scores across the three dimensions—well-being, growth, and achievement—surprise you? If so, in what way?*

- *Are your scores sound and balanced across the three dimensions? If not, are the imbalances caused by deliberate trade-offs?*

- *Which dimension or dimensions hold the biggest potential for you to enhance your overall Return on Ambition?*

PART 2

What Gets in the Way of Your Return on Ambition?

PART 2 FOCUSES on the second main question of the book: What gets in the way of your Return on Ambition? We start by introducing the seven Frenemies—*Convention, Boldness, Independence, Competitiveness, Perseverance, Desire, and Flexibility*—and then devote a chapter to each one as we explore how they can both help and hinder your ambitions. Each chapter includes stories about individuals who have overcome their Frenemies, as well as follow-up questions for personal reflection.

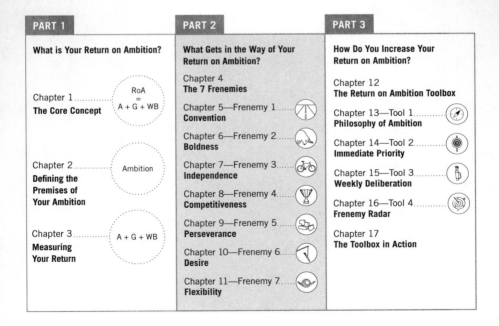

PART 1	PART 2	PART 3
What is Your Return on Ambition?	What Gets in the Way of Your Return on Ambition?	How Do You Increase Your Return on Ambition?
Chapter 1 **The Core Concept** RoA = A + G + WB	Chapter 4 **The 7 Frenemies**	Chapter 12 **The Return on Ambition Toolbox**
	Chapter 5—Frenemy 1 **Convention**	Chapter 13—Tool 1 **Philosophy of Ambition**
	Chapter 6—Frenemy 2 **Boldness**	Chapter 14—Tool 2 **Immediate Priority**
Chapter 2 **Defining the Premises of Your Ambition** Ambition	Chapter 7—Frenemy 3 **Independence**	Chapter 15—Tool 3 **Weekly Deliberation**
	Chapter 8—Frenemy 4 **Competitiveness**	Chapter 16—Tool 4 **Frenemy Radar**
Chapter 3 **Measuring Your Return** A + G + WB	Chapter 9—Frenemy 5 **Perseverance**	Chapter 17 **The Toolbox in Action**
	Chapter 10—Frenemy 6 **Desire**	
	Chapter 11—Frenemy 7 **Flexibility**	

FOUR

The 7 Frenemies

Ambitions can be like friends who help you win, but they can also turn into enemies who insist that you win too fast, too often, or at too great an expense.

WHEN BEYONCÉ FILLED the Parken Stadium in Copenhagen with the lyrics of "Freedom" on July 24, 2016, one listener heard the words in her own way.[1] She felt as if they were meant for her, as she, too, wanted to break her chains and get away.

With her smile and blonde hair, that listener could have been mistaken for any of the thousands of her fellow Danes in the audience, though you might have recognized her from a couple of her recent modeling jobs. Beneath her joyful appearance beat an especially strong-willed heart. She was on a mission. The concert was her last social outing before she was scheduled to leave Denmark the next morning for Brazil.

Half a year earlier, very few people would have believed that Pernille Blume, Denmark's champion freestyle and medley swimmer, would be going to the Rio Olympics. Despite her long-standing dream to reach the Olympic finals, she had been struggling just a short time before. Shortly after New Year's Day in 2016, she told her coach that her motivation had dissipated.[2]

For a while, Blume had been under so much stress that she felt like throwing up when she left home for her daily training sessions. Once, her fierce willpower had compensated for not having the longest arms or legs among world-class swimmers, but that grit had worn out. Her belief in the value of her effort had disappeared. Strong doubts haunted her, especially after her disappointing results at the previous Olympics in London, even though she had reached the finals with two different relay teams.

At the young age of 21, Blume announced her retirement from elite competitive swimming. To make the decision, she reflected deeply about her life. Blume stayed out of the pool for weeks, which is a fundamental change of life for an elite swimmer. Her coach listened carefully to her and suggested a new training program; this gave the young swimmer much stronger ownership of her work and her results. She eventually dove back into the pool again and started regaining her strength. Despite her break, she managed to qualify for the Olympics in Rio at a local swimming competition.

On August 13, less than three weeks after the Beyoncé concert and one-quarter of the way around the globe, Blume qualified for the finals in the Olympic 50-meter freestyle. She was ready to live out the dream she had temporarily abandoned. She was by no means the favorite in the race, and her start was far from the best. But Blume gave it everything she had, and the spectators realized suddenly during the last 10 meters that she was gaining more speed than her competitors. She even surprised herself. She was so disoriented when she surfaced from the water and saw the display announcing her gold-medal win with a new personal best of 24:07 seconds that she turned to the swimmer in the next lane to ask if it was really true.

Blume was not the only one who was shocked. Her little sea-bound homeland has a proud history in swimming, but it had not won an Olympic gold medal in the sport since 1948. Just an hour after her first victory, Blume took part in the 4 × 100 meters medley relay final and added a bronze medal to her collection. She realized a solid return on her ambition, unlike another superb young female Olympian.

Lindsey Jacobellis's extraordinary story played out in the Winter Olympic Games in Turin, Italy, in 2006. Like Pernille Blume, Jacobellis had an unforgettable day and so did the enthusiastic fans of snowboard cross, which had made it onto the Olympic program for the first time. Four boarders race in snowboard cross. They begin side by side in a start box, like horses at a racetrack, and they swoosh down a curved mountain slope with a cascade of jumps. The person who gets to the finish line first wins, and style doesn't count.

"Lucky Lindsey," a member of the US team, had moved smoothly through the qualifying heats. She was a clear favorite, having already won two world championships and five Winter X Games—the most prestigious North American competition—though she was only 20 years old. The final started well. Jacobellis edged in front of the pack in the first turn by perfectly cutting a clean inside line, forcing the others to give her space. From there, she gained the highest speed, establishing a comfortable lead that stretched farther when her closest competitor, Canadian Dominique Maltais, fell and was thrown somewhat dramatically through a safety fence. After the first turn, another finalist also fell, so the race for the gold medal was suddenly left to Jacobellis and Switzerland's Tanja Frieden, who had a much more modest winning record.[3]

Jacobellis was well in the lead as she completed the last turn. She faced a straight line down the mountain toward the goal. She was so far ahead she couldn't even hear the sound of Frieden's board crunching the snow behind her. She turned her head, looked backward, and saw no one. The gold medal was in clear sight.

As she entered the air on the penultimate jump, Jacobellis hung in the air, tweaked out her snowboard, and touched its edge with her hand. The gratuitous trick was a "method grab," which is an aerial maneuver used in freestyle snowboard events where participants compete on style and creativity. Jacobellis embodied the essence of the sport during that elevated moment, but reality hit hard when she landed on her heels at top speed, throwing her board off the track. She recovered quickly, but Frieden came from behind and slid past her across the finish line.

The TV cameras captured the US team's coach smacking himself on the forehead and her parents looking on in speechless disappointment. The picture of her method grab could have become the ultimate symbol of the cool new Olympic sport, but instead it cast a shadow over all her earlier accomplishments.

She had envisioned the 2006 gold medal hanging around her neck. With that vision suddenly shattered, the silver medal didn't seem to weigh very much. Jacobellis had never won gold or reached the top step of the Olympic podium. And she never would.

She ended the 2010 Vancouver Olympics with a disqualification in the semifinal for hitting a post after a less-than-perfect start, and she fell while leading her semifinal in Sochi in 2014. The world's best female snowboard crosser never again reached her 2006 pinnacle—the moment she made the split-second decision to showboat in Turin.

It would be nice if you could accomplish your ambitions with no bumps along the way, but life does not work like that. Everyone faces ups and downs, and the way ambitious people deal with their evolving ambitions over time is a critical factor in their ability to succeed and feel fulfilled. We've seen that few people get very far without ambition, but it can trip you up if you direct it toward the wrong outcomes.

For example, some people mistakenly channel their ambition toward fulfilling their ego and expend energy on things they believe are important but which have negative implications for their overall Return on Ambition. That could be chasing the next promotion, making sure they are "right" in an argument, or working long hours to complete an extra assignment they have requested. Ambition can become so strong that it slows their pace or sparks rapid movement in the wrong direction. In such cases, greater amounts of effort do not always correlate with better outcomes. This paradox can lead to an unnecessarily bad deal for people who overinvest and can even be counterproductive to reaching their desired goals.

In addition, other people's ability to keep up appearances—to look as if they aren't even breaking a sweat—can make your struggles to realize a strong Return on Ambition seem even more burdensome. You can easily blame yourself for not carrying out your ambitions as elegantly as other people seem to be doing. However, appearances rarely tell the whole truth—even the most successful people have hindrances to overcome. Far fewer people lead perfect lives than Hollywood, Bollywood, and Nollywood want you to believe, or are as effortlessly successful as they may portray. The reality is that a deeply fulfilled life requires hard work coupled with continuous close attention to the interplay between efforts and outcomes.

When Friends Become Enemies

In our interviews and work with ambitious people, we've found they share similar mindsets and behavioral patterns that helped them reach their aspirations and become fulfilled. These shared characteristics are typically considered strengths or "friends" of ambition. Examples include the ability to handle complex tasks independently, to adapt to new situations, and to compete and win—all great qualities.

However, the exact mindsets of ambitious people, precisely because they are so ambitious, can also turn into "enemies" of ambition. The result is what we call the "Frenemies" of ambition. We've identified seven of these traits, which you must become aware of before you can overcome their negative manifestations.

These Frenemies of ambition contain gifts, but they have a dark side. For instance, having a strong drive can propel you forward with great speed, but it can undermine you if you push too hard. You must understand these Frenemies and channel them in ways that will serve you and your ambitions.

Pernille Blume had reached her own limit of what she could force herself to do in swimming. She was exhausted. She took a big step back to reflect not just on her sport—after all, she had decided to quit—but on her life as well. Blume needed to create the mental space to think through the return she was getting from the enormous energy and time she was putting into her Olympic ambition. She surprised everyone by announcing her retirement, and then coming back even stronger and more levelheaded about her goals. This time, as a result of her hiatus, she decided to take more ownership of her training.

Lindsey Jacobellis did the opposite when she looked back at the track and decided to show off. She lost her perspective about what looked like an easy finish. Blume carefully created a fruitful space to optimize her Return on Ambitions; Jacobellis faltered at a critical moment and short-circuited her ambitions.

The seven main Frenemies are listed below. This is not an exhaustive list of possible Frenemies, but based on our professional experience, interviews, and survey, we're confident that these seven cover the major Frenemies that beset ambitious people. They are based on psychology, adult development theory, and practice. The Frenemies share similar underlying root causes, so you'll find some overlap, but we've separated them clearly where nuances matter. They are as follows:

1. CONVENTION—The ability to follow a well-trodden path and attain success as judged by society . . . or to get stuck in expectation and routine.

2. BOLDNESS—The ability to move quickly and throw yourself into new, challenging situations . . . or to miscalculate what is required to attain your ambitions.

3. INDEPENDENCE—The ability to get things done by yourself, without help . . . or to fail to include others when needed.

4. COMPETITIVENESS—The ability to outcompete others and be the best . . . or to try to win at all costs.

5. PERSEVERANCE—The ability to go the extra mile and complete challenging tasks, even when you're overloaded . . . or to exhaust yourself frequently and burn out.

6. DESIRE—The ability to push constantly against the limits of possibility and break new boundaries . . . or to chase success for the sake of it.

7. FLEXIBILITY—The ability to adapt adroitly to different people and situations . . . or to be constantly swayed by others.

An underlying mindset drives the root cause of each Frenemy. We challenge you to reflect on those causes as you read each chapter.

When Enemies Become Friends

These seven Frenemies can limit your way of thinking and, as a result, your Return on Ambition. Just having one Frenemy in play can jeopardize your efforts to make a difference and live a fulfilling life, just as a sailor can set a course in the right direction while overlooking a strong current and end up completely missing the destination.

Your Frenemies are inherent to you; the question is, how can you keep them as powerful friends and block their negative manifestations? Some books jump straight to giving you solutions or "recipes" to remove your roadblocks and improve yourself. They may give you tips about what to do differently—for example, how to be a better listener, how to lead a team, or how to manage your time. While helpful, this misses a crucial link in the process: understanding why you need help in the first place and what underlying drivers might be motivating you.

Nobody sets out to limit their Return on Ambition. No one wants to be a bad listener or a poor team leader or become overwhelmed from taking on too much work. The reasons people act in ways that may limit their Return on Ambition are much deeper and are often subconscious. If overcoming your Frenemies were as simple as following a "how-to" manual, you'd already be doing it.

We won't tell you what to do or how to think; nor do we label actions that seem to limit your Return on Ambition as "bad." Rather, we help you explore your underlying drivers so you can reflect on how they might be serving you well or holding you back. We know firsthand that shifting your mindset—especially a mindset that has helped you well in the past—is challenging.

Now let's meet these seven Frenemies and hear some real-life examples of how ambitious people have navigated them.

FIVE

Frenemy 1—Convention

Do you recognize a tendency in yourself to follow a well-trodden path and strive for accomplishments that win praise or approval? If so, how has this helped you? How could it hinder you?

IN SINGAPORE, SUCCESS is summed up in a well-known acronym named the "five C's": cash, car, credit card, condo, and country club membership. Many Singaporeans, with varying degrees of seriousness, seek these material goals as an entry point to joining the elite. Whether taken literally or not, the five C's shape their thoughts and often influence their decisions.

All countries and cultures have some equivalent of the five C's, perhaps in terms of people's education, their career path, where they live, where they play golf or tennis, and the car they drive. In Chinese culture, parents joke that their children can become anything they want, as long as they want to be doctors or lawyers. For some families, it's not a joke.

Many factors can shape your future aspirations, including societal norms, expectations, and pressures. For many ambitious people, the way to "success" is clearly defined in childhood: Get into the right middle school to open the door to the right high school; get good grades and do well on your entrance exams so you get accepted to the right college; get good grades in the right subjects and do the right extracurricular activities to get into the right grad school or win the right prestigious, well-paying job; work hard so you get promoted and receive increasingly bigger pay checks; buy a car and house for your family; and keep working harder so you keep getting promoted and earn more money.

Wow, are you exhausted yet? Remember that ambition is a strong yearning and drive to attain a future state that is different from today's and challenging to reach—but it isn't necessarily a fixed point. If you reflect on your ambitions, they can mature as you do. But the need for speed as you dash forward and follow a conventional path can wipe out reflection. Knowing where to run and how to succeed in the environment you are in is important, and it helps you move forward, enabling many positive outcomes. However, it can also lead to myopic thinking about success.

Many ambitious people feel that they are sprinting along a clearly defined course—similar to a home run in baseball. A sense of urgent competition pushes them so hard and fast that they can't stop to think or change course. They surge forward, sprinting around the bases in a frantic effort to score a home run before getting tagged out, without reflecting on whether they're even playing the game that is right for them. Everyone has felt such pressure at some point, and many people confront it every day.

Take Anish Shah, a New York–based stand-up comedian who produced and hosted a show on Broadway, was selected for NBC's Late Night Writers Workshop, and was named one of the "Top 50 Coolest South Asians." However, his journey was far from orthodox. Initially, it didn't point at all toward making people laugh for a living. "From a very young age, I always thought I would be a business guy," Shah recalls, and he always felt he would do great things.[1]

As a kid, he had a vision of becoming a "good version of Gordon Gekko" (the profit-hungry company raider from the movie *Wall Street*), and he constantly developed business plans. "At one point I had created 23 one-page business plans, which I was evaluating." He flirted with the idea of becoming an actor; it appealed to him deeply, but he didn't consider it seriously. "I used to think that acting was not something real people do. I put blinders on myself."

As a result, Shah pursued a well-trodden path toward business success. In college, he launched a successful venture and built it up until he had 30 employees. Then he headed to Yale for business school, and after graduation he joined McKinsey & Company, the global management-consulting firm—so far so good for a business career. Shah stayed at McKinsey as a consultant for five years, but, to his surprise, he realized he wasn't feeling entirely fulfilled. He enjoyed the work and liked his colleagues, but he felt that something was still missing. He eventually joined the software company SPSS, which IBM soon bought. Shortly afterward, Shah ventured into stand-up comedy for the first time and found his true passion, defying the boundaries of the *Convention* Frenemy: "I started doing stand-up while still working at IBM. I had never viewed it as a serious career option, but I decided to give it a shot at an open microphone night," he recalls. "People laughed. That gave me a huge adrenaline rush, and I was hooked."

Contemplating his future, Shah eventually made a bold decision: He quit his job and moved to New York to give stand-up a serious chance. That was in 2012. "Why did I leave the corporate world to pursue a career in stand-up comedy?" he jokes. "Well, I thought, 'What could I do to disappoint my parents the most?' This is what I came up with and it worked."

While Shah says he's always been comfortable pursuing an unconventional route, it has not always been as easy as it may seem on the surface. "I liked the idea of becoming a partner at McKinsey," he recalls. "That was my goal. Of course, one part of me felt that it would be 'cool' to be able to say I had reached that level. After I left McKinsey to join a relatively unknown tech company, I still introduced myself as someone who 'used to work for McKinsey' and now worked at SPSS. But as I got older, I got an itch to try new things, and I knew I had to make a decision." What he decided was that he'd been running to get to the wrong base and that a healthy serving of laughter is his real sport.

Danica Patrick, the most successful woman in American car racing, was named one of *Time* magazine's "100 Most Influential People" in 2009 and 2010. She also dealt with the pressure of following an unconventional path.[2] At 16, Patrick dropped out of school to move alone to Europe to pursue a racing career. She initially focused on IndyCar racing, the premier level open-wheel (formula car) racing series in North America. Competing in a male-dominated sport, Patrick broke many "firsts" for females, including being the only woman to win an IndyCar Series race. In 2010, when she was the most visible, best-paid driver on the IndyCar circuit, she decided to switch to the bigger stage of NASCAR, the premier stock-car racing (ordinary cars that have been modified for racing) series. Although Patrick arguably would have won more races if she had remained an IndyCar driver, she was determined to take the next step.[3]

Throughout her career, Patrick carved her own route, including launching her own apparel business, Warrior; entering the wine business with the launch of Somnium; writing a book; and shooting provocative ads for her sponsors, drawing criticism from many corners. She movingly recalls the challenges of trying to make a name for herself in a male-dominated industry, especially when filming her attention-getting ads.

"I was always afraid to look too girly," she says in an interview with *Entrepreneur* magazine, "because I wanted to be taken seriously and to make it easy for people to listen to me as a driver and to hear what I'm saying."[4]

Most recently, she decided to retire from motor racing at the relatively young professional age of 36 to focus on her business ventures. She felt she was at the mercy of her sponsors and team, and she was no longer enjoying racing. In making this switch, she chose to bypass the expected, more traditional option of staying put and instead opted to stay true to herself. "I was just over the stress and the judgment," she admits. "I wasn't having fun. And life's too short."

The feeling of running a sprint within defined boundaries does not occur only at a young age. One of the alarming aspects of our professional consulting and coaching roles is hearing successful, hardworking executives confess how little time they have to think about anything—including whether they should stay on the same trajectory and how to find meaning in their lives. Such revelations can be immensely valuable to the people who have them, but we hear them so often from ambitious clients that it's disconcerting—especially when they seem so successful.

These executives often declare that they regret following a direction someone else laid out, running at breakneck speed for no reason, and reaching a midlife crisis beset by the question "Is this all there is?" Often, they undergo a jolting wake-up call before they gain the perspective and strength to ask questions and make new choices.

Jeff Weiner, executive chairman of LinkedIn, the professional social media network, has had similar reflections during his career. Like Shah,

Weiner has an impressive CV. Weiner graduated from the Wharton School of the University of Pennsylvania and rose through the ranks of Yahoo!, a web portal, until he became executive vice president of its Network Division, leading a team of 3,000 people. He joined LinkedIn in 2009 and later became CEO, and, in a 2014 Glassdoor survey, his employees named him as one of the "top 10 CEOs at US Tech Companies."[5]

Weiner says he didn't know what really made him happy or how to lead a more balanced life until he met his wife. Early in his career, he focused only on running fast uphill. "I lacked any semblance of balance before I met my wife. I put everything I had into work and getting the job done, and I was very intense," he admitted during an interview with Oprah Winfrey. He added, "At least I had the awareness to recognize that if I maintained that path for five or 10 more years, I might be successful based on conventional definitions of success, but I wasn't going to be happy."[6]

Do you recognize yourself in any of these stories?

Pursuing an Impersonal Definition of Success

Nothing is wrong with pursuing a conventional career path with a stable trajectory and clearly defined goals. Nor is there anything wrong with working hard to reach those goals. Indeed, the drive that propels ambitious people forward is a strength and often a huge asset. Such ambition enables you to move quickly toward your goal, despite hurdles. Ambition can be like the blinkers attached to the eyes of a racehorse, powering you forward without distraction.

For example, Anish Shah recalls the period at Yale when he prepared for an interview at McKinsey. "I didn't go to classes for three weeks, and I did an insane amount of practice cases."[7] His interviews went very well, and his unbridled focus during this practice period helped him power through.

Ambitious people put themselves at risk, however, when they become so focused on achieving their aspirations that they don't think about whether they're spending their time on the right things and the right bases as they surge for the home run. Sprinting gets you moving quickly—but make sure you're going in the right direction and not simply heading in a direction laid out for you by other people. There is a big difference between living somebody else's idea of success and living your own.

Danica Patrick started running flat out on a clearly defined route at age 10, when entering a go-kart competition introduced her to racing. At 11, she finished fourth in the World Karting Association Manufacturers Cup in the Yamaha Sportsman class. At 12, she won her first championship. By the time she moved to England, alone, at age 16 to continue her development as a driver, she had won 10 regional karting titles and multiple races. At 20, she signed a multiyear contract with Team Rahal, and, three years later, she was named IndyCar Rookie of the Year. Patrick demonstrates that as expectations continue to grow with each success, keeping your foot on the pedal without ever letting up becomes nearly automatic.[8]

What are some of the other symptoms we observe when the *Convention* Frenemy is in play? We see three main signs, all of which are interlinked.

The first is following a well-trodden path and doing what you think others will be most accepting of. Across most domains, society defines success clearly, and it maps out the way for getting "there." Some even argue that the competitive education system prevents students from thinking independently about what's right for them as individuals.

Shah followed a traditional route only temporarily, and he still felt these pressures. From a young age, he had twin desires for careers in business and in acting, but he told himself that business was the only valid path. "I had to check a number of boxes," he says, explaining that he viewed a lot of his early moves as the stepping-stones of a successful career. "I used to see myself as a rebel within a box. I was doing things the unconventional way, but my box was leading me to become a business executive or CEO."

Second, people who are dashing toward a finish line often can't change course, even if they think—or know—they should. Ambitious people often feel torn between a fervent urge to soar into the sky and a simultaneous pull to stay grounded on Earth. While economic realities may be one reason ambitious people allow conventions to hold them back, it's more often fear of failure and an unwillingness to lose power and prestige. Consider the satisfaction someone feels when asked about their background and they're able to name a top-ranked university, a prestigious employer, or an impressive professional position.

Third, the *Convention* Frenemy can result in risk aversion and what we call "playing the options game"—being afraid of cutting off any career choices, no matter how unlikely. While we acknowledge that many ambitious people take risks, others play it safe and get stuck following a well-trodden path, with difficulty narrowing their course. Humans are generally risk averse and give potential negative outcomes much greater weight than potential positive outcomes. It can be tempting to follow a route that minimizes perceived risk.

People may get trapped when they try to keep as many options open as possible rather than choosing a focus. They are afraid of making a commitment and of taking the risk of closing doors. This can include deciding to pursue an MBA to avoid choosing a specific career direction, starting at a large corporation to get access to a wide range of internal opportunities, or pushing to get to the next level on the corporate ladder to maximize the possibility of other attractive jobs in the future. Despite their desire to attain an ambitious future state, many ambitious people paradoxically often make conservative choices. The result is an absence of a meaningful and distinct personal direction.

At some point, you might ask yourself, "What am I keeping these options open for?"

The root cause of sprinting like this may be that you're pursuing an impersonal, societally defined, conventional view of success. Often, a mad dash toward the home plate is driven by the idea that success has only one definition, and if you deviate from that, you'll fail. The *Convention* Frenemy has two possible impacts: It can create a subtle shadow on your decisions and lead to a feeling that you "ought to change," though you never seriously deliberate it. Alternatively, it can dominate your choices so much that you aren't even aware that you're following an outwardly defined path, instead of asking yourself what would give you personal fulfillment.

A number of core beliefs can drive this Frenemy, including "I need to have an important title to impress my friends and family," "I am not good enough and need to prove myself," and "Change is risky." These beliefs may or may not be valid for you; the key is to dig deep and uncover what drives your behaviors.

Oftentimes, this mindset springs from either high expectations or from receiving so much support for a particular track that you plunge ahead without much contemplation. These conventional paths can become rigid channels. Most large organizations spell out in job descriptions, incentive programs, and career ladders what they expect from their employees. When the conventional route is laid out, people are inclined to focus on making the next planned step—marching with their peers—without taking a broader perspective or considering whether they are even in the right parade.

Embarking on a new course can be overwhelming, but you are unlikely to attain outstanding results when you follow the same route as everyone else—even if you start out with a higher drive, more ability, and great ambition—if it's not the right direction for who you truly are.

The negative aspects of *Convention* typically become more challenging as people get older and move up the ladder. The complexity of their lives increases as they advance from the minor leagues, an undergraduate education, or an entry-level position. Professional progress brings more responsibility. Family commitments also tend to increase over time, at least until the children leave the nest. As work becomes harder and your status grows and the kids become teenagers, the risk of mental overload continues to grow.

This Frenemy affects ambitious people more than others because, by nature, they have a stronger yearning and drive to attain a future state that is different and better than today. This future state, however, is not always clearly defined. They are driven to get "there," though they may fail to ask where "there" is. In the absence of a personally defined aspiration, they fall back on accepted notions of a "good" future: prestigious job, big house, fancy car, and so on—the same old five C's pursued in Singapore. In fact, they begin to crave the five C's for no better reason than familiarity: Everyone knows about them and holds them in high regard.

The *Convention* Frenemy affects your well-being, growth, and achievement in different ways. The friendly side of *Convention* shows itself when you are doing well in a system that takes care of you. The expectations placed on you are challenging but not unrealistic. You work hard, but not way too hard. Somebody is there to help if you get into trouble. The system is predominantly supportive, and there are rarely negative consequences for high performers.

However, the enemy part of *Convention* can affect well-being significantly. Realizing that you are going down the wrong avenue can sap your sense of meaning. It might show up indirectly as flashes of doubt about whether the sacrifices you are making to perform at this level are worth it, or in occasional speculation about what you truly want. Considering a career shift can make you feel anxious and stressed.

Another symptom is feeling motivated by what you get out of your effort, but not by your effort itself. You might lose the intrinsic motivation of pursuing your ambition. That may sound like semantics, but research into motivation shows that this distinction is critical for well-being.[9] You can wake up in the morning and get to work to achieve something that lies far ahead in the future. Or you can wake up enthused about what you are going to do this very day. Both types of motivation are important, and each contributes to your well-being.

Your growth is also affected when you're misaligned and swinging for a home run in the wrong ball game. This can happen in different ways.

First, having to build more skills in an area that is no longer aligned with your strengths and passions becomes an increasingly hard slog. Research shows that the absolute improvement in performance is about two times higher when you are building up an existing strength than when you must focus on a weak area.[10]

Second, you may stop pushing yourself to improve if you know you are likely to need different skills in the future. This temporary uncertainty can even cause your dedication to fall and your skills to regress.

Third, your growth might also suffer when you focus on rote learning, leaving little time to be curious and establish your own perspectives on what content or lessons make sense. Learning in a purely "spoon-fed" manner is often less effective than learning when you can experiment through trial and error.

This may not affect your achievement initially, because you have a strong drive and goal orientation. However, you can lose momentum or hit a wall if you realize you're pursuing the wrong path. For example, if you find yourself less in the flow, formerly minor challenges and setbacks may cause larger frustrations than usual. Furthermore, the higher up you progress in many systems, the bigger a risk it can be to continue following expectations without innovating and being creative.

Of course, ambition isn't that black and white. Laying out either-or choices—the right way to do things or the wrong way—is overly simplistic. But our purpose is to provoke you to reflect on your choices. Thinking deeply is the only way to manage the *Convention* Frenemy.

Consider that almost 40% of ambitious people struggle to spend the time they want reflecting on their personal development goals.[11] This pinpoints the scarcity of deep personal thinking about ambition and possibilities. Moreover, people who take the time to reflect about their life's direction are more likely to feel that they are accomplishing their goals across all three Return on Ambition dimensions: well-being, growth, and achievement.

Defining Your Own Rules of the Game

Following the crowd has social ramifications that helped your ancestors survive and may still afford many benefits. However, if everyone needs to run around the same bases or risk being left out of the game, pursuing conventional home runs may feel like a rat race.

Some people, on the other hand, pursue their passion and adapt readily to new knowledge and techniques. They take on challenges and find personal, creative ways to play the game using tactics that suit their strengths and passions. They are shaping the game as much as playing it, and these people report feeling increased well-being, growth, and achievement.

Anish Shah could have been content being the funniest management consultant ever. His easiest option was to stay in the corporate world earning a steady income and professional approval. Indeed, he enjoyed the different roles he had in business, and staying in consulting or tech would have been fine. "But as I grew older," Shah says, "I got an itch to try new things."[12] He felt a strong passion to try something different and decided to take the plunge, starting small with side gigs at night, before finally making stand-up comedy a full-time profession.

Taking a leap requires courage, a willingness to experiment, and the mindset that only you can determine what success means in your life. "I felt uncomfortable in the beginning, especially around the financial instability," Shah says. The payoff, however, can be great. "The box I was rebelling in suddenly became much bigger. I felt a grandiose sense of freedom. What was the worst-case scenario? I would burn through my savings and then go back to the corporate world." As he learned, the risks of making a change are often much smaller than they seem to be at first.

Danica Patrick could have continued her success in IndyCar racing rather than switching to NASCAR. She could have postponed her retirement and stayed in her comfort zone, instead of venturing into new businesses. "I know I'm sort of young for retirement," she says. "It was all sort of unconventional the way it all went down, as far as it being my choice to retire from racing. But what the heck have I done that's been conventional? I feel very good about the way it's gone."[13]

Her upbringing fostered her willingness to take risks. "That seed was planted a long time ago," Patrick says. She grew up believing that owning your own businesses is totally possible and not abnormal. Throughout her life, she has embraced the belief, "If you have an idea, run with it."[14]

Sometimes the change you decide to pursue won't be as drastic as moving from the business world to stand-up comedy, or from professional racing to wine making. You may find that you want to stay in familiar surroundings and your current job for well-considered reasons. Everyone's choices and timing will be different, and the key is to make conscious choices based on your personal awareness of what constitutes success for you.

Michael Rennie, our friend who survived what supposedly was terminal cancer, chose to pursue a long and successful career as a partner and then senior partner at McKinsey. In a similar vein, Jeff Weiner was the CEO of LinkedIn for more than 10 years and is now the executive chairman, and he continues to prioritize what really matters to him. He strongly advocates staying true to yourself and pursuing a path aligned with the difference you want to make in the world. This takes real reflection and conscious inner work. Weiner is candid about the work he did to transform himself from an intense, work-obsessed leader to the more attuned leader he is today. He knows the early days of his career were short on well-being and growth, and he acknowledges that his pursuit of achievement overwhelmed the balance in his life.[15] His thoughtful course correction worked.

Even if things don't go the way you planned, it is important to think through your own broader perspective on life and remain true to yourself and your convictions. In his book *Big Potential*, Shawn Achor discusses a cellist in the Boston Philharmonic Orchestra whose disappointment about being assigned to the eleventh chair outweighed her delight that she had been hired over many other applicants. Then the Boston Philharmonic's conductor Benjamin Zander asked her advice about the best way to approach a difficult passage of a symphony. He used her suggestions and received excellent reviews. As Achor reports, Zander found that the cellist's playing elevated considerably after that. She saw that she was realizing a return on her ambition, even from the eleventh chair. Instead of being frenzied to charge ahead, the cellist was able to reframe her situation, make the most of her present position, and appreciate the way it contributed to her goals, even if she hadn't reached her ambition—yet.

Moving from the field of play to the stadium seats to gain a broader perspective and begin to define your own rules of the game can greatly increase your Return on Ambition. It will develop as you align your investment in energy more closely with what truly matters to you. Conversely, you can increase it by cutting back on frivolous efforts. As you clarify the boundaries of your game, you can cut away nonessential activities and focus more intently on enjoying each play.

OVER TO YOU

Think back on your last five big decisions related to your ambition (e.g., the university you went to, the subjects you chose, your job selections, your big purchases).

- *How many of these were driven primarily by societal or family pressures versus what was most important to you?*

- *Do you ever feel like you have handcuffs on in your pursuit of your ambition?*

- *Do you ever feel like you want to change direction but are not able to? If so, what is holding you back?*

- *How could mastering the* Convention *Frenemy increase your Return on Ambition?*

SIX

Frenemy 2—Boldness

Do you have the ability to move quickly and throw yourself into new and challenging situations without any hesitation? If so, how has this helped you? Has it ever hindered you?

THE 1986 MOVIE *Top Gun* is the story of two daring young pilots, Maverick and Iceman, who continue to push each other as they compete in their F-14 planes. One of the movie's hit songs, "Danger Zone," which plays during the opening scene, is incredibly fitting for a sequence of F-14s soaring into the sky. The lyrics describe the way many ambitious people approach their goals—going as far out on the edge as they can go, burning with as much heat and intensity as they can get, and moving ever closer to the danger zone.[1]

Like Maverick and Iceman, played by Tom Cruise and Val Kilmer, ambitious people often charge full steam ahead with courage, speed, and confidence. Taking off toward their goals, they soar into the sky. They stretch their limits, try new things, and break boundaries, and they often feel most at ease when doing so.

But even the best fighter pilots sometimes move too fast and fail to account for all the challenges lurking in their external environments. Yes, you may have the best training and many hours of experience, but even so you can end up out of your depth, in need of better skills and more personal development, and—perhaps to your surprise—you may not be able to cope.

That's what happens when your friend *Boldness* becomes your Frenemy: You overshoot the runway.

Take Fred Swaniker, a Ghanaian entrepreneur who has experienced the potential peril of moving quickly and with confidence.[2] Swaniker is chairman and founder of the African Leadership Academy (ALA), which aims to transform Africa and develop 6,000 transformational leaders for the continent over a 50-year period. He also founded the African Leadership Network, Global Leadership Adventures, and African Leadership University, which is opening multiple universities across Africa to groom three million local leaders by 2060.

These are grand ambitions for sure, but Swaniker has always been ambitious. "I've always had big dreams," he says. "Even as a teenager, I was always planning and thinking about things that seemed unrealistic, grand, and dreamy. People used to say 'this guy is always dreaming.'" Even then, Swaniker was confident. "I had no doubt that I was going to be successful, and that I was going to achieve something and have impact," he says.

He is well on his way to realizing his ambitions through his ventures, and moving quickly and confidently has served him well. On a personal level, he has been recognized as a TED Fellow[3] and a World Economic Forum Young Global Leader.[4] *Forbes* magazine named him one of the "Top Ten Young Power Men in Africa".[5]

But Swaniker's voyage hasn't all been smooth sailing. He recalls writing ALA's first business plan while he was a student at the Stanford Graduate School of Business. "I have consistently underestimated the amount of money and time it takes to start something. When I started ALA, I had in the business plan that it was going to cost us $4 million to become sustainable. That was 15 years ago. Today, we have raised $100 million so far, and we'll need another $50 to $100 million to become sustainable."[6] A similar circumstance unfolded when Swaniker launched ALA's first summer program, one year after he graduated from business school. "I had projected that we would get 150 kids, each paying $4,000, for a total revenue of $600,000. We ended up getting around 35 paying students. I was way off, and ended up having to let some employees go as a result, which was really painful."

Even the biggest organizations sometimes fall prey to recklessness when they speed along with excess confidence.

Signs reading "Move Fast and Break Things" once decorated Facebook's offices, but that was long before the spread of fake news on the platform and before a scandal that leaked millions of users' data. Today, Mark Zuckerberg admits that the company has to take a more careful approach and do things differently. The signs urging people to move fast and break things are long gone.[7]

Even if you are by nature a hard worker and always keen to improve, you need to understand how your skills match your ambitions so your confidence doesn't outpace reality.

Axel Hedfors, who goes by the stage name Axwell, is an international superstar DJ, member of the Swedish House Mafia, two-time DJ Awards winner, Grammy Award nominee, and the producer of hits such as "Save the World," "Don't You Worry Child," and "One." He's always felt ambitious. "The first time I remember feeling ambitious was when I used to wash my parents' car when I was eight years old. At first, I washed the car for fun. But my dad corrected me and told me how to make it even more shiny, and I was always keen to improve. I always tried to make the car cleaner than the last time. It was ingrained in me."[8]

As Hedfors moved on in his music career, his inner drive remained consistent. "I always want to deliver something to the best of my ability. Good enough is not enough. I have to feel that any song or show is on the next level." To do this, he had to evolve. While making music was originally his hobby, it grew into a side gig and then into a full-time career. At the outset, his goal was to earn enough from music to sustain a living, but as the successes rolled in so did the aspirations.

"I surpassed my dream of becoming a professional musician early on, and from there I kept setting new goals—for example to have a number one hit in the US and in the UK. And to play in the biggest arenas." As his aspirations grew, Hedfors was always confident of his abilities. But he was not blind to reality. "I realized that I had to evolve, too. It was tempting to just continue playing and making hits based on techniques I already knew. But I realized that each time I set a new goal, I had to evolve my skills as well."

Do you recognize yourself in any of these stories?

Skill-Will Mismatch

Maverick and Iceman probably wouldn't have been good fighter pilots if they had lacked boldness. They wouldn't have been able to win so many duels without bravery and faith in their skills. That ability to move with confidence and speed is a real strength. Stretching yourself outside your comfort zone helps you break down boundaries and accomplish incredible feats, beyond the realm of ordinary. The confidence to try new things often leads to unexpected breakthroughs.

The gift of *Boldness* typically brings with it a concurrent urgency to act, which guarantees that something will happen and lead to progress or, at a minimum, new learning experiences. This is in sharp contrast to staying in your comfort zone, which can lead to stagnation as you're left in the same place, holding ambitions you never activate. Real progress requires stretching yourself and challenging convention—to an extent.

Swaniker says that his confidence enabled him to try to build something new where others might never have even gotten started. Nothing seemed like a hurdle to him, even if he had never done anything like it before. "I remember as a teenager, I had an idea to create a satellite dish. I sketched it out, collected some plastic and metal, and made a dome with wires and a transmitting device—it didn't work since I knew nothing about electrical engineering or telecommunications. It was just me playing around. I also had ideas about designing and building helicopters."[9]

But moving with too much speed and confidence can also get you killed or, at least, set you back significantly. Flying an F-14 jet at a top speed of more than 2,000 kilometers (1,200 miles) per hour is a dangerous business and can lead to painful lessons. Any new venture requires a fine balance of confidently trying something novel, yet understanding the limits of your abilities. Numerous ambitious people have failed to recognize the direct connection between the level of their ambition and the experience and skills they need to succeed. You can't expect to succeed in any venture without the necessary education, preparation, personal growth, and reflection.

This is the risk of the Frenemy *Boldness*, which compels ambitious people to plunge in full steam ahead without slowing down to amass the skills and information they need. Ambitious people can struggle with this Frenemy in three main ways:

First, they don't think about personal growth. Many ambitious people reach impressive positions with their youthful efforts, and they believe that they will continue to climb. They think that because they know about a problem and have an idea of how to fix it, their remedy will work. However, many iconic entrepreneurs have misjudged what it takes to establish a business. Consider the countless examples of free-spirited enthusiasts who quit their day jobs to set up a yoga retreat, a music production studio, or a social media marketing agency. Many such businesspeople struggle once reality sets in and teaches them that their ambitions require more than participant-level skills, passionate energy, a business card, and a website. There is a fundamental difference between boldly venturing forth and exploring areas in which you do not yet have what it takes—just ask Swaniker during his early foray into satellite-dish making.

Second, and along similar lines, people who are excessively bold may seek shortcuts or take unreasonable risks. If you see a gap between where you are now and where you want to go, you may be tempted to seek risky solutions and shortcuts to bridge it. You convince yourself that success hinges on finding that one magic ingredient, rather than on doing things in new and different ways. This could have been one of the reasons that Facebook initially struggled to identify and stem fake news on its platform.

Third, you may recognize that you need to grow and learn but underestimate what it takes to do so. Swaniker specializes in leadership development and personal development, so he understands his own path: "Whenever I have failed as a leader," he says, "it is because I have had blind spots, so I am on a constant journey toward self-awareness."[10]

One blind spot obscured some of the realistic issues he needed to deal with in business planning. "When I first started out," he recalls, "I had a strong belief that the market would behave a certain way, that all the people we hired would work out, that I would get the capital we required, and that the products and services we designed would work . . . I was perhaps too optimistic." Swaniker learned from his experiences. "I'm still optimistic about everything I do, but I've become more aware that even my best assumptions are sometimes not correct, and that I need to constantly learn."

Similarly, Hedfors notices that some young musicians don't make enough effort to improve. "Many talented artists lose out because they don't work hard enough," he explains. "They don't fully realize that the music industry is constantly evolving, and that they must evolve with it. Having one hit doesn't mean that your next song will be successful too."[11]

The root cause of a *Boldness* shortfall—when the friend becomes an enemy—is a mismatch between your level of ambition and the experience and skills you need to succeed. Ambitious people rarely have a gap in their yearning and drive to achieve. However, as they venture with speed and confidence into new environments, their skill level may not always keep up, and they may take unnecessary risks or fail to acknowledge the need for further development.

It can be difficult for ambitious, competent, and successful people to admit that their capabilities do not match their ambitions and eagerness to succeed. Their underlying mindset often is, "I don't need to improve to realize my ambitions" or "I can keep doing what I've always done." There is a belief that reaching your ambitions will be smooth sailing, and a tendency to underestimate what it truly takes to get there.

Psychology teaches about the hazards of this fallacy. The so-called "overconfidence effect" is a cognitive bias in which people's subjective belief in their abilities is not accurate; an objective appraisal shows that their skills fall short. This cognitive bias can lead to three pitfalls: overestimation of your performance, overplacement of your performance relative to others, and over-precision in your certainty about the accuracy of your assumptions.[12] In studies, test subjects' confidence levels systematically exceeded their actual abilities. For example, when they were 100% certain of their answers on a general knowledge test, it turned out they had given the wrong answers a whopping 20% of the time.[13]

This is perhaps best (and most entertainingly) illustrated by the Dunning-Kruger research on experience and confidence. The Dunning-Kruger effect is a cognitive bias in which people believe they are smarter and more capable than they really are. As self-awareness and experience with a subject increases, confidence typically declines to levels more reflective of one's actual level of skill. The researchers illustrate the phenomena with the 1995 criminal case of McArthur Wheeler, who robbed two banks in Pittsburg without wearing a disguise. He was caught later that day thanks to CCTV footage and was flabbergasted that the police had found him so quickly, as he had covered his face with lemon juice, which he believed would blur his image on the cameras. Wheeler was not short on confidence but was unable to accurately recognize his level of readiness to rob a bank, and he was therefore found rather lacking in terms of capabilities. A more experienced robber might have realized that they were setting themselves up for failure with the lemon juice approach and gone back to the drawing board to devise a new plan.[14]

Ambitious people may be more prone to overconfidence than others, since they have achieved success often in the past and are used to winning. Studies on animals show that winning increases testosterone and self-confidence, leading to a self-reinforcing cycle.[15] While this feedback loop can be positive, it can also lead to hubris if you start believing the hype about yourself, and it goes to your head. Even just believing you have won something (think of snowboarder Lindsey Jacobellis) may be enough to trigger a surge in hormones and confidence.

Another reason this mindset may be more prevalent in ambitious people is because *Boldness* is exciting. By definition, ambitious people are going somewhere—typically quickly. Many of them enjoy running uphill at a rapid clip much more than stopping to focus on personal growth or extra training. Moving fast administers an energizing adrenaline rush.

Left unchecked, *Boldness* can affect your Return on Ambition in a variety of ways. As you might expect, the biggest limitation the *Boldness* Frenemy imposes on the three dimensions of your Return on Ambition is that it hampers your growth. Neglecting this area for too long can lead to stagnation or even a regression in your required skills, as your level of ambition continues to increase. In the long run, this Frenemy can have a massive negative impact on achievement, especially when your external environment steadily becomes more demanding.

Achievement and growth must go hand in hand. Although you learn by doing, you must expend a conscious effort to learn and grow that is as massive as the future state you aspire to attain. For example, while many musicians play gigs all the time, rocking over and over to the same songs, improvement requires a different kind of practice. While many athletes play matches every week, they spend the vast majority of their training time honing and further developing their skills.

Boldness may not directly affect their short-run well-being, which might even increase for those who prefer constant full-throttle action. But over the medium and long run, well-being is likely to wane when growth and achievement begin to suffer.

What Got You Here Won't Get You There

Many ambitious people would have a hard time if they were forced to behave opposite to their inclinations—if rather than being fast and bold, they were forced to be slow and tentative. People in this sort of halting, hesitant state seem to be surrounded by static. They don't make progress. They're out of touch with their convictions and filled with hesitation. Staying in your comfort zone and doing only things you already know how to do can be stultifying.

But you don't need to move more slowly just for the sake of moving slowly. Instead, be sure to combine speed and confidence with continuous development. People with a high Return on Ambition constantly strive to improve themselves and the way they work on accomplishing their goals. They actively take the time to reflect on where they are compared to their ambitions and whether they would benefit from stopping and doing things differently once in a while. They are aware of their skill gaps and learning curve and make conscious efforts to address them.

"I do a lot of self-reflection about myself as a leader," says Swaniker. "I try to recognize patterns and learn from my mistakes, such as talks that went badly or investor meetings that could have gone better . . . I never believe I have 'arrived' as a leader. I am always developing." Like many ambitious people, Swaniker is extremely demanding of himself. "I have very high standards, especially for myself. I am always seeking to get better."[16]

People with a high Return on Ambition ensure *Boldness* includes a parallel drive to improve constantly. They remain aware that "what got me here won't get me there." They recognize that the right skills are always contextual and that every individual has areas that call for more personal development. They know there are no shortcuts to success.

To pursue his personal development, Swaniker constantly asks for feedback. "The way I develop is to try new things and ask for feedback. When things fail, that's often the best learning opportunity. As long as you are open to receiving advice and feedback, it can be very powerful."[17]

The best-selling author of *Grit*, Dr. Angela Lee Duckworth, is a professor of psychology at the University of Pennsylvania and renowned expert on resilience. She talks about the importance of constant self-development and advocates combining resilience, ambition, and self-control in pursuit of your long-term goals. This philosophy was ingrained in her in childhood. She recounts in an interview with *Quartz*, "My father would literally say things like 'You're no genius,' to me . . . The blessing of all this is that I never did think I was a genius . . . I did grow up to be someone who is ambitious, but also someone who never had the self-concept of being a genius or someone who is gifted."[18]

The key here is to pinpoint the areas you most need to develop and pursue that development in a focused way. This means trying new things, being deliberate about it, and pushing yourself beyond your comfort zone. The psychologist Lev Vygotsky terms this the "zone of proximal development,"[19] and entering it requires consistency and hard work.

"Today, anyone can set up a DJ studio," Hedfors says. "When I started playing around with music when I was 13, I had to save up to buy an Amiga 500, an early computer with only a few sounds and music functionalities. I had to work hard to make the tunes sound good, but I loved it. I was a nerd. Today, you can download an app on your smartphone and begin mixing tunes. It is a totally different era."[20]

From an early age, Hedfors was a keen student of music. He practiced hard. "I don't think I was talented at all. Rather, I worked on music all the time. Sometimes 24 hours a day. I always tried to build development into my schedule. For example, in the breaks in between shows, when I was feeling exhausted from performing, I would be learning about new tools, new software, and new theories, and watching the shows of other musicians to learn. Sometimes I had to get up early in the morning to fit it all in, but it was necessary to keep getting to the next level."

Another example of someone who is always looking to improve, despite achieving an array of success, is football (soccer) star Cristiano Ronaldo. He's won the *Ballon d'Or* (football player of the year) five times, has won more than twenty-five trophies, and is Real Madrid's all-time leading goal scorer. Ronaldo approaches his development as a football player with intense effort and a great deal of humility. He is bold and confident, but at all the clubs where he has played, his teammates and coaches consistently say that he is the hardest worker on the team and always wants to improve. He shows up at training one or two hours before his teammates and is often the last man to leave the training field, staying to work on his technique, dribbles, free kicks, and physical fitness.

Ronaldo's former fitness coach Giovanni Mauri reports that the football star followed a unique fitness routine. "We are talking about a world class player who, when we returned home at 2:00 a.m. from a Champions League away match, would not jet off home in his car. No, he would stop at the training center for at least an hour for various recovery exercises and cryotherapy."[21]

Even at the tail end of his career, Ronaldo had no intention of letting up. When he joined Juventus in the summer of 2018 at age 33, the club's doctors said he had the fitness level of a 20-year-old.[22] He quickly became the most dedicated person on the club's training field, impressing his new teammates. One player explained, "It is impossible to follow Cristiano Ronaldo in training. When we arrive, he is already training; when we leave he is still training, I have never seen a player like that."[23] Ronaldo could have gone to Juventus and said, "I've made it," but, instead, he is pushing himself to even higher levels of performance.

Being bold and moving with speed and confidence—keeping them in perspective—continues to remain a friend of ambitious people throughout their careers. Swaniker, Ronaldo, Duckworth, and Hedfors have not slowed the pace of their achievements; at times, they have even sped up.

As a result, the impetus to improve their skills continues to drive them. High-achieving people don't slow down their learning until their ambitions dwindle, which often happens to them only when they fully retire.

To master the *Boldness* Frenemy, you must understand yourself, your abilities, and your need to keep growing and learning. People with a high Return on Ambition have a keen sense of their current skills and the future skills their ambition will require.

Duckworth finds that the happiest, most successful people have a metacognitive self-understanding. "They can look at themselves and honestly understand what they're doing well and what they're not doing well . . . Eventually, they will mediate their weaknesses and raise their strengths. People who have no self-awareness, they're the ones you really worry about; they may be okay on certain dimensions, but they're never going to grow."[24]

Increasing your Return on Ambition also involves pushing yourself to the edge. Know that if you keep jumping off increasingly higher cliffs, your parachutes and technique must keep getting better. Indeed, you not only need to close the gaps you identify, but you also need to open new learning opportunities constantly. "As soon as I'm in a comfortable place, I make myself uncomfortable again," Duckworth continues.[25] This pursuit of self-development requires getting comfortable with ambiguity and realizing that in this increasingly complex and fast-paced world, the questions you will face in the future have not yet been posed, and the answers haven't yet begun to be formulated.

"Even when I don't know how I will figure something out, I am confident I will figure it out," says Swaniker. "You have to remain optimistic. The last thing ambitious people should lose is their optimism and faith. When in doubt, roll with the punches. If this were easy, others would have done it. Don't beat yourself up about having tried something and failed. Give yourself a pat on the back for having tried—and move on."[26]

OVER TO YOU

- *Have you ever been in this Frenemy's danger zone, where you moved forward boldly and neglected your blind spots? What pulled you into this zone? Could you have avoided it?*

- *How do you think about your own learning and development?*

- *How many hours a week do you spend on dedicated practice toward fulfilling your personal development goals?*

- *How could mastering the* Boldness *Frenemy increase your Return on Ambition?*

SEVEN

Frenemy 3—Independence

Do you have a penchant for getting things done by yourself, without the help of others? If so, how has this helped you? How could it hinder you?

THE TOUR DE France, the oldest, most prestigious bicycle race in existence, is the world's largest annual sporting event.[1] There have been over 100 editions since its founding in 1903. Riders compete through more than 20 days of racing (in "stages"), covering more than 3,000 kilometers (1,850 miles) in total. Some stages are as much as 230 kilometers, requiring more than 5 hours of biking.

Typically, more than 20 teams compete, each with 8 riders. Each team has one or more "protected" riders, who have the best chance of winning the overall race, winning a stage, or accumulating points. The other riders, called *domestiques*, do whatever it takes to support the protected riders, whether that means helping them climb a mountain by shielding them from the wind, cheering them on to raise morale, fetching water from the team car, and, in some cases, even sacrificing their bicycles to the lead rider if his suffers a mechanical failure. In addition, each team has two support cars, one of which carries the sporting director (similar to a coach) to provide instructions, and another carrying drinking water and spare bikes.

However, you cannot rely solely on your team to win. Moments come in every stage where an individual rider must step up and break free from the other riders if he is to cross the finish line first. This can entail a lung-busting ride up a mountain, safeguarding the lead against challengers who are attempting to pass you, or a host of other scenarios where the rider has to fight by himself. In addition, some of the stages in the Tour de France are individual time trials, where riders start one by one a couple of minutes apart and must complete the stage without the support of others. These time trials can have a significant impact on the overall and aggregate standings. Winning the Tour de France calls for a superb team, coupled with the ability to win alone when the situation requires it.

You may be wondering why we are talking about bicycles. Chances are, you aren't an elite racer and don't have seven support riders flanking you. But you can still understand the challenge of riding solo versus riding with a team. In fact, many ambitious people prefer to ride solo and feel that they must keep working independently to reach their goals. With or without teammates (co-workers), doing things by yourself can be tempting, especially when you believe you can do them quicker and better than other people. However, the solo hero strategy has its perils, and you must be aware of when the *Independence* Frenemy can emerge.

For example, take Ashkan Pouya and Saeid Esmaeilzadeh, who left Iran as kids in the 1980s during the Iran-Iraq War. When Pouya was 10 and Esmaeilzadeh was 8, they moved to Sweden as refugees. They vividly remember the move and the challenges of entering a country where they did not speak the language or even understand the alphabet. But they were eager to integrate, and they also remember looking forward to starting school and meeting new friends.[2]

Growing up, they had big dreams. Pouya had a three-part goal: build a body like Swedish model Marcus Schenkenberg, learn to fight like Bruce Lee, and become as successful as Bill Gates. Esmaeilzadeh, too, was always striving. At university, he studied not only medicine and chemistry, but also philosophy, history of religion, and logic and argumentation. Instead of partying, he took evening classes. One summer, he studied seven days a week for seven weeks in a row. Coupled with the credits from his evening classes, keeping that pace enabled him to complete his graduate degree one and a half years early. Immediately after, he began working toward his PhD.

Initially, the two friends found a great deal of individual success. Early in his career, Pouya pursued jujitsu and judo with great fervor. Competing as a professional martial arts athlete, he won several Swedish gold medals in both disciplines and a world championship medal in combat jujitsu. After completing his graduate studies in economics and innovation management, he switched his attention to entrepreneurship.

Esmaeilzadeh stayed on the academic route, pursuing a PhD in chemistry at Stockholm University. He graduated with a thesis on the "Crystal Chemistry of Manganese Tantalum Oxides" in 2000, and in 2002, at age 28, still at Stockholm University, he became Sweden's youngest associate professor.

"We were both very ambitious," Pouya says. "We would never have managed to constrain ourselves to nine-to-five jobs."

Esmaeilzadeh adds, "As a researcher, sometimes I would work all night, even though I wouldn't get paid extra. I was driven to finish my experiments more quickly, to see the results."

Pouya and Esmaeilzadeh were doing just fine independently, with impressive accomplishments and promising careers before age 30. Continuing as independent acts would have been tempting, but, in 2003, the childhood friends decided to join forces.

Their story began in Esmaeilzadeh's lab at midnight. He was crouched over an experiment he had been preparing for days, heating a carefully measured mixture of silicon nitride and additives up to 1,800 degrees. Then he left it to cool slowly on the oven overnight to form crystals. Happy with his midnight labors, he went home.

When he entered the lab the next morning, he quickly sensed that something was wrong. The oven was off and the cooling liquid had leaked onto the floor. The mixture had cooled rapidly, instead of gradually, congealing into a yellowish shard. Dismayed, Esmaeilzadeh stuck it in a box and put it away. He felt frustrated, since getting a new oven and redoing the crystallization experiment would take months.

Later, however, he began to think about the shard that had come out of the experiment. Looking at it under the microscope, he observed that it did not have a crystalline structure. It was amorphous like glass but much harder and almost as tough as a diamond. Esmaeilzadeh realized that he had created a new material and that he could be onto something significantly bigger than an academic paper. It took him a year to re-create the results. During that time, he called in Pouya, who immediately saw the product's commercial potential, for example, in automobiles, windows, and even contact lenses.

In 2003, the duo launched Diamorph, which now sells a wide range of advanced material solutions. In 2004, they founded Serendipity Innovations, now part of Serendipity Group. Their business model focuses on marrying leading academic research with rigorous business commercialization, perfectly blending the two men's core competencies. Since its inception, Serendipity has founded or invested in more than 15 technology companies. In 2019, its portfolio had a market value of about $400 million. In 2010, His Majesty King Carl XVI of Sweden awarded Pouya and Esmaeilzadeh the Swedish Årets Nybyggare Pionjär—Pioneers of the Year—prize.

Just the year before, the pair had faced a tough decision. Lund University offered Pouya the position of director of innovation to help it fulfill its vision of becoming Europe's leading university in fostering companies based on cutting-edge research. The offer tempted him, and the duo discussed it back and forth. They decided that Serendipity was a mature company and could survive with only Esmaeilzadeh at the helm. Pouya took the offer, and they parted ways.

The separation was short-lived, however. Both men felt stretched in their new roles—with Esmaeilzadeh managing the whole business and Pouya splitting his time between the business and the university. After nine months, they realized that they were missing the central ingredient of their success—their combined energies—and decided to reestablish their full-time partnership and run the business together.

Sanford Biggers is another ambitious person who has felt both the gift and the strain of *Independence* during his career.[3] Biggers is an interdisciplinary artist who works across painting, film, video, sculptures, music, and live performance. His work draws on a large range of influences—including African-American ethnography, hip hop music, African spirituality, Buddhism, jazz, and American icons—and he often adds political undertones to create awareness about contemporary issues. He has been presented internationally, including at the Tate Modern in London, the Renaissance Society in Chicago, and The Kitchen in New York.

Biggers grew up with numerous role models. "Everyone in my family is in medicine—my father, my brother, and my sister. The standard set in front of me was very high, and I therefore grew up with a high bar for achievement. My family never demanded that I follow a certain path," Biggers says, "but there was always an expectation that I would be successful, like my brother and sister."[4]

He recalls the pep talks his father used to give him. "'Regardless of what you do, you need to give it your all,' my father used to say. As a result, I always felt that I had to be above average, and that regardless of what I do, I had to get to a new level, because everyone around me has."

He gravitated toward art at an early age. "Because my siblings are eight and nine years older than me, I grew up alone a lot of the time. In early elementary school, I discovered art and used to paint at home for hours. It was a very solitary activity, because that's how the work gets done. But I also found it calming and therapeutic."

Art was not an immediate professional aspiration for Biggers. "I didn't know if I would become a professional. I didn't know where it would go." When he enrolled in college, he thought he was going to become a psychologist. "I had no idea that I could make it as an artist, and that it could be a viable career option. Therefore I needed a Plan B," he says.

By the second year of college, he had dropped Plan B, and he pursued an education in art, going on to obtain a master's in fine arts. He continued the mostly solitary practice of creating art throughout college. "After graduation," he says, "I focused on making art. I continued to do it the same way as before, and recognition came along the way. The stakes grew, but my principles for creating art stayed consistent." While some of Biggers's colleagues chose to set up a studio and hire a team of people to work with almost immediately after graduation, Biggers says he was "anti-that," maintaining a strong belief that he would be sacrificing authenticity if he went that route. He wanted to maintain his independence.

As Biggers became more recognized and the demand for his work grew, he began to feel the tension. "At one point, I was teaching at university for six hours a day and would then go to the studio for another eight or nine hours, to work on art. It was essentially two jobs, and I felt stretched." While Biggers acknowledges that the hectic schedule was fun for a while and gave him an adrenaline rush, it also meant there was little time for anything besides art. "I basically never slept," he says, and he had little time for a social life. He eventually saw that what he was doing was impractical. "I realized that to keep up with the pace of the industry, I had to make some changes. I had to start letting people in."

Do you recognize yourself in any of these stories?

The Lone-Wolf Syndrome

To win a bike race, a rider must be able to break free from the pack at exactly the right moment and sprint to the finish line. At some point, ambitious people, too, must ride independently if they wish to break new ground.

Being able to sculpt your own path and forge ahead is an important strength. In interviews, many ambitious people highlight pivotal moments where they shunned conventional wisdom and pursued their goals alone. Such grand ambition often requires just a little lunacy. It calls on you, by yourself, to see and believe in a future that does not exist—and to pursue it anyway.

Pouya and Esmaeilzadeh have developed numerous new products and processes that were completely unknown to the market when launched. They would be nowhere without the confidence and drive to pursue— together—what they believe in. And Biggers nurtures a gift of vision and imagination to create masterpieces that break the mold of what is possible.

The challenge comes when you believe that riding solo is not just an occasional sprint, but is also, in fact, the most efficient way to ride. This Frenemy has numerous manifestations. One manifestation is that ambitious people come to believe that they alone have to solve all the obstacles in their way. As a result, they don't ask others for help.

Biggers acknowledges that he had a romanticized view of art and the artist, which held him back from working with and through others. "I felt that my art had to be done by me. I believed there was a magic in me putting my intention behind every brush stroke, and even every email that I sent." Biggers felt he had to be involved in everything, to guide it in the right direction. "I wanted to be responsible and accountable for whatever came out of my studio."[5]

A second manifestation is perfectionism. Some ambitious people think that if others can't do things exactly the way they envision, they must do it themselves. They often set high standards, but knowing how to accomplish something yourself requires different skills than teaching, enabling, and supporting others to do it. When ambitious perfectionists realize that others will not or cannot meet their standards, they often believe the only solution is to take on the work themselves and work harder. This not only burns them out, but it also can leave their colleagues, friends, and family feeling sidelined and unworthy.

Third, what often happens (inadvertently or not) is that people with *Independence* fail to include those around them in their ambitions, as if they are running a different race where everyone else is irrelevant. Ambitious talents who want to progress quickly through the organizational hierarchy often fall prey to wanting to be the lone, heroic action figure. They don't think that they are doing anything "wrong," but they are disrupting the status quo—and not always in a good way. Their colleagues may begin to resent their ambitious nature and constant desire to "fix" things as if they alone hold the secret to every solution. Leaders who fall from this height—when teamwork could have saved them—deal their careers a terrible blow.

Another example emerges when the realization of an ambition has multiple constituents. The pitfall here is that important stakeholders—many of whom have to support the ambition in one way or another—are brought into the race too late. And, as a result, they either reject the request for support, make negative comments, or even begin to actively or passively sabotage the initiative.

For leaders, in particular, this can result in what some people call "solo leadership." This is leadership without the support of your team or constituents. The leader begins to call all the shots, without involving or consulting the other people involved. This risks making the ambition synonymous with the leader, rather than with the organization. Solo leadership may work (and even be the desired approach) with simple and more routine challenges. However, the moment a leader faces more complex challenges—challenges where people around the leader need to change what they're doing—solo leadership falls short.

The root cause of this behavior is the "lone-wolf" syndrome. This syndrome can compel you to take charge of everything yourself with the conviction that it's the quickest and best way forward in all situations. This can result from a number of core beliefs, such as "I know best and can achieve my ambitions by myself," "Asking for help is a sign of weakness," "Involving others in my ambitions will slow me down," and "Helping others is a waste of my time."

This mindset can have many triggers. One common cause is having a family upbringing, societal view, or corporate culture that stresses the importance of independence. You grow up believing that, to succeed, you need to "go out and get it." Biggers admits that he felt additional pressure because his career path was not the same as his father's or siblings', who all became doctors. "I had a lot to prove," Biggers says. "I didn't want to be the broke-artist son. This made me work like crazy, to show the world that I could succeed on my own. I felt that getting help in my studio was a sign that I was not organized and not able to handle the workload."[6]

A second common trigger is the experience gained working in teams. Ambitious people often have experienced group projects where some people didn't pull their weight. In fact, many ambitious people chafe against situations where other people slow them down because their job requires them to coordinate with others and incorporate their opinions.

Early on, Pouya and Esmaeilzadeh recognized the challenges of working together. "We had extremely different working styles, given our different backgrounds," Esmaeilzadeh says.[7]

Pouya continues: "I remember the first time that Saeid reviewed what I had put together for Diamorph's business plan—he crossed out half the text because it was forecasts for the future, and it wasn't grounded in confirmed facts!"

Esmaeilzadeh was driven by the pursuit of knowledge—money was just a means to get there—while Pouya was focused on business planning and generating a profit. They agree that if they hadn't been childhood friends with a deep connection, the cooperation could have ended the day they reviewed the first business plan.

A third trigger can be hubris, similar to the Frenemy *Boldness*. When people are overconfident in their abilities and feel that they know best, *Independence* limits their willingness to listen to others.

Finally, *Independence* can be involuntary. Ambitious people may find themselves in a situation in which no one else believes in their visions, or their associates are against the changes they are making. The Renaissance-era astronomer Copernicus was ridiculed and even threatened with death for contradicting the Catholic Church, when he postulated that the sun, rather than Earth, is the center of the universe. Misunderstood geniuses often have to go their own way until others recognize that they were right all along.

In such situations, some ambitious people adopt a "with me or against me" mindset, dig into their trenches, and push even harder by themselves.

Why does this affect ambitious people more than others? In today's world, speed matters. Ambitious people often have defined goals and believe speed is essential in achieving their objectives. "I know where I need to go," you may be thinking. "Now it's just about getting there fast." The desire to realize your ambitions right now can be like riding downhill on a bike where you don't notice anything or anyone except the road ahead—but if you feel tempted to forsake relationships for short-term gain, consider the long-term consequences.

Another reason the *Independence* Frenemy is more prevalent in ambitious people is that they've often experienced early successes where they accomplished certain goals relatively independently with little or no external support, whether that meant getting good grades in school, setting up a business at a young age, or creating music or art. This starts in school where children benefit from a system that rewards individual merit. Thereafter, it can lead to early career successes. Extrapolating this into the future, they believe they can continue to solve challenges on their own, even as the complexity and scale of those challenges grow. "Ambitious people often believe that their vision is the best and that we know everything," Biggers says. "We think we can control not only the ship, but also the wind that directs its course."[8]

Pouya and Esmaeilzadeh had great success in their individual careers before deciding to join forces. Although they were better together, each man knew that he would always be able to fall back on his individual merits—and they were each tempted to do that during their brief stint apart.

Independence can undermine the three dimensions of your Return on Ambition in multiple ways. Your race to achievement can hit a wall when you are no longer able alone to solve all the challenges that come your way because you have piled too much on your plate. Or you can crash when you stop having all the answers and realize you require different expertise and more diverse knowledge and experience. Or the crash can come when people around you are no longer willing to support you in your perceived individual pursuit.

As noted, being able to ride solo in a sprint and accomplish things quickly on your own is a key strength. However, often you'll face a trade-off between short-term gain from sprinting away and longer-term losses, when the main pack of riders catches up to you and threatens to surpass you.

Solo riders may also find that having fewer collaborators can visibly affect their well-being. Solo riding can be lonely, and the loss of support, brainstorming, and collegiality can undermine the lone warrior's motivation. In addition, performance challenges can have a spillover effect, leading to solo riders feeling stressed and overwhelmed. Biggers certainly felt this strain, as demand for his art grew, and he was forced to work harder to keep up.

Growth is an interesting facet of the balance between going it alone and working with a team. *Independence* can stretch you and put you in a multitude of new situations that require you to grow. However, everyone has their limits, more so in today's increasingly complex and fast-moving world. "I felt that continuing to do everything myself was stunting my growth as an artist," Biggers says. "As my ideas were getting bigger, I found that there were things I couldn't do, and skill sets I didn't have. It was humbling, but that realization was a pivotal moment in my growth as an artist."[9]

Going it alone, you also lose the opportunity to learn from others, and you risk not taking the time to reflect properly on where you truly need to grow.

Riding in a Pack

People with a high Return on Ambition often prove to be highly independent and able to carve out their own path in life. They set goals and seek to reach them. They are courageous and dare to be different. At times, it seems like personal ambition and being self-driven are synonymous with being independent and going it alone. If you've found your voice and carved out your direction, it is only natural to seek to maintain as much independence as possible. And if that describes you, you'll probably do just fine.

But if you want to maximize your Return on Ambition, it doesn't stop there. No one wins the Tour de France without a team. Even when a rider breaks free from the pack, the support cars and teammates are by his side. The conductor has the orchestra. A Formula 1 driver has a whole cavalry of support—just watch any pit stop. Athletes (and increasingly nonathletes) have coaches. We almost never hear a successful person say, "I did it all by myself." Rather, those who truly succeed are highly interdependent with others. Oscar thank-you speeches are long for a reason.

Moving from independent to interdependent requires the conviction that you are stronger in a pack than by yourself. Consider the analogy that it is easier to break one stick than a whole bundle. This mindset rests on several core beliefs: "Other people can help make me stronger," "Seeking help is a sign of maturity and strength," and "Helping others enlarges the pie."

"I definitely had a shift in mindset," Biggers says. He points to when he lived for three years in Japan, where he experienced a seamless integration of cultures and spent time in a Zen temple. Regular meditation helped him gain more self-awareness, and he realized that he did not always have the answer and that there is always a gray zone.

"I began feeling more comfortable in the gray area, and realized that I'm fallible, like everyone else," Biggers says, explaining his decision to establish a team and begin to partner more broadly on his creations.

For example, when he aspired to create a gigantic Black Power fist as the headboard of a king-sized bed, he was introduced to an artist who had done similar work before, and he decided to collaborate. "I realized that I didn't need to reinvent the wheel each time. If I had done it myself, it would have taken three or four times longer." Biggers describes his new mindset as knowing he is blessed to have a team. He acknowledges that he can't reach his goals without the help of other people.

The shift to a collective point of view can be uncomfortable. You may feel as if you're giving up control, power, and speed. Collaboration requires humility and the underlying conviction that life is a team game with enough to gain for everyone and that, despite initial challenges, a diversity of resources and views will lead to better outcomes.

Biggers admits it was uncomfortable to give up control and that he had to start seeing his art more as jazz, which is all about improvisation, instead of classical music, which is meant to be played as it is written. "I've allowed some wiggle room for my art to take on a different shape, through collaboration."

For some people, moving from independent to interdependent means building a support network, but remaining firmly in the driver's seat. For others, it means partnering, like Pouya and Esmaeilzadeh.

Sometimes, avoiding the *Independence* Frenemy calls for rallying people around you so that they are engaged in your ambitions in one way or another. Since ambitious people stick out, you can easily—and sometimes inadvertently—ruffle the feathers of those with a vested interest in the status quo. You need to bring your various stakeholders on board, rather than pretending that they do not exist or are simply hurdles you must surmount.

However you assemble your formal and informal teams, the effort is usually worth it. "A big part of Serendipity's success comes from the energy we create when we are together," Pouya explains. Esmaeilzadeh adds, "We are often compared to the chipmunks Chip and Dale, who do everything together. Some even say that we look very alike! The different skills we bring to the table are critical—one with a business mindset and one at the forefront of research. In addition, we know we have each other's backs . . . we back each other up. When things are challenging, we are able to maintain perspective and focus on the next steps."[10]

Conquering the *Independence* Frenemy has two prongs: You must be strong on your own and united with your support network. Moving away from solo riding does not mean shunning it completely. The key is to establish the proper support structure around you and to hang on to your important stakeholders and supporters, even when taking solo sprints. Maintaining a mindset of collaboration rather than conquest can greatly increase your Return on Ambition, since it provides cover when you're cycling up the mountain, positions you to take occasional strategic sprints, and keeps you motivated even during the worst thunderstorms.

Biggers says that he still needs to spend a lot of time alone to gather his thoughts and take a step back. He still has the urge to do things independently but says he has found a "wiser way of working" by focusing on the things he is best at and which he enjoys the most. The result? "I can do more work, and better work," Biggers says. "And I have more time for family and leisure."[11]

OVER TO YOU

Take each one of your major ambitions one by one.

- *Who do you have around you who knows the details of your ambition?*

- *Who supports you and provides motivation?*

- *Who serves you with inspiration or as a sounding board?*

- *Who actually helps you progress toward this ambition?*

- *Who else might you need to involve? To get a second opinion? To ask for help?*

- *Who do you want to keep in the loop or bring along the way?*

- *How could mastering the* Independence *Frenemy increase your Return on Ambition?*

EIGHT

Frenemy 4—Competitiveness

Do you have the desire to outcompete others and be the best? If so, how has this helped you? How could it hinder you?

IN 2006, ONE of modern-day football's (soccer's) biggest corruption scandals unfolded in Italy. *Calciopoli* (translated as "Footballville" or "Footballgate"), as it was called, involved the biggest football clubs in the country. A prolonged police investigation, including wiretaps, uncovered systematic match rigging. Recorded telephone calls revealed that the leaders of certain football clubs were pressuring the officials in charge of Italian referees and attempting to influence referee appointments and, thereby, win games. There were even allegations that the culprits locked noncooperative referees in team dressing rooms. The results hit five of Italy's biggest football clubs hard, most notably Juventus, which officials stripped of its 2004 and 2005 Serie A titles and relegated to the second-tier league.[1] The teams involved had been prepared to win at any cost, and it backfired spectacularly.

Many ambitious people recognize a similar tendency to compare themselves to others. They wonder how to be better than anyone else, even when beating them has nothing to do with furthering their own goals. That's what happens when they let *Competitiveness* take over, making them overly focused on winning. They may believe that realizing their ambitions is a zero-sum game, where their success depends on getting a larger share of a limited pie—and cutting other people out. This can include not only accomplishing higher achievements, but also becoming better known and more popular. It can furthermore include the need to "be right" at all costs.

Magnus Olsson was on that path when he went through a journey of developing more self-awareness and choosing his battles in order to become a better leader, husband, and father.[2] Olsson is the co-founder and chief experience officer of Careem, a Dubai-based transportation company with operations in more than 100 cities in the Middle East, Africa, and South Asia. Uber acquired the company for $3.1 billion in 2019, just seven years after it was launched.

Olsson has always felt ambitious. As a child he was driven to learn and understand how things work. But, he says, his ambition never focused on winning; rather he always wanted to do something meaningful for the world. He calls his ambition his creative force.

Nonetheless, he still has felt the tension and pressure ambition can generate. First, he noticed an emerging pattern in his work and his personal life of having a strong reaction whenever people challenged his point of view. In a meeting, a colleague once argued for approaching a business challenge in a different way than the one Olsson advocated. While the discussions focused on making a business decision, Olsson took the disagreement personally. "I felt that my intellect was being challenged, and my first reaction was to fight back and assert my superiority."[3] He launched a bombardment of facts and logical arguments to showcase his intellectual dominance.

"Even after I had made my points, I continued to pinpoint things the other person had not thought about, thereby undermining his credibility . . . and making myself look and feel better." Olsson quickly regretted smothering his colleague so badly, but it was too late. The colleague was left deflated and the damage was done.

Such situations happened a couple of times, but Olsson's real wake-up call came a few months later. A business trip put him in a different time zone than his Dubai-based colleagues. He woke up one morning to find numerous missed calls from a senior colleague and a message saying, "Call me, it's urgent." Due to the time difference, however, Olsson couldn't reach his colleague.

"I got extremely anxious. I was focused on myself, and I kept wondering what I could have done wrong." Olsson passed eight anxious hours before he received a call back from his colleague. "The urgent news was that our latest round of fundraising had hit a snag, and it was in jeopardy. This was terrible news for the company, but initially I felt elated that I was not the problem—it wasn't about me! I realized that this was sick: I was more worried about my image and about being found to have done something wrong than I was about the immediate future of the company. That's when I knew I had to change."

Throughout her tennis career, Li Na has also felt the gift and pitfalls of being fiercely competitive—a story she recounts honestly in her autobiography. Li is the most successful Chinese tennis player ever and was the first Asian-born player to be inducted into the International Tennis Hall of Fame. She achieved a career-high ranking of second in the world and won nine Women's Tennis Association (WTA) singles titles. This included two Grand Slam singles titles at the 2011 French Open and 2014 Australian Open, making her the first Grand Slam singles champion from Asia.

For Li, the need to be competitive started early. She began playing badminton as a child, but her coach, Xia Xiyao, of the local Wuhan youth tennis organization, convinced her to switch to tennis, a bigger and more lucrative stage. However, to make the change, she had to win. In her memoir, she recalls Coach Xia telling her, "If you want to get onto the school's team, you must first defeat one of my players."[4] Li knew her father also was determined to have her join the team, and she felt heavy pressure to win, which she did. She was eight years old.

When Li was 11, she was one of several classmates from her local amateur sports school who was invited to train with the more competitive province-wide team. Coaches told the players that only one spot was available, and she knew she had to work very hard to make it. She was the youngest player in the group, and although she worked hard, she did not make the cut.

"This was the first time in my life that I really understood the meaning of the word 'competition,'" Li says.

Li continued to train hard, and she was eventually successful. When she was 15, she won the National Tennis League finals in China, becoming the youngest champion ever in the adult division. She soon got the opportunity to further her skills by attending a tennis academy sponsored by Nike in the United States. She moved to the United States for 10 months despite never having been there before and not speaking any English. After she returned to China, things started developing more quickly, and Li turned professional in 1999, before she became 18. She won a host of local tournaments and also competed in prestigious WTA Grand Slam tournaments. By 2002 she reached the rank of number 296 in the world.

Behind her tough exterior, however, Li was struggling. She had always sacrificed some degree of well-being in the name of achieving her goals, including feeling immensely homesick while she was away from her family and enduring tough coaching methods from an early age. "Under the shining banner of achievement," Li recalls, "any means were quietly permitted." She admits that she experienced many negative effects from this method. She had been feeling the pressure to perform accumulating inside her since she was 11.

In 2002 she reached her tipping point. The mental and physical strain led to a stress-related disorder linked to her menstrual cycle. As her symptoms got worse, she reached the point where she was unable to train both in the mornings and the afternoons as she was accustomed to doing.

"No matter how much I loved tennis, I wasn't going to let it ruin my health and happiness," Li recalls. In 2002, at only 20, she retired from the sport.

Throughout his life, serial entrepreneur Peter Thiel similarly learned important lessons about the nuances of competition. Thiel co-founded PayPal, an online payment system, and was the first outside investor in Facebook, the online social network giant. He has earned billions from starting various companies and making successful investments in early-stage technology start-ups. He founded the Thiel Fellowship and wrote the best-selling book *Zero to One: Notes on Startups, or How to Build the Future.*

"When I look back on my younger self, I was insanely tracked, insanely competitive," Thiel says during an interview on Tim Ferriss's podcast show.[5]

He attended Stanford University for his undergraduate studies and then

Stanford Law School. He went on to join the prestigious Manhattan law firm Sullivan & Cromwell. However, he quickly realized that he had joined the firm for the wrong reasons and that his primary motivation—beating others—was seriously flawed.

"Looking back at my ambition to become a lawyer," Thiel recalls, "it looked less like a plan for the future and more like an alibi for the present."

Thiel lasted only seven months in the firm before he decided to quit. He was not done competing, however.

"Just as I was leaving the law firm, I got an interview to compete for a Supreme Court clerkship. This is sort of the top prize you can get as a lawyer. It was the absolute last stage of the competition. But I lost. At the time I was totally devastated. It seemed just like the end of the world."

In hindsight, however, it was a valuable life lesson: Thiel learned the importance of being competitive with both eyes open. "If I hadn't lost that last competition . . . I never would have left the track I'd laid down since middle school. I wouldn't have moved to California and co-founded a start-up. I wouldn't have done anything new."[6]

Do you recognize yourself in any of these stories?

Creating a Fictitious Stage

The seeds of ambition are often sown in childhood. School makes children chase good grades and accolades in a setting where doing well depends on being compared to each other—if you win, your friends lose. Adults tell little kids to follow victorious role models and to pursue competitive ideas of success. This drive starts early, led by well-meaning parents who adorn kids' rooms with swimming medals, attendance certificates, science fair blue ribbons, and football trophies. It makes children and their parents proud. While many of these competitions are worthwhile, they also shape a child's mentality.

To be sure, *Competitiveness* can be a fabulous quality, and it can generate grit, determination, and persistence. Competitive people often have an iron will to win, even when the going gets tough. In addition, they tend to have a heightened ability to understand their rivals and to read them well—a great edge, especially in head-to-head combat. By nature, humans are competitive and apt to compare themselves with others, traits our ancestors undoubtedly found handy.

The challenge arises when the desire to "beat others" and to prioritize your relative achievements or status—rather than your absolute achievements or status—clouds your thinking. While that's human nature, it doesn't always lead to optimal outcomes. One study illustrated this point and showed that what makes people happy is less related to their total wealth (how much they can buy with their money) and more attuned to their relative wealth compared to other people—which is another form of competition.

Researchers tested study participants in pairs.[7] Side by side, they had to individually carry out the simple task of counting dots on a screen. Based on their performance, they received a reward of 30–120 euros. Each participant also learned how much money their counterpart received.

Researchers performed brain scans on the subjects throughout the test, paying special attention to monitoring the ventral striatum, the region of the brain activated by rewards. As expected, when a player completed the task correctly, that activated the ventral striatum. Its activity subsided when the person gave a wrong answer. However, the biggest spurt of brain activity registered when someone got a right answer *and* his or her colleague was wrong. In short, regardless of your absolute wealth, your money seems more rewarding to you if those around you have less than you do.

Interestingly, the pain of having less wealth than one's counterparts was stronger than the joy of having more. People have an innate drive not just to be socially superior, but also—even more so—to avoid being deemed inferior.

The ability to understand the playing field you're on, and to compete and win against others, is clearly important. But given that we've told you *Competitiveness* is a Frenemy—part friend, part enemy—you could see this caveat coming: If you have too much competitive drive, it will work against you—and it can be downright harmful.

In the "counting dots" experiment, the subjects perceived their reward to be more valuable (regardless of its face value) only when they did better than their counterparts, even though the other people were their neutral peers in this instance and not their rivals. While these participants agreed that more wealth is, naturally, more desirable than less wealth, the experiment points out the potential pitfalls of focusing on relative gain (outperforming your neighbor) rather than on what is truly important to you.

The *Competitiveness* Frenemy can get the best of even the most well-grounded people, either in fleeting moments or over longer time periods. It can play out in four major ways:

First, at a macro level, you may compare yourself with others and concentrate on beating them rather than on pursuing your ambitions. Relative gains become more important than absolute progress toward your goals.

Thiel says this need to triumph over others is one of the biggest dangers of competition. "It focuses us on the people around us, and while we get better at the things we're competing on, we lose sight of anything that's important, or transcendent, or truly meaningful in our world."[8]

Second, at a more micro level, you feel you must win every battle and that everything always must be done your way so you can be perfect. You see every outcome—win or lose—as a direct reflection of your self-worth. This can extend beyond your individual sphere as well; we've encountered ambitious leaders who believe that their team's accomplishments are a direct reflection of their worthiness as a leader and as a person. These leaders fear their team members' potential mistakes, and, as a result, their desire for perfection goes into overdrive. This can lead them to exercise an overbearing management style where they double-check their team members' work and correct their mistakes harshly.

The third manifestation is a perception that someone is monitoring every move you make. The workplace is rife with constant comparisons and constant perception management. For example, certain colleagues write office emails late at night or over the weekend to make sure their manager sees "how hard they are working" compared to other people. Or you help your colleagues, but you make sure to copy your managers on the resulting email. It's as if you're saying, "Look how smart and helpful I am." Interestingly, people often have a blind spot in this regard. While they don't believe they would resort to this type of behavior themselves, they immediately notice similar conduct in their team members or subordinates.

Fourth, constantly competing with and comparing yourself to others can have an influence on you outside your professional sphere. This Frenemy plays out on a much more regular, subtle basis in the way you interact with your friends and colleagues. Ambitious people we interviewed admitted that they sometimes find themselves hoping that their friends will do well but not too well. Even with friends, people often think about how they compare.

At times, you find "serial one-uppers" who always have to do one notch better than other people. "I went rock climbing during my vacation," says Friend Number One. "That's nothing; I went skydiving and that's way more extreme," says Friend Number Two, offering Friend Number One absolutely no acknowledgment or excitement, in fact, barely listening at all. "One-upping" becomes a game that ambitious people play in social settings, often without realizing they are playing it at all.

The root cause of this facet of the *Competitiveness* Frenemy is what we call "creating a fictitious stage." It emerges when ambitious people focus more on comparing themselves to others than on their own work. This behavior's underlying mindset is often, "I need to be better than others," or, more comically, "Second place is the first loser."

This can manifest when your self-worth, or even your identity, is tied directly to your external achievements. You see your accomplishments as a zero-sum game. Your goal isn't to achieve; it's to beat others. Coupled with insecurity and some doubt that you have what it takes to achieve your goals—a prevalent theme in our interviews and our work with ambitious people—this Frenemy can become especially forceful.

"I've always felt that I was nobody special," Li admits.[9] Her coaches focused on her weaknesses rather than her strengths, and Li never felt she could do anything right, even as a child. She developed a strong internal critic, her "internal referee," who did not let mistakes slip by unnoticed.

Thiel also recalls colleagues who felt unable to leave their jobs as lawyers, even though they were unhappy. He remembers their disbelief when he quit his prestigious law firm job just seven months in.

He explains, "All you had to do was go out the front door and not come back. But psychologically this was not what people were capable of, because when their identity was defined by competing so intensely with other people, they could not imagine leaving."[10]

If this is your approach, you will never be truly happy or effective in realizing your ambitions. If you associate every move with your image, you push yourself into a situation where you care more about stroking your ego and maintaining your status than accomplishing your goals. At one extreme, life can become just a series of events where you need to prove your self-worth, like a constant beauty pageant. You need to look better than the others; if you're not the best looking, then you are a failure. You create a fictitious stage where you're always on the runway.

Competitiveness is often more prevalent in ambitious people, and it is easy to see why:

First, they are driven to become more than they are and to accomplish grand visions. They often feel as if they need to prove themselves. This intense drive and desire for success can spur you on, but it also can lead to a fixation on some particular goal and the fear of not achieving it. Ambitious people can become so consumed by such a goal that they will stop at nothing to get it.

Second, higher-status people with greater degrees of wealth and social position are more prone to making competitive social comparisons since they feel they have more to lose. They eschew perceived downward mobility. Because of their lofty ambitions, they are more competitive and more risk averse.[11]

Third, when researchers evaluated students against meaningful, well-known standards (such as class rank), their competitiveness increased as their proximity to the highest performance standard increased. In other words, when ambitious people are closer to the top in terms of social definitions of success, they become increasingly intent on achieving the peak.[12]

Fourth, in ambitious environments where everyone is bent on winning (including those already at the top), playing along may be the easier alternative. Feedback loops are often rapid, and mistakes do not go unnoticed.

Competitiveness can help you reach your ambitions, but it can also become a liability and ultimately hurt your Return on Ambition. Although your achievements may benefit in the short run from your ability to compete, constantly comparing yourself to others can weigh you down over time. You can harm your growth if you develop the wrong capabilities by focusing on outshining others, instead of focusing on what truly matters and what makes you distinctive. You can also undermine your well-being, since always having to win can be exhausting. You will get drained if you approach each day as a new battle, and focusing on the wrong contests can weaken you when it really counts.

Playing Your Part

You may feel that the world is indeed a stage and that you need to be better than others and maintain a certain self-image. In many ways, *Competitiveness* is a strength that can take you far. You never want to be blindsided by competition, and you shouldn't hide the good work you do. However, people who gain a high Return on Ambition have learned to temper their competitive drive. They set aside the goal of beating others merely so they can feel superior or just for the sake of it. Rather, they measure themselves against their own standards and focus on continually improving themselves.

This requires having an underlying mindset that you are on your own path toward your goals and that others' successes do not lessen your accomplishments. With this attitude, you can maintain a clear path toward your objectives and celebrate your achievements in a genuine, humble way.

To understand this, Thiel had to undergo the devastation of losing a job he badly wanted. Olsson had to endure eight anxious hours and a phone call that awakened him to his misaligned priorities. Similarly, Li had to go through painful health problems and take time away from tennis in order to reach her ultimate potential.

To cultivate this mindset and avoid a painful wake-up call, learn to pick your battles instead of getting caught up in the heat of the moment. Avoid continuing a fight just because you started it. Chapter 16, "Frenemy Radar," will provide you with a powerful tool for this kind of restraint. Another way to beat the *Competitiveness* Frenemy is to demonstrate humility and to let go of always being in charge or always having to be right. This can be challenging, yet the payoffs are often great.

Research has confirmed that humility leads to better decision-making and a stronger intuition about when you might be wrong.[13] In addition, those who don't have sufficient humility are more likely to overreact in conflicts.[14]

Magnus Olsson recalls how he realigned his focus. "Whenever I over-reacted, I would regret it and wish I had acted differently. To overcome my reactive tendencies, I focused on pausing in the moment, during discussions and meetings. At a deeper level, I explored why I was being triggered, and I had to learn how to let go of the need to always appear intellectually superior."[15] Olsson confirms that this was a long, deliberate process. While he can still get triggered to overreact, that pattern emerges to a much lesser degree than before.

As a result, the energy during his company's meetings has completely shifted. He explains, "Today, success in a meeting is that we make decisions, that there is progress, and that there is a feeling of excitement in the team. I am no longer focused on leaving the meeting with everyone thinking that I'm the smartest guy in the room."

Olsson acknowledges that his team now makes better decisions because everyone is able to contribute fully. Meetings are more productive, and the team environment is warmer. "It is exhausting and unnecessary to try con-tinuously to maintain a self-image and certain perception of yourself. The sooner you can realize this and let it go, the better," he says.

He also learned that humility and achievement are not trade-offs. "You don't have to give up your ambition just because you decide not to define yourself based on your achievements. It's two different things. In fact, I would argue that reducing your ego and letting go of the need to win for the sake of winning will help you focus on the right things and, as a conse-quence, you will be more successful."

Another facet of a more balanced view of competition is seeing it for what it is and not letting it define your life. Li went from playing tennis *to prove* herself to playing *for* herself. After a two-year hiatus, she rejoined tennis with a new mindset: "Don't put too much pressure on yourself. . . . Just do your best."[16]

Continuous self-awareness can help too. Says Thiel, "I've become much more self-aware over the years about the problematic nature of a lot of the competition. I deliberately take time to think, and ask myself daily 'How do I become less competitive in order that I can become more successful?'"[17]

Becoming aware of and better managing *Competitiveness* can have an important impact on all three elements of your Return on Ambition. It can strengthen your relationships with yourself and with others, as it helps you develop more authenticity and trust. It relieves the pressure of always having to win. And it keeps you focused on the things that really matter to you.

OVER TO YOU

- *Do you sometimes focus on winning and beating others, just for the sake of it?*

- *If so, where does this urge come from?*

- *Will the battle you are fighting be worth it five years from now?*

- *How could mastering the* Competitiveness *Frenemy increase your Return on Ambition?*

NINE

Frenemy 5—Perseverance

Do you often commit yourself to going the extra mile and completing challenging tasks, even when you're overloaded? If so, how has this helped you? How could it hinder you?

A ZEN STUDENT went to his teacher and said earnestly, "How long will it take me to attain enlightenment?" The teacher's reply was casual: "Ten years." Impatiently, the student answered, "But I want to get there faster than that. I will work very hard. I will meditate 10 or more hours a day if I have to. How long will it take then?" The teacher thought for a moment and replied, "Twenty years."

This story may remind you of many ambitious people who are in constant overdrive and work themselves to the bone. Sometimes, the dream of a more compelling future can spur you to try to sprint a full marathon. You may feel that you must operate nonstop to reach your goals. Although this can help you move quickly, even if you can maintain this pace for an extended period of time, it carries risks and can trip you up.

Arianna Huffington, successful entrepreneur and best-selling author of more than 15 books, knows this better than most. She found it out the hard way while working as the co-founder of the *Huffington Post*. Two years into the launch of *HuffPost*, she collapsed from exhaustion. "I broke my cheekbone and needed four stitches over one eye." She says she was doing well by outward measures, but on the inside, things were not well. "I collapsed from exhaustion, burnout and sleep deprivation. . . . By any sane definition, if you find yourself lying in a pool of blood on your office floor, you are not 'successful.'"[1]

Elon Musk, one of today's most ambitious and successful entrepreneurs, has also fallen prey to this *Perseverance* Frenemy. Musk has ambitions to change the world and help humanity. His ventures include producing the Tesla electric car, making space tourism mainstream, improving solar energy, and creating ultra-fast travel through Hyperloop trains. Very few people come close to his degree of ambition. He has a jaw-dropping resume: founded X.com, which merged with Confinity to become PayPal, the online payment platform; founded the space technology company SpaceX; and co-founded Tesla and Neuralink, a developer of implantable brain-computer interfaces. And he certainly doesn't need to work for the money; he has an estimated net worth of more than $80 billion, making him one of the 10 richest people globally in 2020.[2]

Musk's achievements and bold ambitions are inspiring. However, he is extremely busy and has in the past attempted to balance two CEO jobs with the development of new ventures, as well as spending time with his family, which includes six children. And it doesn't always work. Musk admitted in a *New York Times* interview in 2018 that he was working 120 hours a week, feeling overwhelmed with stress and, sometimes, taking medication to sleep. He said that the past year had been the most "difficult and painful year of my career," and admitted that he hadn't taken off more than a week since 2001—when he caught malaria.[3]

"There were times when I didn't leave the factory for three or four days—days when I didn't go outside," he said. "This has really come at the expense of seeing my kids. And seeing friends." He says on his 47th birthday in 2018, he spent 24 hours at work. "All night, no friends, nothing." During the interview he was clearly emotional and teary-eyed. At times, he had trouble mustering the words he wanted to say.[4] However, slowing down is not easy, and Musk believes he has "no option" but to keep working this hard to keep his companies afloat.

Ambitious people can find it extremely hard to stop pushing themselves, since they are so set on achieving their dreams. Often, like Musk, they see no other path. If the going gets tough, they work harder.

Amelia Boone, attorney turned endurance racer, also felt the imperative to work nonstop. She is one of the globe's most successful obstacle course racers, with three World's Toughest Mudder titles, one Spartan World Championship, 50 podium finishes, and multiple race victories. These races require competitors to compete on foot and overcome various physical challenges—such as jumping over brick walls, swinging across monkey bars, and crawling under barbed wire—and some races are longer than a marathon.

Boone juggles a full-time corporate law job at Apple with vigorous training. She works 8–10 hours a day and still manages to run 70–90 miles per week, as well as doing regular CrossFit workouts. Fans have dubbed her the Queen of Pain and the Michael Jordan of Obstacle Course Racing.[5]

"I'm so numb to pain, I stopped registering my body's warning signs of injury," she says. Then one day, during a 25-mile training run, she ignored a nagging tightness in her inner thigh. "Then I felt a lightning bolt of pain." An MRI showed that she had fractured her thigh bone. Overtraining had left its mark, and Boone was forced to rely on crutches for three months and then embark on a rigorous rehab program after that. She could not run again for months after the injury.[6]

Do you recognize yourself in any of these stories?

Karoshi Paradox

Being a hard worker is often a virtue. How much you work is one of the elements of life that you can control, whether you are preparing for an exam, training for an endurance race, or delivering a project with a tight deadline. People rarely achieve success without hard work. Your strength lies in having the energy to pursue your ambitions, being able to push yourself even when you are exhausted, and never giving up. Don't take these gifts for granted. Study after study shows that grit, persistence, and sheer determination are often greater predictors of success than innate talent.

Huffington and Musk would not be pioneers if they confined themselves to working from nine to five. Boone, who has something resembling a nine-to-five job, would not have won so many titles if she wasn't prepared to train hard and race hard.

However, the *Perseverance* friend becomes an enemy when it is uncontrolled and begins to run counter to the natural laws of the brain and body. Every endeavor has a tipping point where more work begins to have decreasing returns, and a further rupture where more work starts to have a negative impact. When you push yourself too hard and operate nonstop, your efforts begin to work against you, and the midnight oil can burn your house down.

Three related types of behaviors emerge when the *Perseverance* Frenemy takes hold:

First, many ambitious people mistake activity for progress and simply push themselves too hard, often on a daily basis. Huffington admits she was working 18-hour days while building the *Huffington Post* website, and that led to her collapse. When Boone got injured running, her first instinct was to work harder and come back stronger. "To prove to everyone that I wasn't a statistic, that I wasn't broken, I was going to come back quickly," she says. "So I cross-trained like a fiend, vowing to make a triumphant return by the end of the season. The day after I was diagnosed, I was in the pool swimming with a buoy between my legs for as long as my bored mind could take, staring at the line on the pool floor through tears in my goggles. I'd get on an Assault stationary bike and work my arms and one leg, and then I'd get on the SkiErg [a cardio machine that simulates cross-country skiing]—it's brutal—and use it sitting down, sometimes for an hour-plus every day. I did pull-ups until I couldn't do any more and push-ups on one leg. Somewhere along the way, I came up with the brilliant idea that crutches could be a form of exercise. At Western States [Endurance Run], I crutched around for eight miles."

Boone was secretly proud of her progress, but she failed to appreciate the incredible toll it took on her body. "I did all the things I wasn't supposed to do. I clung to fitness in every way possible. What I didn't realize was that through the intense cross-training, I was building really bad habits and imbalances. Three weeks after I got off crutches for the femoral stress fracture and started to return to running, I ended up with a sacral stress fracture—a crack in the bone at the base of the spine—on my left side, where I was doing all that biking, standing on one leg, and hopping on one leg crutching around. Then I knew I had completely screwed up. A six-month sentence of no running suddenly doubled to a year."[7]

For some, being busy becomes a habit, regardless of the work at hand. You find things to do, even when there are no urgent tasks, and you feel guilty if you take time off. Whenever someone asks you how your day or week has been, your first response is "busy."

Second, we often see ambitious people taking on too many things, either by saying yes to everything or by picking up new tasks on their own unprompted. Musk, who runs multiple billion-dollar companies and who is known to break his workday into five-minute intervals, is at one extreme. Each endeavor is part of his grand vision to change the world and humanity, but is it too much at once?

From a business performance point of view, you could argue that he might have gained a higher return on investment if he had reduced his number of ventures or found a way to gain more leverage, for example, by hiring a few more capable people to handle some of his responsibilities. A heavy workload also affects your ability to think clearly. Musk has admitted that there are days when eight cans of Diet Coke and several large cups of coffee keep him going, with negative consequences. "I got so freaking jacked that I seriously started to feel like I was losing my peripheral vision."[8] From a personal point of view, Musk admits that the work has taken a heavy toll. Such a workload is clearly not sustainable, even when you love your work.

Not everyone is trying to run multiple businesses. However, ambitious people often push the boundaries of what is possible. You might be trying to succeed in a full-time job while wanting to spend time with your family, launch a side business or project, stay in shape, and learn Spanish at the same time. These different initiatives all contribute individually toward a higher Return on Ambition for you, but taken together, they counteract one another. Each initiative begins to compete for your time, yet each one also feels starved for attention. The result is that you're not happy as you struggle to keep all the balls in the air, many of which you added to the mix yourself.

Finally, many ambitious people are perfectionists who are unable to leave something until they feel it is flawless. In these instances, they ignore both that the marginal returns of their efforts diminish and that there is an increasing opportunity cost of spending time perfecting a piece of work instead of spending that time on something else. When you do that, you're eating up precious hours you could be spending with your family and friends or on hobbies, or even working on other initiatives.

The root cause of this friend turned enemy is what we call the "Karoshi Paradox." Karoshi is a Japanese term that translates to "overwork death." Death from working too much—though the final blow is often administered by a heart attack or stroke—is a real issue in some parts of the world. Ambitious people often have an inherent conviction that they have to work harder and harder to succeed. They believe that life moves quickly and so must they. But this leaves them feeling that they don't have time to stop even for a moment. Their underlying beliefs are typically that "the harder I work, the more successful I will be," "I don't have time to prioritize," and "I need to get everything done." The paradox is that the more they push, the less likely they are to succeed, and perhaps the more likely they are to experience a work-related death.

The *Perseverance* Frenemy has two main triggers, which are more prevalent in ambitious people. The first is the sheer size of the ambition. If the ambition and timeline you have set for yourself require an overwhelming effort, be cautious. Often, people who set grand ambitions and want to quickly hit their goals become locked in a situation where more work begins to be a necessity rather than a choice. These pressures are thus self-imposed, leaving people feeling that they must keep going.

Second, many people have an underlying belief that their work or achievements define their self-worth. This belief is often more prevalent in ambitious people, who by nature want to accomplish something important. Given that the amount of work you do is an input you can control, the temptation is often to take on more things, say yes to more things, and work more in order to reach your goals. At one extreme, you risk becoming an insecure overachiever, riddled with the unfortunate cocktail of working extremely hard to prove yourself, but constantly feeling self-doubt.

Boone admits that she felt enormous pressure to keep working hard and winning. "The night before every single race pre-femur break, I was a crying mess. What if I don't get on the podium? Are my sponsors going to drop me? I felt so much external pressure to keep winning. You have to keep winning, Amelia. You have to keep winning."[9] The higher the degree of ambition and accompanying insecurity, the more fatal this cocktail can be.

As mentioned, this Frenemy bears a gift that is often a crucial ingredient in pursuing all three dimensions of your Return on Ambition: It can lead to higher achievements, more growth, and greater well-being, when all your ducks are in a row. But overused, *Perseverance* becomes an enemy that can reduce each element—well-being, growth, and achievement—of your Return on Ambition.

Each of those elements has a tipping point, and taken together, too many initiatives can become overwhelming. Short-term imbalances do sometimes occur. But if they keep occurring, or persist for an extended time, the issue is likely structural and often can cut down on your Return on Ambition until you make significant changes.

For example, achievement suffers when you are unable to manage everything you have taken on. This often results in being overwhelmed and stressed and, perhaps, even leads to burnout. You are unable to think clearly, and instead of you finishing one initiative and moving on to the next, your many initiatives linger half-done. Not only that, but the output from your efforts is often low as well. The bar for competence and achievement is high in competitive environments, and doing just enough across many initiatives rarely suffices.

Growth also suffers when you try to grow too much, as paradoxical as that may sound. Your body and mind have a finite capacity for absorption, and continuously adding new things to learn or do can lead to a lot of activity but no progress. Boone felt this urge even when she was in physical therapy rehab. "If you are like me, and I'm assuming lots of athletes out there are," she says, "you want a solution to the problem, and you want it now. And if you hear that ART [Active Release Technique, a muscle rehabilitation technique that treats your body's soft tissue by combining manipulation and movement] and acupuncture and ice baths can help, then you are going to take it to the limit and do all of those things, in every spare waking minute you have (which is a lot more than you usually have, since you can't spend that time training). But, just as your body needs rest from training, it needs rest from rehab."[10]

Well-being, if prioritized, can experience a boost amid the *Perseverance* Frenemy. But prioritizing your well-being is a double-edged sword. Friends and family do not like feeling as if they are one more "to do" on your check-list. Even if you can balance it all, it can be difficult to hide the fact from the people you are making time to see that even your personal well-being has become a strategic initiative that you time-box and manage.

In addition, well-being is often the area of life that suffers most when ambitious people are overwhelmed. It can seem easy to reduce family time or postpone a hobby, but in the long run the delay is rarely worth it. Very few people like to work that hard. Leisure time is rapidly becoming a new form of currency, yet many people realize that only when it is too late. Serious damage can happen if you push yourself too hard and begin to recognize any of the red flags that we laid out in Chapter 3, for example regular exhaustion, anxiety, or an inability to enjoy your hobbies or other leisure activities.

Re-Adjusting the Dials

Ambitious people may find it impossible to focus on only one thing at a time. Perhaps the right number for you is three. And times will surely come along when you are much busier than you like to be. But doing three things in a high-quality distinctive way is very different from doing five things in an average way. And you will find a big difference in pushing yourself hard for a period of time and then resting, versus burning yourself out. You can work less hard than you do now and still achieve grand ambitions, though there will be trade-offs in terms of how you spend your time.

Those who realize a high Return on Ambition manage their *Perseverance* Frenemy in very different ways, rather than letting it take over. The under-lying mindset for managing this Frenemy centers around understanding that you can do anything but not everything. The underlying beliefs that support this mindset include "Prioritizing will make me more effective," "Balancing the different areas of my life will make me more successful," "I can say no to things," and perhaps even "My work does not reflect my worth as a person." Similar to action video games, where gamers compulsively monitor the health of their avatars displayed in colorful status bars at the top of their screens, ambitious people understand the importance of longevity and being cognizant of their "life dials."

With this mindset, new opportunities arise.

One possibility is to increase your clarity of thought and your well-being by pacing yourself more effectively. When asked if she could have built the *Huffington Post* if she hadn't worked so hard, Arianna Huffington is clear in her response: "I would have been as successful, if not more so. Who knows what else I might have done if I hadn't paid such a price in terms of stress, anxiety, and the impact that it had on my health and my relationships?"[11]

Another important possibility is focusing on what really matters. This doesn't mean setting run-of-the-mill checklist priorities but, instead, engaging in hardcore prioritization.

Elon Musk has learned to be a relentless prioritizer. "Focus on the signal over noise," he says. "Don't waste time on stuff that doesn't actually make things better."[12] For him, the "signal" is product development, to which he dedicates the majority of his attention.

Firm prioritization requires planning and reflection. Often when you get stressed, you are overwhelmed and lose sight of the forest for the trees, focusing on finishing the next task instead of taking a step back. At that point, you need an elevated perspective and perhaps external counsel from someone who can see what is going on. You also need the inner confidence to say no. And, often, you may need better energy management to alternate between peak performance and periods of rest.

Boone says she previously "just didn't understand the concept that you may need 'rest' every once in a while." Today, she has learned the hard way and has a new attitude. She has also released her self-imposed expectation of perfection. "Racing through my fears as I rebuilt from my injury, I learned something: There's freedom in being humbled and realizing that your expectations are only constructs in your own head . . . And despite the fact that, on paper, I no longer have the same unblemished race resume, I find myself more at peace. I'm a stronger runner, athlete, and racer—physically, mentally, and emotionally. And that's mainly because I feel more confident from being open and vulnerable."[13]

The principles that athletes follow are equally important for nonathletes. Huffington wrote an open letter to Musk, urging him to ease up on the long hours at work. "Working 120-hour weeks doesn't leverage your unique qualities, it wastes them," she wrote. "You can't simply power through—that's just not how our bodies and our brains work."[14]

Musk says he now prioritizes sleep. "I find if I don't get enough sleep I'm quite grumpy . . . I could drop below a certain threshold of sleep, and although I would be awake more hours, I would get less done because my mental acuity would be affected."[15]

Huffington explains, "We used to think that there was a trade-off: You had to sacrifice your professional success in order to attain inner peace. Now we see, no, not at all. The science is so conclusive."[16]

Your Return on Ambition will benefit greatly if you understand and manage the *Perseverance* Frenemy. Typically, mastering this Frenemy calls for cutting away excess initiatives and simultaneously focusing your extra energy on maximizing your priorities. Every unit of energy you expend has an opportunity cost, and you have to think about where you are getting the biggest return on your ambition and where you can pursue opportunities for enhancement. For some, this allows the same level of achievement with less effort. Others find they are able to reinvest their freed-up time toward higher levels of achievement. Mastering this Frenemy almost always increases well-being and growth, since it gives you time to invest in these areas of your life. Either way, your Return on Ambition will go up.

OVER TO YOU

- *Do you sometimes push yourself past the point of exhaustion in the pursuit of your ambitions?*

- *If so, what is driving this behavior?*

- *How could mastering the* Perseverance *Frenemy increase your Return on Ambition?*

- *Are you able to reach the same returns with less effort? Or could you increase your returns while holding your efforts steady?*

TEN

Frenemy 6—Desire

Do you feel a hunger to constantly strive for more and to push the limits of what is possible? If so, how has this helped you? How could it hinder you?

THERE IS A Buddhist parable about a demon with a long and thin throat and a large belly. The long and thin throat can only consume a small amount of food at a time, while the large belly keeps crying out for more food. Because of this mismatch, the demon is always hungry and never satisfied. Its whole life is spent looking for food, trying to fill its appetite. It is a bottomless pit that can't be filled, but that doesn't stop the demon from trying—leaving it perpetually unfulfilled.

Similarly, many ambitious people have unrealistic expectations about their ambitions and are constantly on the lookout for more heights to scale. While the *Desire* Frenemy can spur them on, it can also do more harm than good.

Take Khalid Alkhudair, for example. Alkhudair is a serial entrepreneur, a board member of numerous organizations, and founder of Glowork, which has helped thousands of women in Saudi Arabia gain employment. He has been named a Young Global Leader at the World Economic Forum, received the Chaillot Prize for Human Rights from the European Union, received the King Salman Award for Entrepreneurship, been named Endeavor Entrepreneur of the Year, been ranked the third most powerful Arab under 30 by *Gulf Business* magazine, and is the first Saudi Ashoka Fellow, joining a network of the world's leading social entrepreneurs.[1]

Alkhudair was always driven to achieve great things.[2] From an early age, he felt his friends and family doubted him and his abilities. Stubborn and eager to prove them wrong, he left Saudi Arabia at 16 to study in the United Kingdom, supporting himself financially and paying for his own education.

He recalls a gloomy day in London, when he was 18 or 19: "I was having the worst day possible—I was lacking money, it was raining, and I accidentally locked myself out of my house. I thought to myself 'one day, this has to change,' and I set myself the goal of becoming a millionaire by the age of 30."[3]

Alkhudair accomplished his goals. After taking odd jobs as a DJ and working in restaurants, he returned to Saudi Arabia and joined KPMG where, after five years in marketing and communications, and a short stint at Deutsche Gulf Finance bank, he was promoted to chief operating officer for the region. "I was 28, and had achieved my financial goal. I asked myself, 'What's next?'" Never one to settle on an easy target, Alkhudair's next goal was career driven. He wanted to make a difference in Saudi Arabia. "I thought it would be really interesting to take the hardest thing in this country and make it successful." He landed on the topic of female employment. "No one was talking about this topic. It was almost a taboo subject. However, I did my own research and spoke to companies, and found out that many were open to hiring females, but just didn't know how."

Alkhudair launched Glowork in 2011 with a goal that was completely unthinkable at the time: to help 50,000 women obtain employment. As of 2019, the company has placed more than 41,000 women in jobs, has helped change employment laws in the country, and has played a major role in changing societal perceptions of female employment. Alkhudair felt he had achieved his stated goal and stepped down in 2018, handing over the reins of a well-functioning organization.

Constantly striving for more has driven Alkhudair toward his many achievements. However, the work took a toll. "I got to a point in my life where I realized that constant, continuous striving wasn't healthy at all. Despite material success and career recognition, I wasn't happy. I had to take a big step back, take a hard look in the mirror, and re-evaluate my priorities."

Continuously increasing expectations about your ambitions can go beyond the need to keep setting newer, higher goals. Your expectations also can affect how you experience day-to-day living and the way you balance many different facets of your life.

Pia Mancini can confirm that wholeheartedly.[4] Mancini is a democracy activist, co-founder and CEO at Open Collective, chair of the DemocracyEarth Foundation, and mother of a young child. Her TED Talk, "How to Upgrade Democracy for the Internet Era," has been watched more than one million times.[5]

Mancini was born in Bueno Aires, Argentina, and politics filled her life even as a child. "Politics was a very common topic of conversation in my house," she says. "We discussed it at almost every meal."[6] Since then, she has worked most of her life in this area. She is driven by a deep belief that we are 21st-century citizens who interact with 19th-century-designed institutions, built with the information technology of the 15th century.

"We need to design the political and economic system for the internet generation," she says, "with technology that makes politics a conversation rather than a monologue, and unlocks a whole new economic system."

She co-founded DemocracyOS, an open-source platform that allows citizens to debate and vote on proposals that their political representatives are discussing. They also can propose new projects and ideas to their representatives for consideration. She hopes this will help foster more open and participatory governments. In a similar vein, she has also co-founded Open Collective, which enables groups to set up collectives quickly, raise funds, and manage them transparently, leveraging open-source technology. "We're building a new set of institutions, or at least the scaffolding for new institutions to be built on, to allow people to organize and govern themselves in the internet era."

Big challenges like this do not come easy, and Mancini admits that your ambitions can easily take over your life, if you let them. She recalls, "When I was a campaign manager, I was working 24/7, campaigning in the slums of Argentina, running a foundation, and constantly engaging in public speaking. I would throw myself into everything with full steam ahead." She has experienced firsthand how challenging it can be to balance everything at once, and she's learned that doing so requires thoughtful choices. "If you're not making the trade-off," she says, "someone is making it for you."

Do you recognize yourself in any of these stories?

The Ambition Treadmill

The big bellies, small throats, and resulting insatiable appetite for achievement that many ambitious people feel aren't all bad; in many cases, you can channel that appetite into being a strength. *Desire* can keep you striving and running fast; it can act as an underlying engine for your ambition. Mancini recalls always being ambitious. "I was always looking for ways to engage in local and global issues, even at a young age. My sister calls me 'the ultimate activist' because I'm always after one thing or another."[7] Her ambitions and vision for more transparent and democratic political and economic systems help keep her motivated, even when there are obstacles or challenges.

And there is no doubt that Alkhudair's constant hunger to conquer the hardest goals he could find helped him break old boundaries and set new paradigms. The 41,000 additional women now in employment in Saudi Arabia would surely attest to his stellar achievements.

But as is often the case, there is a flip side. *Desire* can make you lose perspective. It can begin to take on a life of its own and thereafter consume you. It can leave you prioritizing the wrong things in life, exhausted, and ultimately unhappy. It may frustrate you often. You face the risk that the running will never stop and that you will never be fulfilled.

What symptoms will you experience when the *Desire* Frenemy is in play? Look for three main manifestations. First, you keep raising the bar higher, so you have to run faster and faster. You have a constant yearning for more, and your ambition keeps growing.

Alkhudair felt this energy at the height of Glowork's success. "I kept receiving awards and recognitions on a weekly basis. It was crazy. As a result, I kept asking myself 'what's next?' I kept setting new targets, and I kept accomplishing them. For example, I helped open female gyms, which also was a taboo subject. I helped change laws to make it happen."[8] Alkhudair kept striving for the next big thing, often focusing on the most difficult challenges he could find. "Nothing was ever enough," he says. "I started being harder on my employees, asking them to do more. And of course, I kept doing more myself."

Second, ambitious people may feel that others progress with greater ease than they do. They begin believing the stories of people who are so-called overnight successes. They envy others' successes and begin to feel entitled to successes of their own. They forget that life deals people different hands, and they misunderstand the role of luck, telling themselves, "If those people reached their achievements, I should have reached mine by now as well."

Third, you may feel an innate drive to do "more" but lack a clear understanding of why you are pushing so hard. Mancini recalls that a close friend once asked her why she was running so fast, and she didn't have an answer. "The feeling wasn't that I was pushing a particular boundary. I was on a rolling stone and I couldn't get off. I was moving forward on my projects, but without a sense of purpose."[9]

Ambitious people are often accustomed to running fast, and their ambition can continue to push them forward almost blindly. Mancini admits that she felt the pull of strong inertia with her ongoing initiatives, and the easiest thing to do was keep going. "I wasn't really questioning if that was the right thing to do. I was hitting the floor running every time something new popped up. When my friend asked me why, it stopped me in my tracks. It was a wake-up call."

The root cause of this constant striving and frustration is what we call the ambition treadmill, a machine that keeps running, forcing you to keep up. Once ambitious people are on this treadmill, they often feel perpetually behind. They are haunted by the idea that they should have achieved much more by now. They believe they'll be able to relax once they achieve the next milestone, just as they think their big break is just around the corner.

The *Desire* Frenemy often affects ambitious people more than other people; that has to do with the nature of ambition itself. Remember, ambition is a yearning to attain a future state that is different from today. That concept has striving baked into it, and it is linked to the dimension of time.

Speed is almost always of essence. You're trying to get somewhere that is more attractive than where you are now, so why wait?

For many ambitious people, the quicker they can make things happen, the better. At a deeper level, many ambitious people believe that their self-worth is tied to their accomplishments. If you feel that you'll be worth more as a human being if you achieve more, you'll probably run faster to get there. And once you get there, you'll be tempted to raise the bar again.

Desire naturally affects the three dimensions of your Return on Ambition. The most noticeable impact is often on your well-being. When you desire what is not yet in sight, you do not always appreciate what you already have. You may be regularly frustrated and slightly off-center. At the peak of this Frenemy's grip, you may even be miserable.

"When I started looking at my life," Alkhudair says, "I realized that I was missing the basics. On the outside, everything looked fine. But on a personal level, I was missing meaningful friendships. I realized I didn't have anyone I could truly call a close friend, anyone I could open up to. And I hadn't nurtured my family relationships—it had been all work, work, work. I realized I wasn't happy."[10]

Your growth dimension can suffer if you de-prioritize it. Much like a company that is chasing next quarter's results and, as a result, cuts back on research and development, you can begin living milestone to milestone and neglect your personal development. It is tempting to plan your tasks around the activities that will get you to your goals as fast as possible, and the ambitions treadmill can lead you to focus only on short-term gains. However, you must plant the seeds now for the crops you wish to harvest in the future.

The *Desire* Frenemy initially can boost your achievement level, as it propels you forward. However, the returns quickly diminish. As consultants, we have seen many ambitious people run too far, too fast and, at times, in the wrong direction, ending up depleted and exhausted. Especially when you combine *Desire* with *Boldness* and *Perseverance*, the consequences can be severe. The resulting burnout and lengthy recovery can take you out of the game for a substantial period of time, which will hold you back from meeting your goals. Too much craving is bad for you—and for your ambition.

Grounded Striving

Ambitious people who can channel the *Desire* Frenemy in the right way attain an interesting balance of striving and being grounded. They maintain their level of ambition and their drive. You don't have to turn down the flame of your ambition, but people with a high Return on Ambition forge a different relationship with their ambition. They see it in a different light. They are equally (or more) ambitious than anyone else, but they also understand what is important for them across the different dimensions of their lives.

Alkhudair recalls the moment he decided to reevaluate his life. He was at Davos, speaking with a gentleman who had impressive accomplishments, someone he respected immensely. He was surprised to learn that behind the man's smiling exterior was a difficult life and a great deal of unhappiness. "I remember thinking, 'This is a guy I have always looked up to, and he is going through the same crap as me.' I realized that I could not wait until I was too old to enjoy life to think about what was really important. I decided to relax more, spend more time with the people I care about, and enjoy life a little. Before that, it was all work and no play."[11]

Asked if his new perspective on life would slow him down, Alkhudair vehemently replied, "It will not slow me down in reaching my goals. I still have a big goal in my job. I set myself big KPIs [key performance indicators] and personal targets. I want to not just achieve, but overachieve, in the context of everything I do and wherever I go. My goals are always very ambitious. But also focusing on other areas of my life gives me balance and makes my striving sustainable. I have found a way to allocate time for myself and I'm much more content on a daily basis."

Attaining a healthy equilibrium of grounded striving requires cultivating the mindset that you are exactly where you need to be. It requires acknowledging that you've already achieved a great deal and understanding that there are no shortcuts to meaningful success. Accepting that life doesn't always follow your plans will help. Believing that it should, and getting frustrated when it doesn't, is a sure path to misery. This does not, however, imply that you stop striving. On the contrary, ambitious people strive incessantly. Yet even if you give 110%, you'll need to be able to release yourself from the outcomes, whatever they may be, and accept where you are.

Mancini realized the importance of being extremely deliberate in her decisions and conscious of the trade-offs she was making. "I don't think you can have it all, at least not at the same time," she says. "There is almost always a trade-off, and that is okay, but if you have unrealistic expectations about what is possible, you will always be unhappy."[12] Mancini says she has had short-term imbalances in the past, for example, giving up aspects of her social life to develop and grow professionally, but she knew it was what she needed to do at the time to achieve her professional aspirations.

Becoming a mother has further heightened Mancini's sensitivity to the importance of making deliberate decisions and balancing different areas of her life. "I haven't become less ambitious, but my perspective has changed. I'm much more conscious about the time I spend away from my daughter." She is still striving to change the world, but her notion of "success" has become broader, and now it includes being the best mom she can be. "Being fulfilled in life starts off by knowing yourself and knowing what it is that will fulfill you in the first place. There's nothing worse than not being aware of what's going on in your life, or harboring unrealistic expectations about what is possible for you."

People who manage the *Desire* Frenemy this way reap bountiful rewards across all three dimensions: achievement, well-being, and growth. By taking a more holistic approach to your ambitions, you can attain more grounding and mental clarity, rendering you more effective in the present. Forget the hungry demon's insatiable appetite and reframe your reality so that your ambition and your energy—the fuel that feeds it—live in healthy balance. Do all you can and then, instead of stressing about the future, let the results unfold.

OVER TO YOU

- *Is your hunger for success helping or hurting you? Are you on the ambition treadmill?*

- *Do you ever feel a deep frustration about where you are in life? Is there a mismatch between reality and your expectations?*

- *What is keeping you from attaining more balance and grounded striving? Can you make a change?*

- *How could mastering the* Desire *Frenemy increase your Return on Ambition?*

ELEVEN

Frenemy 7—Flexibility

Do you find yourself adapting significantly to different people and situations? If so, how has this helped you? How could it hinder you?

AESOP WAS A Greek storyteller who lived around 600 BC. In one of his fables, an old man, a boy, and their donkey were going to town. The boy rode on the donkey and the old man walked beside him. As they went along, they passed some people who remarked that it was a shame that the old man was walking and the boy was riding. The man and boy thought maybe the critics were right, so they changed positions.

Later they passed another group of people who remarked, "What a shame! The old man is making the little boy walk." Hearing this, they decided that they would both walk. Soon they passed more people who thought they were both stupid to walk when they had a decent donkey to ride. So they both rode the donkey, until onlookers scolded them by saying how awful it was to put such a heavy load on the poor donkey. The boy and man said they were probably right, so they decided to carry the donkey. As they crossed a bridge, they lost their grip on the animal and the donkey fell into the river and drowned. "That will teach you," said an old man who had followed them. "Please all, and you will please none."

This chapter is about a Frenemy that affects many ambitious people. It pertains to constantly changing your colors and what you stand for to try to please everyone. While adaptability can be immensely valuable in an increasingly dynamic world, it can also trip you up.

Yoga teacher Rachel Brathen wrote the *New York Times* bestseller *Yoga Girl*, founded the nonprofit 109 World, and has garnered more than two million Instagram followers. She felt the strain of the *Flexibility* Frenemy early in her career.

Brathen discovered yoga in her late teens, fell in love with it, and started teaching it shortly after. Within a few years, she was teaching it full time on Aruba in the Caribbean, where she had moved with her then boyfriend, now husband.

In a speech she gave at TEDx Aruba, Brathen told a story about the importance of being who you are—not just a people pleaser.[1] She recounted posting her first Instagram photo in 2012, a picture of her dog sticking his head out a car window. Initially, she used her account to post selfies and photos of breakfast on the beach. She quickly saw that pictures of yoga poses got a much bigger response than any other posts.

Brathen started making daily posts that fit the themes of yoga, balance, health, and happiness. The pictures showed yoga poses on the beach, green smoothies, and sunshine—depicting, in her words, "a perfect life." On Instagram, every day seemed perfect, even if Brathen was actually having a really bad day.[2]

Her wake-up call came on a "crappy day" at the end of a long week. After a quarrel, she and her boyfriend went out to dinner. Brathen ordered a shot of tequila with her meal and uploaded a photo of her dinner to Instagram with the hashtags #tequila #reallylongday. The next morning, she was bowled over by the impact of what she had done. Upset followers had posted many angry comments, accusing her of being a hypocrite and a fake yoga instructor. Brathen hadn't been completely honest in the presence she projected and had unconsciously angled her account to fulfill people's image of her as perfect and happy in order to build her following. When she showed a bit of her true self, she got slammed.

The corporate environment is also rife with the *Flexibility* Frenemy, not only in terms of pleasing others, but also when it comes to projecting a persona you believe will benefit you on the job.

Bing Chen, a digital media pioneer and entrepreneur, has been recognized as a *Forbes* magazine "Top 30 Under 30 Leader" and as one of the *Hollywood Reporter's* "35 Under 35 Next Gen Leaders" and "Agents of Change." Chen is the founding architect of the multibillion-dollar You-Tube creator ecosystem. He has a vision of building a platform that will enable people to self-actualize more rapidly. In the course of his rapid ascent, he learned the importance of having a consistent set of principles and standing up for them courageously.[3]

Chen recounts, "I remember when I was an intern at the Walt Disney Company, and I met with Rich Ross [then president of the Disney Channel] for the first time. He asked me how I was, and I proceeded to recite my full resume to him, telling him about all my achievements, and how great I was doing. I still remember his words . . . He said, 'Bing, do you know what your problem is? You try too hard to be impressive and not hard enough to be liked.'"[4]

Chimamanda Ngozi Adichie, the award-winning author of *Purple Hibiscus*, *Half of a Yellow Sun*, and *Americanah*, also has spoken out about the importance of being true to yourself and finding your own voice. *Time* magazine listed Adichie as one of its "100 Most Influential People" in 2015, and she is a recipient of a MacArthur Fellowship, commonly called a MacArthur "Genius" grant.[5] Born and raised in Nigeria, Adichie had an early love of reading and writing. She experienced adapting to a persona that differs from her true self at a young age, driven more by a lack of awareness of what was possible and less by conscious choice.

"I was an early reader, and what I read were British and American children's books. I was also an early writer, and when I began to write, at about the age of seven, stories in pencil with crayon illustrations that my poor mother was obligated to read, I wrote exactly the kinds of stories I was reading: All my characters were white and blue-eyed, they played in the snow, they ate apples, and they talked a lot about the weather." This is what she wrote even though, as Adichie says, in "Nigeria we didn't have snow, we ate mangoes, and we never talked about the weather, because there was no need to."[6]

This demonstrates how impressionable and vulnerable we are when we don't know better, especially as children. Only when Adichie discovered African literature did she begin to believe that the characters in her books could, in fact, be people with whom she could identify. That helped her find a more authentic voice.

Do any of these reflections or situations sound familiar to you?

Chameleon Syndrome

A chameleon can change the color of its skin and blend into its environment. This unique ability allows it to camouflage itself and sends social signals to other chameleons. Like a chameleon, some people have a tendency to adapt their behavior to blend in with their environment, often so that others will like them. Typically, they are not trying to manipulate or trick people but just to please them in order to get along.

Such people often are good at solving conflicts, maintaining social harmony, listening deeply, and adapting to new and multi-stakeholder situations. These abilities can help them reach their ambitions since they can maintain strong connections with a diverse set of people.

However, this strength can turn into a Frenemy when it leads people to change their ways with the direction of the wind. If you sway too much in the breeze in order to please people, you can end up focusing more on pleasing them and maintaining the status quo than on making progress toward fulfilling your own ambition.

When this Frenemy is in play, two main types of behavior emerge. The first is an emphasis on avoiding conflict or shying away from challenging the status quo. Brathen did not change her colors back and forth. Instead, she maintained a specific, not fully authentic, persona to appease her Instagram followers. She saw firsthand what happened when she posted something contrary to their image of her, so she knew what would happen if she did it again. As a result, she knew she could avoid a backlash by continuing to post idyllic beaches, gourmet brunches, and blissful yoga poses.

We see the same game playing out in the workplace. Ambitious people who are prone to this Frenemy might shirk difficult conversations, whether that means avoiding updating their colleagues on a faltering project, giving the boss bad news, providing feedback that is candid enough to be useful, or saying no.

It can be tempting to dodge a challenging conversation, even when you know you should deal with it. Chen is still rueful about a challenging situation early in his career when he was not vocal enough. "A senior colleague who had asked me to make a change to our website threw me under the bus," he remembers. "During a meeting, he saw that our boss was unhappy with that change, so he lied about having told me to make the change. Back then, I didn't say anything to my boss. I had a really strong gut feeling that I should, but I was scared. I will never forget that. It was a turning point for me."[7]

You can also succumb to conflict avoidance and be unwilling to challenge the status quo when you place limits around your ambitions—based on how you view the world and your definition of what's possible. In many cases, you can end up conforming to current paradigms but sabotaging yourself.

Adichie explains, "Because all I had read were books in which the characters were foreign, I had become convinced that books by their very nature had to have foreigners in them." At the time, her paradigm didn't include the knowledge that characters in books could be African. Only when she discovered such writers as Chinua Achebe and Camara Laye did she begin to see what was possible.

"I went through a mental shift in my perception of literature. I realized that people like me, girls with skin the color of chocolate, whose kinky hair could not form ponytails, could also exist in literature. I started to write about things I recognized."[8] Many ambitious people face similar challenges when they try to break new ground but find themselves unwittingly conforming to limited paradigms.

Second, the *Flexibility* Frenemy plays out when ambitious people try to please others by changing their opinions, behaviors, or values depending on their circumstances. They often say yes even when they don't concur.

In the face of daunting ambitions, changing your colors like a chameleon can be tempting. But if you shift around too much, you will spin in circles and often confuse other people. Being wishy-washy indicates that you may lack strong values. This lessens you in the eyes of your colleagues and puts you at risk of making poor decisions that don't support your ambitions or your personal principles.

"Another example of changing who I am to fit in happened when I was at YouTube," Chen recalls. "I was getting pulled into more executive meetings with senior stakeholders in the company. I realized that I was starting to behave very professionally . . . and I was being very proper. I was using certain diction and not making certain jokes. I was talking to people only about work. I felt like I was being fake. Then I got feedback from my two bosses, who both said something along the lines of, 'I know why you're doing this. Just be yourself.' I was fortunate to receive some very direct feedback in both instances, and it was only after that thoughtful feedback that I made a conscious decision to just be myself."[9]

The root cause of this Frenemy is focusing on fitting in and keeping the peace, rather than focusing on the process of realizing your ambitions. Often, underlying beliefs such as "I must maintain harmony so people like me" and "I must fit in and do what people expect" drive this behavior. Acting this way implies that you must always avoid conflict, even at the cost of your true, authentic identity.

Time and again, ambitious people fall into a contradictory pattern where, on the one hand, they are incredibly driven and even overly controlling, while on the other hand, they feel a strong urge to maintain harmony. This paradox is incredibly difficult to manage: How can you change the current situation when you want to keep things the way they are? At a deeper level, people in the grip of this dilemma believe that if they disturb the status quo and say or do things that might upset other people, they will lose the regard of those around them and either not get the support they need to succeed or end up dejected and alone. Their ambition and their peacekeeping urges are united by their—partly subconscious—fear of loneliness.

This Frenemy is prevalent in ambitious and less ambitious people alike. However, certain subtleties can affect the ambitious in different and, at times, greater ways. For example, many people want others to like them. However, for the less ambitious, this may not cause tension, as they usually aren't trying to change the status quo.

In contrast, ambitious people have a concurrent drive to change things. The greater your ambition is, the greater the likelihood that you want others to do things differently. You are likely to have to convince someone (or many people) to share your ideas or promote your project in order to reach your ambitions. The status quo is not your ally, yet some people may be worse off if the status quo is disrupted, and people in general dislike change. As a result, ambition leads to more scope for social disharmony. For ambitious people pleasers, this triggers the uncomfortable and countervailing forces of disruption and harmony, a balance that is impossible to sustain.

This Frenemy affects all three facets of your Return on Ambition in interesting ways. In the short run, *Flexibility* can appear to enhance your well-being, since it looks as if you're maintaining excellent relationships with your friends and acquaintances. Often, you enjoy being well liked, and you are extra vigilant about keeping things that way. However, this can easily turn sour.

When ambitious people get "caught" in their inconsistencies—say if people find out that you haven't been telling the truth about where you stand or if you end up backing both sides of an opposing argument—the result is not pretty. Your previous glow dissipates, and the situation quickly turns negative and damaging. Once you break people's trust, mending it can take long, serious effort.

At a personal level, you could feel extremely uncomfortable being torn between the twin forces of ambitious change and the need to maintain harmony, especially when you know you should be doing one thing, not the other, but you can't change course or be the messenger of difficult news. This can leave you emotionally drained and with a nagging feeling of not being fully authentic and true to yourself.

Similar to your sense of well-being, it can seem that your level of achievement is doing fine in the here and now, since everything seems to be sailing smoothly along. You may be tempted to convince yourself that you can maintain this façade indefinitely as long as you can cover the cracks of your inconsistencies, and that you "just" need to get through the next few hurdles so that everything will come together.

This rarely goes as planned. In the short run, you may focus on achieving the wrong things, going on tangents to appease certain people. In the longer run, people will begin to see through your competing priorities, leading to an inevitable crash in achievement.

Too much *Flexibility* can affect your growth. When you center yourself more on people pleasing and less on your destination, you risk failing to capitalize on relevant, necessary learning opportunities along the way. You may even pursue certain paths just to impress others and risk spreading yourself too thin. Picking up insights and information here and there might make you a jack-of-all-trades but a master of none.

In addition, you risk losing opportunities to hone your personal set of principles and values—and adequately develop the skill of judgment. As a person with strong ambitions, you need a sturdy backbone to support you as you climb to higher ground. Consistent good judgment and solid decision-making are skills that you sharpen over time. They require a strong moral compass, not just going along to get along.

Staying True to You

We are not saying you should avoid taking others' feelings and viewpoints into account. On the contrary, you should explicitly seek to understand where people are coming from and what opinions they hold so you can make a conscious decision about how to interact with them. That's not people pleasing; that's informed engagement.

In some situations, standing up for your beliefs may lead to conflict. People with a high Return on Ambition understand that they will always draw critics and that some people will always disagree with their course of action. Stand firm anyway. You can make your case as respectfully but clearly as possible—even if you ruffle some feathers—just as long as you are consistent and fair and consider other people's opinions and options. Healthy conflict is part of that tripod of growth, well-being, and achievement.

Today, yoga expert Rachel Brathen has become a leader in her industry. She worked hard to define her profile and says that her Instagram feed has become much more authentic than when she first launched it. Now, it includes pictures of her activities outside of yoga, photos of her family, and discussions of her real feelings. The image of herself she shares now is a far cry from the perfect lifestyle she depicted in her initial posts.

In 2014, when Brathen's best friend died just as Brathen herself was admitted to the hospital for appendicitis, her posts suddenly became very personal. She began opening up about the sadness she was feeling. Her change in tone cost her 100,000 of her 670,000 followers, but surprisingly enough, Brathen says, their desertion was a good thing. It cleaned up her online community. "I've always wanted to inspire people to find self-love and healing, practice yoga and live a healthy, accepting life . . . When I went through that trauma, I lost all the followers who weren't genuinely interested in who I was; they had no interest in seeing someone's grief."[10]

Brathen says that every time she posts her less glamorous feelings, she loses 2,000–6,000 followers. But she believes that her authenticity is one of the big reasons why her Instagram account, @yoga_girl, has achieved explosive success. "When people stuck around through that crisis, it created this bond that's way deeper than any regular social media person. You can't fake that. You can't market that. You can't create it or stage it."[11]

Brathen cautions people to not believe everything they see on social media, though she now focuses on being 100% genuine. "When I'm authentic, I get authenticity back and it's the most powerful thing."[12]

While you may choose to engage indirectly with people in some situations, at other times you may decide to engage directly, to be persuasive, and to try to bring about change. A chameleon can't do that. You must maintain the sturdiness of an anchor, not the flimsiness of a flag flapping in the wind. Standing up for what you believe can help guide your decision-making and lead you to do what you know to be right. This requires a consistent set of values and principles.

"I was sick and tired of pleasing people," says Chen, "so I made the decision to just be myself. And to have the confidence to stand up for what I believe is right, even if people don't like to hear it. I've always had integrity, but the difference now is having external courage with that integrity. I now trust my gut much more and I speak up when something doesn't feel right.

"For example, I've spoken up against a colleague who was constantly going behind people's back and taking credit for their work. He would lie about small things all the time. He was later fired for embezzlement. In another situation, there was a suspicion that a colleague was being sexually harassed, and I had no hesitation about addressing it head on," Chen says. "It turned out to be true, and I'm glad I had the confidence to take action."[13]

Brathen, Chen, Adichie, and other people with a high Return on Ambition have a fundamentally different mindset than your average chameleon. Like them, you must understand that if you are to realize your ambitions, you won't be able to please everyone. Indeed, having vocal critics, as well as supporters, often signals that what you're doing is making a difference. You will see that you often need to break down old paradigms and that people are just as much a part of the process of change as the goal itself. Goal-related and people-related change must go hand in hand.

Rather than being a victim of the two countervailing forces—change and harmony—you can manage them with awareness and conscious choices. Realize that you need people's respect, but not everyone is going to like you.

"I'm here to accomplish things, not please people," Chen explains. "Pleasing is sacrificing yourself and your potential for short-term, individual satisfaction. Serving others by living a consistent set of values has the most impact in the long term. If you live your life for others, you aren't actually living your life for yourself. Whatever you end up doing will fit their version of success, not yours."[14]

"Forget about likability," Adichie says. She vehemently disagrees with the common idea that likeability is essential, especially for aspiring writers. "Instead, focus on your story. Focus on the unique magic you bring to paper. The fact that while, yes, there are many writers . . . no one will ever be able to tell your stories the way you do if you commit to staying true to yourself."[15]

When you stop focusing on pleasing others, life becomes easier. You spend less time stressing about what people might think, and, instead, you live by your values and principles. Pursuing your ambitions will begin to feel more effortless. Who wouldn't want that reality?

OVER TO YOU

- *Think back to the last five major decisions you made at work or in your private life—to what degree did you make the decisions based on what people might think of you?*

- *Have you ever encountered a situation where you knew you should do one thing, but you did something else in order to maintain harmony with someone? If so, what drove this decision?*

- *How might engaging in healthy conflict enhance your Return on Ambition?*

- *How could mastering the* Flexibility *Frenemy increase your Return on Ambition?*

PART 3

How Do You Increase Your Return on Ambition?

PART 3 HELPS you answer the third key question of the book: How do you increase your Return on Ambition? We introduce the Return on Ambition Toolbox, which is a practical set of four tools. Then we dedicate one chapter per tool, where we describe and illustrate the approach in practice. At the end of each chapter is a self-coaching guide to help you apply the discussed tool in your quest for a higher Return on Ambition.

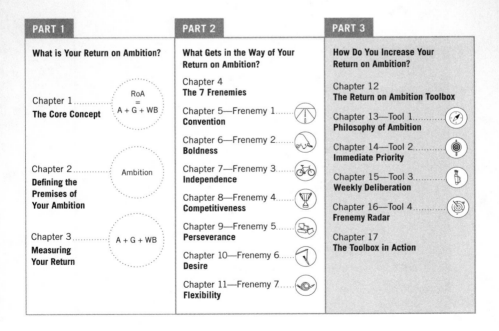

TWELVE

The Return on Ambition Toolbox

Becoming more aware of yourself and your surroundings is only the first part of your future journey. You must also choose your direction and move toward it with a willingness to learn and adapt along the way.

IT'S TIME TO put what you've learned into practice—in your work and life, in how you use your time, and in the way you think and relate to your feelings.

This chapter lays out the Return on Ambition Toolbox, which will come in handy as you scale your mountain of ambition. The toolbox consists of four main tools:

- Philosophy of Ambition

- Immediate Priority

- Weekly Deliberation

- Frenemy Radar

We will teach you how to manage yourself as an asset and increase your Return on Ambition by investing a mere 1% of your waking hours—no more than one hour a week, or an average of eight and a half minutes a day.

In Chapter 1, you met Bella (ambitious art student), Jitesh (stalled, formerly fast-tracking young corporate manager), and Nora and Alexander (professionally and socially successful young parents). We'll now follow their journeys as they learn about and apply the Return on Ambition Toolbox. Imagine they've been reading this book with you, and here's what they're thinking now.

Bella is curious about how to make more progress with her artwork by exerting the same amount of effort yet having greater focus and a more mature sense of purpose. She has talent but she needs depth. She's been having sleepless nights as she thinks about leaving grad student life and having to make her way as a professional artist—with serious ambition and communicating a real message.

Jitesh, still concerned with how his subordinates aren't turning in good work, decides to go for a run to clear his head. This helps him realize he isn't growing and advancing anymore, certainly not as quickly as before. He needs to bring his leadership skills up to his company's standards—and his own.

The self-assessments prompt Nora and Alexander to have a new discussion about how they could enjoy everything they have without letting work exact such a heavy toll on their relationships with each other and with their kids—Jean, Michele, and Liam. Nora suggests, finally looking away from the screen where she was checking her email, that they should take the kids to the mountains for a picnic, where they could spend time roaming the woods instead of staying home surrounded by electronics and work. As she silently asks herself if she could get up early enough to get some work done before the excursion, Alexander agrees—though he wonders if his smartphone would get a signal in the forest.

As they read about the seven Frenemies, Bella, Jitesh, and Nora and Alexander recognized how each one helped them, but also made their lives difficult. They were inspired but also frightened by the idea of shifting away from being managed by their Frenemies and toward managing them. Like you, the four of them are ready to learn how to get the best Return on Ambition for their investment of time and talent.

Investing 1%

If you are an ambitious person, your most valuable asset is yourself. Yet most ambitious people fall far short of dealing with themselves as an asset. Reading a book, complaining about how busy you are, or even making a to-do list don't count.

Investing in yourself as an asset requires time, energy, and other resources, and like any investment, it is important to continually track your returns. To experiment with being an intelligent investor of your time and abilities, ask yourself the following questions:

What share of my time do I spend contemplating how best to invest in myself and my ambitions and managing the outcome?

What tools or approach do I use, and how effective are they?

The art of investing is time consuming. Fund managers typically charge a small share of your assets for this service. Investors believe the cost is worth it. Likewise, investing in yourself can be time consuming and worth paying a small "fee." The difference is you get to pay yourself!

We're offering you a deal: You can manage yourself as an asset and get a considerably higher Return on Ambition at a charge of 1% of your waking hours. Carving out *one hour per week* will change you.

That small price might sound too good to be true, but it works. And, for the sake of transparency, we must mention that to achieve a truly life-changing impact, you'll also pay a "sign-up fee" of three hours. This fee comes from carrying out a self-coaching session at the end of each of the next four chapters. The first two self-coaching sessions are an hour apiece, while the last two are half-hour sessions.

Each chapter—and thus every self-coaching session—covers one tool in the Return on Ambition Toolbox. Figure 12.1 gives you an overview of the four tools, the self-coaching sessions you'll conduct as you go through the rest of the book, and the process you'll use to follow up afterward to ensure an ongoing high Return on Ambition.

	Tool	Use during reading	Use after reading
Manage yourself as an asset	**Philosophy of Ambition** Your guiding principles for the future that you evolve during life	One-hour self-coaching session after Chapter 13	A contemplation every 1–2 years
	Immediate Priority Your focus for the next 1–3 months with a note on what Frenemy to look out for	One-hour self-coaching session after Chapter 14	Approximately one-hour contemplation every 1–3 months
Perform as your asset	**Weekly Deliberation** Your intentions for three opportunities over the next week and lessons learned	Half-hour self-coaching session after Chapter 15	Half an hour each week
	Frenemy Radar Your evolving map of where and when your Frenemies cause sensations and friction	Half-hour self-coaching session after Chapter 16	Five to ten minutes to process each of approximately three sensations per week
Total	*The 3-hour sign-up fee*	*The 1-hour weekly fee*
			+ refreshing your Immediate Priority and Philosophy of Ambition as needed

Figure 12.1—The Return on Ambition Toolbox

The bottom line? You commit one hour every week to managing your investment in yourself, and soon you'll see results that far outweigh the "cost" of that hour. After a few weeks of practice, you will start replacing much of your usual worries and self-doubt with intentional contemplation and conscious learning, and you'll begin operating with an increased sense of purpose and effectiveness. Those are the kinds of returns you want!

The Three-Hour Sign-Up Fee

To begin to put your intentions into action, we encourage you to open your calendar right now and schedule four self-coaching sessions in the form of two one-hour sessions and two half-hour sessions. You might even write the name of each tool (outlined below) you will address after reading the chapters.

- **CHAPTER 13: TOOL 1—PHILOSOPHY OF AMBITION.** Take one hour to formulate your Philosophy of Ambition, your guiding principles. Hold this session at a place where you are at peace with yourself—perhaps in a park or in your favorite armchair.

- **CHAPTER 14: TOOL 2—IMMEDIATE PRIORITY.** Take one hour to define your Immediate Priority for the next one to three months. Coordinate your efforts on your calendar; write down what you expect to achieve and when you hope to achieve it.

- **CHAPTER 15: TOOL 3—WEEKLY DELIBERATION.** Take half an hour for your first Weekly Deliberation. Ideally, hold this self-coaching session at the end of the workweek or right before beginning the next one. Routinely sitting and thinking in a place where you would naturally find yourself at the end or start of the week will help you begin instituting this new ritual.

- **CHAPTER 16: TOOL 4—FRENEMY RADAR.** Take half an hour to reflect on three intense events from the past week where a Frenemy was at play, and what caused it to appear. This will help refine your radar so you can more quickly pick up on the presence of your Frenemies in the future.

You don't have to do this alone; in fact, we encourage you to involve others. Often after we hold coaching sessions with leaders, they go home and tell their spouses about the lightning bolts of self-realization they felt and receive a surprise: "I could have told you that long ago for free." Your partner, friends, relatives, or colleagues can provide invaluable feedback and support as you embark on your journey. This is especially relevant now that you are ready to convert your learning experiences into action. Those who are close to you may notice your Frenemies more than you do or see areas where you aren't living up to your potential. When wisdom arrives, it doesn't matter what messenger brings it.

The One-Hour Weekly Fee

After reading the book and conducting all four self-coaching sessions, you'll continue to put in less than an hour each week relating to the third and fourth tools (Weekly Deliberation and Frenemy Radar). In a typical week, you'll spend . . .

- **30 MINUTES ON YOUR WEEKLY DELIBERATION (TOOL 3)**—Identify three tasks or events offering you the opportunity to make progress on your Immediate Priority in the coming week. Then formulate your intention for each one. If you did not reflect on your insights from each of last week's opportunities immediately after finishing the associated activities, then you have time to do this within the 30 minutes as well.

- **5–10 MINUTES TO REFLECT ON EACH OF THE WEEK'S TOP 3 SENSATIONS TO FINE-TUNE YOUR FRENEMY RADAR (TOOL 4) (TOTAL 15–30 MINUTES)**—After they occur, think abut the strongest sensations you felt in the past week, using the Frenemy Radar method. Dig deep to uncover the underlying mindsets that caused them, and how you can manage them better in the pursuit of your ambitions.

That adds up to 45–60 minutes per week. By all means, take longer if you like, whenever it's helpful for you during the week.

This chapter introduced you to the four tools that make up a simple, incredibly powerful toolbox you can use to take your Return on Ambition to a new level. Let us now dive into each tool one by one.

THIRTEEN

Tool 1—Philosophy of Ambition

Your Philosophy of Ambition is your set of guiding principles for the future, which evolve as you continue to learn.

WELCOME TO THE toolbox. Let's get started with the first tool, which is called your "Philosophy of Ambition." As the name implies, it calls for defining a set of principles to guide your Return on Ambition and to help you evaluate your life and work as you progress. Having a philosophy is far more important than simply having goals.

Goals as Ends—or Means

A goal can make you run faster, but it won't necessarily make you better or give your life more meaning. This chapter and the next one will walk you through the limitations of isolated goals and offer you an alternative, more effective approach that puts your goals in context.

In Part 1, we mentioned the sports psychology study showing that 78% of those who engage in sports and exercise enhance their performance by setting goals. It's fairly simple: You set a goal for how much faster you want to run a regular route and start timing your runs. The struggles that emerge as you try to meet your goal will force you to be creative about your strategy for meeting it. Maybe you dedicate certain days to practicing speed or endurance. You could use a heart-rate tracker to see if you're giving it everything you've got and then see how your heart rate improves.

Goals can help you but are unlikely in themselves to make a big difference in your Return on Ambition. Even Jim Collins's famous concept of "Big Hairy Audacious Goals" is not a panacea for improving something as far reaching as this.[1] Sure, a goal can boost your regular running pace, but every goal is just a small blip in the greater scheme of things.

Think of an ambitious person you know who has had the luck, skill, or stamina to achieve a surprisingly impressive goal. No matter how overarching that goal was, no longer having to pursue it frees up an enormous amount of energy that the person can now direct toward new aspirations. Once conquered, goals become part of your new baseline, a foundation from which to move forward. We have seen numerous examples of ambitious people who achieve their goals and then—sadly—find themselves in a void.

Falling short of a goal is not the end of the world either, though it might feel that way for a while. Sooner or later, you will encounter new windows of opportunity. Your setbacks prepare you to identify those openings and jump through them more elegantly. Life is not a single hit-or-miss contest. If you don't bag what you shoot at the first time, you'll get new chances. In either case, keep an eye on your ambition as a whole.

Have you ever lost the sense of how your goals fit into the broader picture of your life? Have you seen this happen to friends or family members?

Take economic independence as an example. If you suddenly don't need to work, you'll free up a lot of space in your life. But how well does economic independence work as a goal?

We have an impressive acquaintance—let's call him George—who has been highly successful financially. His track record includes cashing out of two big start-ups, which catapulted him into becoming a private investor, a board member of multiple hot start-ups, and a significant voice in the political debate about entrepreneurship in his home country.

Therefore, his confession over a drink was surprising: "To be honest, I'm quite bored," he said. Despite the admiration showered on him, his exposure to brilliant people, and the lasting economic independence he earned for himself and his family, he missed the buzz of being in the middle of a start-up and the excitement of its ups and downs. Simply put, George could not find his old passion after he arrived at the dream destination of financial freedom.

This missing piece is similar to the feelings reported by lotto multimillionaires. A study shows that the majority of those who won major lottery prizes say that despite their win, they find themselves feeling worse off than before they bought that lucky ticket, and they wish they'd never bought it in the first place.[2]

To lift himself out of his boredom, our friend George threw himself into a new breathtaking social entrepreneurship project six months after his late-night confession. He rekindled his passion for making a hands-on difference. Now George's work is an integral, personally nourishing part of his life, and each initiative he takes on is in line with his broader aspiration.

Your goals are ends that you want to meet, but they also have the potential to illuminate your path as you seek to accomplish and be fulfilled by something beyond those goals, something bigger and more meaningful. This is where the Philosophy of Ambition tool comes in handy.

Your Philosophy of Ambition is a short list of statements that outline the future states you yearn to achieve and what you wish for the journey. By formulating these principles, you state explicitly what you aspire to. While writing them, debate with yourself about what matters today and how you would like your purpose to evolve.

Your work to fulfill your ambitions is your biggest investment in your life. The clearer you can envision your desired return, the more effectively you can guide your efforts—while remaining aware of what you would like to enjoy along the way.

The Power of a Philosophy: The Financial World

To see the power of a philosophy, we now move to the tangible world of heavyweight investors Eugene Kleiner and Tom Perkins, who started an investment firm, Kleiner Perkins, in 1972 in what is now Silicon Valley.[3]

When you start an investment firm, you set goals for how much capital you want to raise, how quickly you want to grow, and how big you want to become compared to other funds. But your investment philosophy goes beyond the numbers. What kind of investments do you want to focus on? How do you want to do business? Kleiner and Perkins put their attention on early-stage start-ups (recently founded companies) and kept concentrating on them even when such investments temporarily fell out of fashion a few years later during a financial downturn.

Kleiner Perkins's philosophy focuses its partners on being of "the highest value of service for entrepreneurs." The firm's goal is "to invest in an ethical and moral manner, and to figure out investments in large and growing marketplaces." Its motto is "Someone you don't invest in today might be your best investment tomorrow."[4] The managers whose funds achieve the highest returns stick to their specific philosophies. That allows fund managers to focus and give their investors the comfort of knowing that they are experts in their specialty area. The firms Kleiner and Perkins invested in, earning outstanding returns, include such successes as Amazon, Electronic Arts, Google, Genentech, JD.com, and Twitter. Kleiner Perkins is legendary today.

When you work with Kleiner Perkins, you know what to expect and what is most important to do. Its philosophy helps the firm attract investors and determine whom to hire, how to train, what to focus on daily, what to invest in and when, and when to exit. It continues to evolve as a living organism and is continuously guided by its historic principles.

John Bogle and Ray Dalio, who each founded a firm around the same time as Kleiner and Perkins, also illustrate how important steady philosophies are to investors. However, their respective philosophies could not be more different. While Bogle and Dalio's firms both invest widely in stocks and bonds, what sets them apart is their approach to trading.

Bogle grounded his philosophy in his studies at Princeton University in New Jersey.[5] Investment fund managers bet on the future, and their success depends on the fate of individual companies or markets. The general stock market has always been and continues to be on a long-term, upward trajectory driven by the general economy's tendency to grow. Bogle compared the general returns on stocks over time with the performance of managed funds, after deducting management fees. He concluded that investing in a broad portfolio of stocks with no special intelligence was more profitable than paying somebody to pick individual stocks and bonds for you.

The philosophy for the company he founded, The Vanguard Group, is to spread investments widely so their returns follow the general market while minimizing the costs of managing their money. Vanguard invests extensively in specific markets to achieve its aggregate results, and it doesn't take much of its investors' money for doing so.

Today, The Vanguard Group has more than $6.2 trillion in assets under management.[6] The size of the fund is larger than the entire annual gross domestic product of Japan, the world's third-largest economy. The Vanguard Group is the globe's largest provider of mutual funds and the second-largest purveyor of exchange-traded funds. Its 17,600 employees invest money cost consciously. Bogle was always consistent in his philosophy and so are the leaders who succeeded him at Vanguard, though Bogle occasionally disagreed with them. His philosophy inspired a whole segment of investment firms to do business in a similar manner.

Ray Dalio did more or less the opposite of John Bogle. He started his career trading commodity futures with a special focus on agricultural products. Geography somewhat restricts agriculture's demand and supply sides, allowing a better idea of what's likely to happen. You can more easily make a model of this marketplace than of the general stock market, and that enables more meaningful predictions of future prices.

Dalio took this experience with him when he founded Bridgewater Associates in his small apartment in New York, not far from Bogle in New Jersey. Some of the firm's early earnings came from advising major buyers of agricultural products such as McDonald's, the fast-food chain, and Nabisco, the snack manufacturer. Over four decades, Dalio and his associates built many more models to illuminate upcoming developments in commodities and, later, also in stocks, bonds, and currencies. After starting as an advisory firm, Bridgewater raised funds and invested based on its analyses and innovative approaches. Its instruments helped it hedge its investments by allowing it to manage downward risks while harvesting likely upsides.

The concept that you can beat the market without making overly risky gambles is central to Dalio's philosophy. The firm's predictions up to the subprime mortgage meltdown and credit crunch in 2008 made it famous beyond the global investment community. Today, Bridgewater is the world's largest hedge fund with $160 billion under management and 1,500 employees.[7]

These stories show that you can greatly increase your return over time by considering, articulating, and evolving a set of principles that guides you beyond simple goals. Legendary investors, who outperform almost everyone else in the ultracompetitive financial industry, guide themselves by steadily applying their philosophies. A guiding philosophy is helpful whether you are investing other people's money or the energy and vigor of your own life.

Example of a Philosophy of Ambition

To illustrate the power of principles, consider Vivienne Ming, the data scientist and serial entrepreneur who turned down a dream job—an offer from Amazon founder Jeff Bezos, the world's richest man.[8] Bezos asked Ming to become Amazon's chief scientist, the well-paid top explorer of one of the world's biggest, fastest-growing data repositories. She turned him down.

The role failed Ming's guiding principle to "live a life that makes other people's lives better." She recognized that Bezos had the same intention, but she applied a different interpretation.

To stay true to her guiding principle, Ming set an ultimatum for accepting another offer. When the leaders of Emozia, a start-up analyzing mobile phone data to gauge users' emotional states for marketing purposes, asked her to join the board and become the firm's chief scientific advisor, Ming said she'd join only if she could use the company's data to help people with bipolar disorder, previously called manic depression, predict their next manic episode. She saw a huge potential for improving—and perhaps saving—many lives. One out of four sufferers of severe bipolar disorder go on to kill themselves, and Ming believed predicting episodes would allow people to seek help early.

Emozia accepted her conditions and succeeded in creating algorithms predicting manic episodes—and to predict them well ahead of time. How far in advance was possible? The jaw-dropping answer is that one of the algorithms created by Ming for Emozia could predict bipolar episodes three weeks in advance, significantly earlier than any previous indicator. Three weeks' notice enables sufferers to reach out for support to avoid or reduce the impact of the episode.

An admirable, extraordinary person in many ways, Ming became who she is only by clinging to her strong sense of purpose, which helped her through unnerving difficulties. People don't usually choose their own first and last name, but she did. "Ming" is an amalgam of Smith, her original surname, and Chang, the last name of her love in life, Norma Chang.

"Vivienne" is another story. Ming was born as Evan Smith, the privileged son of caring parents in sunny California, talented in both math and sports. The circumstances fostered high self-expectations in little Evan, but at just 11, he started feeling a sense of wrongness—an early indication of what became a living nightmare. This dread transformed into what Ming calls "a deep and profound self-hate, the kind of thing that robs you of not just your happiness but of the feeling of ever doing anything worthwhile in this world."

He eventually dropped out of college, became homeless, and started living in his car. His anxiety and insomnia often did not allow him to close his eyes before sunrise. He debated ending his life. He spent one particularly long night on the brink of that decision with a loaded gun by his side, but after myriad considerations, he concluded that he would live to make other people's lives better. Smith decided not to allow his deep sadness to steal his worth. He believed he could make a difference.

He managed to pull himself together. He earned outstanding test scores that got him accepted to Carnegie Mellon University, where he met Chang. Smith's newfound compassion made their love story possible, but he still fought his sense of internal wrongness, especially late at night after Chang fell asleep. It became impossible not to confess. Smith did what few men have ever done to a beloved fiancée. He told Chang, "I wish I were a woman." And Chang did what few fiancées have done in that situation; she understood.

In time, Evan became Vivienne. They married and now have two children (biologically theirs, with the help of modern technology). The Mings co-founded Socos Labs, an independent think tank focused on using technology to unleash human potential. One area of focus is how parents can "robot proof" their kids. It's all about making other people's lives better.

Vivienne Ming gives you a perspective on the power of being guided by an overarching philosophy and a clearly defined set of personal principles. Without it, she would perhaps have pursued short-term solutions or gone down a path that was not aligned to her aspirations in life. Instead, she was able to overcome significant challenges and stay true to her definition of living a life that makes other people's lives better.

Before we move on to the first self-coaching session, let's check in on our four friends from Chapter 1.

Bella's ambition is to use her art to change people's consciousness about how humans affect nature. This is her guiding principle during nearly sleepless, intense work sprints. In defining her Philosophy of Ambition, she says she wants her audience to appreciate her art not just momentarily but also to have the experience stay with them. Her art is not the end product; her goal is to maximize its result. Bella wants to inspire people to think and act differently. She is willing to live her life at a fever pitch, as she does now, for at least five years to see her dream begin to come true. As she emerges from being a student artist to being an independent professional artist, she wants to approach her creative work in the spirit of hope and purpose, not fear.

She understands that sometimes she will exhaust herself—and fall victim to her *Perseverance* Frenemy—so she promises to stop and rest before jeopardizing her health. She eventually shapes these reflections into her Philosophy of Ambition principles:

- Change people's consciousness about how humans affect nature through my art.

- Create art that is an aesthetic and intellectual experience that stays in the mind of the audience.

- Contribute to making people think and act differently.

- Dedicate at least five years to working extremely hard to see my ambition bear fruit.

- Learn to work in a spirit of hope and meaning.

- Maintain my good health by listening better to my body.

- Pay attention to my relationships, especially with my supportive parents.

Puzzling over his current problems with his team, Jitesh welcomes the opportunity to reflect, look ahead, and see the big picture. He knows he has a long way to go with his team to get back on track, but taking the long view builds his sense of perspective and renews his optimism. This elevated perspective helps him see that getting his current team to function better is a challenge on the road to his success, not a barrier. Jitesh takes 10 deep breaths to center himself, and then formulates his Philosophy of Ambition:

- Build my leadership skills and develop a reputation for helping people to become more productive and creative.

- Become a CEO of a Fortune 500 company before age 45.

- Build a network of like-minded people who can make a difference in the world.

- Meet a woman I can love and become a caring husband and father.

- Continue to work out to stay strong and healthy—and start running half marathons regularly.

continued

Nora and Alexander struggle to find the time to reflect, but they recognize how important it is to control their swirl of activities and to have an overarching purpose. They discuss whether to formulate individual sets of principles, but they recognize that the most important priority is their marriage and partnership. They start by formulating their shared Philosophy of Ambition:

- Spend proper, rested quality time with each other, as well as with our three children.

- Take risks in our careers and trust that better options are available when one of us is not happy about work.

- Use our expertise and quest for outdoor family time to embrace and help protect the natural world.

- Live healthily to experience and savor our children's years as kids and teens and, eventually, to be here to enjoy our future grandchildren.

- Stay young in mind and be more playful and less consumed with work.

They also share their individual aspirations. Aside from her corporate plans, Nora has a practical project in mind: She wants to reengage more deeply with her daughter Michele by working with her to redesign her girlish pink bedroom now that she's almost a teenager. Alexander feels drawn to address the climate crisis, either through an environmental nonprofit or through his company. Both parents agree that their immediate challenge is to spend more one-on-one time together and with each child.

Reflecting on the exercise they have just been through, Bella, Jitesh, and Nora and Alexander initially found it difficult to define their principles. However, as soon as they were able to find a quiet spot and calm their minds, their aspirations began to emerge. They acknowledge that focusing on the principles of their Philosophy of Ambition has expanded what they believe they can accomplish, and they are enthusiastic about bringing the principles to life.

OVER TO YOU—YOUR FIRST SELF-COACHING SESSION

You have now arrived at your first self-coaching session, your opportunity to formulate the principles of your Philosophy of Ambition. You may have a lot on your mind and in your heart. Take a walk, breathe some fresh air, and open your mind and senses before you get started. You can even conduct the whole self-coaching session while walking, as long as you can sit down and take notes occasionally. Or you might wait until tomorrow morning as you remain in bed thinking. Choose a location that works best for you, but make sure you're focused and can carve out an uninterrupted hour. Ideally you bring along a set of pens in various lively colors and at least two pieces of paper.

You are welcome to reflect longer—in fact, once you get started, you may find that you wish to think deeply about your life more often—but spending an hour alone to formulate your Philosophy of Ambition is a good beginning. When you formulate multiple attractive principles, you might find that some of them do not support each other. This will help you bring more attention to how to balance them, from which you can learn. You can always go back and review and revise the principles in your first draft.

The box below contains all the guidance you need to have an effective self-coaching session about this subject, and you can use its techniques whenever you face an issue you need to reflect on. There is space to capture your notes at the end of this self-coaching guide.

TOOL 1: PHILOSOPHY OF AMBITION

WHY

Your Philosophy of Ambition helps you define the guiding principles for living a meaningful life. It provides a frame of reference for assessing how satisfying your Return on Ambition is for now. Make sure your ambitions move you in the right direction and don't undermine your joy on the journey.

WHEN

Defining your Philosophy of Ambition is the start of your effort to work more consciously and competently to realize your Return on Ambition. Pause anytime to reflect on whether you're living in accordance with your philosophy. You will become much wiser as you apply the entire Return on Ambition Toolbox. As you move on, you can always edit or expand your Philosophy of Ambition.

Reserve one whole hour for your first self-coaching session. This is part of your entry fee, so embrace it. Chose a harmonious location. In solitude and free of distractions, contemplate the ideas and goals you think will be most important to you for the next couple of years and throughout your life in general.

Make sure that you have pens and paper.

HOW

This self-coaching session has three rounds. In the first round, you explore the art of the possible. In the second, you start drafting your principles. In the third, you select and define your principles. Here's the agenda:

ROUND 1: REFLECTING ON THE ART OF THE POSSIBLE

Please make sure that nothing will distract you for the next hour. Put your phone on flight mode. Place yourself in a quiet spot. When you are ready, relax your body.

Take a couple of deep breaths. Inhale slowly through your nose and all the way down filling your lungs. Relax your stomach and let it expand naturally as you breathe in. Do not rush. Notice the calming effect. Breathe out, in a relaxed way, through your mouth. Do this four more times.

Read one question at a time. Don't write anything down yet. Just wonder about the possible answers and explore your thoughts while you try to sense what feels most right for you. Notice the sensations in your body. Take a few minutes to reflect on each question before you go to the next.

- What am I most grateful for in life?
- When and how am I most truly alive?
- How would I describe my true self?
- What am I most excited about in my future life?
- Who means something special to me?
- Who might be special to me whom I have not yet approached or even met?

continued

- What do I want to do for the people who are special to me?

- What do I want to do for others beyond them?

- What difference do I want to make?

- Right now, what is most important to me?

- Am I completely honest with myself?

ROUND 2: DRAFTING THE FIRST PRINCIPLES

If you are in a flow state of mind, please just continue with the questions below. Note your answers on paper. Go through these questions, feeling free to jump back and forth among them. The most important thing is to allow yourself to be introspective about each question.

- While reflecting on my answers to the above questions, do I notice any common themes?

- Do I notice any outliers?

- Is there a universal truth that will always guide me—and if so, what is that truth?

- What do I aspire to achieve for myself, my closest loved ones, and the world around me in the next three years? The next 10 years? Throughout my lifetime?

- What role should personal growth play in how I aspire to develop and how I value learning?

HOW

- What gives me the most energy in enjoying the present moment and in recharging my body and mind?

- What are absolute musts for me in my everyday life, and what am I willing to let go of to enable these musts?

ROUND 3: SELECT AND DEFINE YOUR PRINCIPLES

Glance through your notes so far and reflect on what is most important to you and what you have not yet captured fully. Choose and articulate one or a couple of principles—not more than seven—and capture each one in a single, self-explanatory sentence. You can refer back to the principles Bella, Jitesh, and Nora and Alexander wrote as an illustration of what they could look like.

If you feel creative, take a clean sheet of paper and start writing out your new principles with colorful pens. Maybe even add a few simple illustrations. Artistic rendering can help bring your new principles to life and make them more personal, inspiring, and memorable. You can even frame the page afterward and hang it up in a place where you'll see it every morning before starting a new day.

continued

WHAT

List one to seven self-explanatory one-sentence statements that, combined, make up your Philosophy of Ambition:

_____

_____

_____

_____

_____

_____

NOTES

What reflections and insights do you have from this self-coaching session beyond the outcome of listing your principles? What do you now know about yourself that you didn't know before? How could this help you in the future?

_____

_____

_____

_____

_____

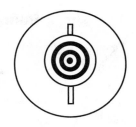

FOURTEEN

Tool 2—Immediate Priority

Your Immediate Priority is your focus for the next one to three months, including a note on what Frenemy to look out for.

WITH YOUR PHILOSOPHY of Ambition defined, you can start formulating the first goal in a sequence of goals that will move you toward a higher Return on Ambition. The second tool is simply called Immediate Priority. Yes, it's singular—one priority. That might sound unambitious at first glance, but as an ambitious person, you will have a myriad of other obligations with success criteria in various shapes and forms taking place in parallel. A singular goal related to your Return on Ambition enables you to maintain the required focus and dedication, before moving on to the next goal.

We begin by helping you understand why most personal goal-setting strategies don't work and how the Immediate Priority tool addresses these shortcomings. Then we review the underlying components of the tool: a qualitative objective, several quantitative measures, a Frenemy Watchlist, and a one-to-three-month timeline. At the end of the chapter, you'll be ready to conduct your second guided self-coaching session.

The Three Sources of Poor Personal Goal Setting

People struggle with the goals they set for three significant reasons: They set too many goals. The goals are too long term. And they are too superficial.

TOO MANY GOALS

Trying to do too much is a common, untreated disease among ambitious people. It has a lot to do with having too many explicit and implicit goals. People prone to this problem often accomplish less than they expect of themselves, and it can weigh down their mood and weaken their relationships. Today's frenetic pace of life reinforces this tendency.

A few decades ago, the world was simpler and moved at a slower pace.[1] People read one newspaper, based on their political views or their location. National borders limited your number of television channels, which aired for only a few peak hours. The nightly news, delivered by newscasters with gravitas, was the last word. Mainstream fashion shifted gradually, and trends traveled slowly. Calling someone required both of you to use a phone plugged in with a wire. Mail took days to arrive. Travel was expensive and limited to big-city airports. Daily life had a more or less predictable rhythm.

Today's urban life is a sizzling, fizzling pot of options and interruptions. Seemingly, anybody can become almost anything. The world is wide open with infinite opportunities, as change accelerates too fast to filter or absorb. There is constant information overload. Spouts of contradictory advice confuse people about whether to eat this but not that, to exercise one way or another, to say this and not that—and the Twitter and Instagram arbiters greet every possible answer with both honor and shame. Reporters' reputations soar based on the number of clicks they receive, so they make their stories sensational. Influencers spin their tales. And everyone can comment instantly on everyone else.

The availability of multiple possibilities is fantastic, but having so much choice challenges human beings, especially when time is scarce and decisions have to be made quickly. The more opportunities you have relative to what is possible, the higher the risk of stressing over your decisions, making bad choices, or procrastinating about making good ones. Take a deep breath.

Are you trying to do too much?

It's easy to get caught in one of the most pervasive tendencies of modern life: an overwhelming drive to do too much. The symptoms include chronic busyness, widespread untidiness, a feeling of inadequacy, and sleep deprivation. It might help explain why your Chapter 3 self-assessment scores on achievement, growth, or well-being were not as high as you would have liked. Striving for too much limits the potential for thriving.

The Immediate Priority tool will help you gain and maintain laser-sharp focus on the opportunity that will make the biggest difference for your Return on Ambition right now. That makes it relevant for you to look again at your sources of dissatisfaction and address the area with the biggest potential for improvement.

GOALS THAT ARE TOO LONG TERM

Did you wake up this morning feeling energized by a significant milestone that you have carefully crafted for yourself, one that demands you do your best in the coming days?

What a difference it makes to answer "yes." Having to answer "no" or even "maybe" could indicate that you're wasting your potential. You alone are responsible for framing your priorities in ways that make you jump eagerly out of bed every morning.

The Immediate Priority tool has a one-to-three-month time frame. It will guide you to define at least two quantitative accountability measurements to track your progress and pace yourself to achieve your goal on time. No matter which Frenemy tries to either help or get in your way, defining and owning your priorities will help you activate your accountability for your life, your work, and your Return on Ambition.

GOALS THAT ARE TOO SUPERFICIAL

The third mistake in setting goals is to set superficial objectives. Extensive research shows that this helps explain one of the greatest modern mysteries: How can so many people make New Year's resolutions and so few live up to them?[2]

Say you want to lose weight. Joining a fitness center, using a step-counting app, and going on a big-bang shopping tour for healthy food can help. But you are unlikely to lose much weight or to maintain a lower weight over time unless you understand what inner tensions this aspiration might cause.

Have you in the past set goals that faded away after a short while and were eventually abandoned?

As you learned in Part 2, Frenemies can act against your intentions and ruin your plans. For example, *Flexibility* is very effective at ruining a new diet. You can commit categorically to your diet, and *Flexibility* will, at first, help you arrange your life to accommodate your new regime. But as the days and weeks pass, and you lose some visible weight, you might find yourself in unforeseen situations. Say that you are invited to a family gathering. It's inconvenient, but you put on your party best and show your appreciation for the festive food and wine by consuming what is served. *Flexibility* helps you through this short sequence of social obligations, which your friends and family wouldn't have enjoyed as much if you insisted on not eating or drinking anything fattening. Without your old Frenemy *Flexibility*, you wouldn't have been yourself. It's been a part of you for as long as you can remember. It kept you polite. But as a result, you have violated your diet so severely that it's impossible to continue in the previous diet spirit on Monday. Could you have gone and just quietly avoided the foods you didn't need to eat? Maybe—but not without managing your Frenemy.

The Immediate Priority tool helps you contemplate which Frenemy carries the most significant risk to each new aspiration, and how you can ensure it does not get in your way.

Effective Goals:
Practical, Precise, Personal, and Passionate

Football (soccer) is extremely popular in part because the objective is clear. To win, a team must put the ball into the goal, guarded by the opposing team, more times than their opponent. Football is easy to understand, is suspenseful, and often ends with close, nail-biting moments that send fans into passionate frenzies.

In daily life, the power of the Immediate Priority is like that of football. You want to counteract the tendency to create too many goals, especially ones that are too long term or superficial. Instead, you want goals that are practical, precise, personal, and which you are passionate about.

The obstacles you face in preparing to tackle your goals are likely much more sophisticated than a game of football made up of three simple poles on opposite ends of the playing field. To help you codify your Immediate Priority, include four crucial elements, each of which we will walk you carefully through:[3]

1. One qualitative, aspirational objective.

2. Between two and five quantitative and aspirational measurements.

3. One Frenemy on your watchlist.

4. A time frame of one to three months.

Let's go through the four elements in an order that follows their natural flow. At the end of the chapter, you'll find a thorough guide to your next self-coaching session. Don't worry about taking specific steps before the self-coaching session. For now, focus on getting an initial sense of how this powerful new tool will work for you.

ELEMENT 1: ONE QUALITATIVE AND ASPIRATIONAL OBJECTIVE

First define a single, qualitative, aspirational goal with the largest, most imme-diate potential for increasing your Return on Ambition. Select an objective motivated by and consistent with your Philosophy of Ambition. Typically, it would relate to increasing your achievement, growth, or well-being, or a com-bination of them at the same time. Do not pick something that will happen almost by itself. You want something that stretches you so it will spark your excitement and impel you to move with determination.

"Qualitative" means that you can't hide your wish behind a number. Peo-ple express genuine passion through emotions, not numbers. "Aspirational" implies an affirming wish to achieve something, as opposed to wanting to avoid something. The difference can be as subtle as that between wanting to stop smoking, which is avoidance, and committing to live healthily and do intense physical activity every single day. A desire to avoid makes your brain pay more attention to what could go wrong, while an aspirational objective lets you focus on what is desired.

Once you have a single Immediate Priority, nail it down by reflecting deeply about what is the biggest possible difference you would like to see in one to three months.

Now Bella, Jitesh, and Nora and Alexander must work through their Immediate Priorities. This requires a thought process different from that used when formulating a Philosophy of Ambition. To craft their Immediate Priority, Bella, Jitesh, and Nora and Alexander will need to cherry-pick the area with the most significant, short-term potential for improving their Return on Ambition.

Bella takes a long, thoughtful walk, immediately grabs a pen upon returning to her apartment, and writes:

I will approach opportunities with openness, courage, and opti-mism in my art and life.

Jitesh feels a need to reach out to his colleague in the Human

Resources department before defining his Immediate Priority. He admits to being lost with the team he's managing and emphasizes his commitment to become a more effective, successful leader. That goal is quite broad, so his HR partner helps him zoom in. Jitesh's goal becomes the following:

I will help at least two members of my team become significantly more productive and better able to deliver work on time, according to our collective expectations.

Nora and Alexander struggle a bit about when and where to begin. It took a week after they'd agreed to move ahead just to find the time to sit down together to discuss their Immediate Priority. As they share a couple of glasses of wine one evening, their objective emerges by itself:

We will do what we must get done professionally in less time to allow more time for each other and our children.

Notice that each goal statement starts with "I will" or "we will." That's no coincidence. You will connect better with your passion and confront yourself more completely when you say, "I will" instead of watering down your promise by omitting "I" or by saying, "I want to" or "I would like to."

ELEMENT 2: BETWEEN TWO AND FIVE QUANTITATIVE AND ASPIRATIONAL MEASUREMENTS

To fulfill the second element of the Immediate Priority exercise, put "quantitative" trackers in place to see if and when you are progressing with your qualitative objective. Be aspirational and use numbers. You can use "done" and "not done," the binary equivalents of 0 and 1, or you can use the entire numerical scale. Your measurements should reflect what you are actively and productively doing, not something that you want to stop doing.

The quantitative measures are feedback mechanisms that help you gauge if you are truly progressing. The more precise and granular your feedback mechanisms are, the better your chance of knowing where you could do better and when you are about to achieve your objective.

Create no more than five measurements so that you will be able to remember them all by heart and to keep them manageable. And you should have at least two measurements for two reasons: awareness and quality of thought.

The first of these two reasons is related to the so-called "Moonwalking Bear Phenomenon." It's quite puzzling if you haven't seen it; just type "basketball awareness test" into YouTube.

Eight basketball players are on the court, four wearing white shirts and four wearing black shirts. A voiceover asks, "How many passes does the team in white make?" Each team starts throwing its basketball around. Watch carefully while counting just the white-shirted team's passes. But as viewers are intently counting the players' moves, few of them notice— especially since the phenomenon has not been introduced by name—that a man in a bear costume is moonwalking right across the basketball court as the teams throw the balls.

That's exactly the risk of a single performance measure. You get so focused on that target that you don't pay attention to anything else. You don't see the bear that you're not looking for or expecting. Applying two or more measures in parallel will make you more observant and give you a better sense of what's going on—and you won't miss a dancing bear.

The second reason for having at least two measurements is that you might define the first measure with ease, but you may struggle to find the second one. To see what we mean, try this simple thought experiment:

- You and your assistant are paid $1.1 million in total.

- You are paid $1 million more than your assistant.

- What is your assistant paid?

You can quickly figure out that the assistant must get $0.1 million. *Right?*
No, that's actually wrong. The correct answer is half that: $50,000. You

received $1 million more than your assistant. The sum of what you and your assistant get is twice your assistant's pay plus $1 million and should equal $1.1 million. That can only be the case if your assistant gets $50,000.

Around four out of five smart, well-educated people get a puzzle like this wrong when they have the impression that it is easy. Nobel laureate Daniel Kahneman and the late Amos Tversky, his long-time research partner, formulated such thought experiments to prove that people are less rational than they believe they are.

The practical message from their research is that you can get smarter by thinking more slowly about something difficult. The little quiz looked easy, but it consists of two equations with two unknowns. That's not advanced math, but getting the right answer requires most people to slow down their thinking a notch. Getting the puzzle wrong has more to do with thinking too fast than with mathematical abilities. If you think, "Oh, this is simple subtraction," you'll get it wrong. If you got the correct answer, then you took a little more time than most people—or you've done so many double equations with two unknowns that they have become second nature. And if you had known in the first place that it was tricky, you would have thought a little more slowly and had a higher chance of answering correctly.

This explains the second reason for formulating at least two quantitative measures. Something that looks easy doesn't compel you to slow down and really think. The first measurement is typically straightforward, while the second or third should require more thinking. To enhance your contemplation, keep adding measures until it gets difficult to define another meaningful gauge. Your debate with yourself will help you clarify what you really want and don't want, and then you can measure what you want to accomplish. You will notice issues you otherwise would not have faced until you were well into pursuing your goal. Now, you are already making progress because you are visualizing your future effort.

You can base your measurements on performance or practice. Ideally, you want at least one measurement for each. Performance-oriented measures relate to your outcomes, while practice-oriented measures relate to what you do to create desired outcomes.

Outcomes are essential but not the only thing that counts. You can go to five job interviews poorly prepared without a plan for what to say and still get the job in one of them. Alternatively, you could prepare and strategize better than anyone else and yet not get a job, though you are as qualified as the other candidates. You control how you practice, but other factors influence your results, like how someone else perceives you and your performance. By measuring both practice and performance, you increase the odds of doing your best and securing a successful outcome. Even if you don't succeed, you enhance your learning and increase your chances of success in the future.

Define performance-oriented measures in one of two ways:

- **ACTUAL RESULTS:** How many goals will you score? How big will the deal end up being? Will your direct reports come to the meeting prepared? What test grade will you get? How fast will you run the half marathon?

- **RATINGS BY OTHERS:** Will your teammate rate you as the top player in the match? How high will your colleagues rate your effectiveness? What grade will your professor give you for your verbal participation in courses? Will your children say you are becoming more attentive?

Your performance measure will help you stretch your motivation to break old thought patterns. Ideally, create a measurement where you feel stretched but not overwhelmed. That's exciting, but it reduces the risk of elevating unhealthy levels of stress and anxiety.

In some situations, stretching to meet a performance goal isn't relevant. An example could be whether you get that dream job or not. There is no room to stretch. Either you are hired or you aren't. It's binary, 0 or 1. However, don't limit your motivation to that one measure. Add an extra performance criterion. For instance, listen for your interviewers' feedback and notice what you've done well. Your second output measure could be that your interviewers give you feedback afterward that confirms your aspiration: "I showed that I'm enthusiastic and passionate instead of staying inside my introverted shell." That extra performance measure means that you are not setting yourself up just to pass or fail. You've created room to make progress within what otherwise would have been an either-or situation.

Practice-oriented measurements help you track your effort and institute new habits, which overrule older, less productive ones. For these measures, the real challenge tends to be just living up to your newly defined standards and maintaining new habits.

You can turn to two types of practice-oriented measures:

- **COMPLETED TASKS:** How much distance will you run during a match? Will you deliver your project? Will you submit your master's thesis? How many times will you join your family for an entire dinner?

- **ADHERENCE TO NEW HABITS AND ROUTINES:** Will you ask yourself every time you get the ball whether the team benefits most if you pass or try to score? Will you gather weekly feedback from your colleagues on what you did well and what you could do better? Will you pause and think before answering any questions? Will you meditate for half an hour at least three times this week?

Define practice-oriented measures in terms of observable behaviors. Don't leave anything up to debate or interpretation. "I will become more creative" is not observable or measurable. Tweak it to an observable alternative: "I will write one unique new idea every day," or "Each day, I will identify one question that is relevant to my work but for which I do not know the answer."

Bella must find ways to measure whether she is focusing on opportunities with openness, courage, and optimism or not. That's a bit abstract, but eventually she lands on borrowing the mathematics term "possibilistic"—meaning what is possible—to express her future scope. She is proud of herself for being creative in devising these measurements:

continued

- Conceptualize one piece of hopeful and possibilistic art every week.

- Ask myself every morning, "What fear will I defeat today?"

- Have two of my professors, unprompted and independent of each other, give me feedback that they see a significant leap in my artwork.

Jitesh found it easier to define measures after talking with his HR colleague. He identified two team members to work with and continued to add measures until he struggled to come up with a meaningful fifth measure:

- Work with Sarah and Mateo until they each become punctual and self-manage the completion of their tasks. (Recognize them when they perform well or show up on time.)

- Conduct half-hour, weekly one-on-one sessions with them to discuss what they're learning and how to tackle their upcoming challenges.

- When I'm with them, listen instead of talking at least half the time. Use curious questions in at least half of my comments.

- At the end of the week, discuss with Sarah and Mateo what each of us has done well in our interactions and what we could do even better next week.

Before they create measurements, Nora and Alexander fill their empty wine glasses. They're puzzled about how to get everything done in less time. Nora starts laughing after sipping her wine: "Alexander! We're letting the work rule instead of letting our time rule. Why don't we decide how much time to make available for work, and then reverse engineer our schedules to focus on what matters most to do in that time?" Alexander thinks a moment and then toasts her with his lifted glass: "Let our calendars rule, not our to-do lists!" They end up with a set of measures that are a bit nerdy, but they're both excited about them:

- Score ourselves on how well we keep our work (when not traveling) between 7:30 a.m. and 6:00 p.m. on workdays, with no more than 2 nights a week with work between 8:00 p.m. and 10:00 p.m. Work no more than four hours total during the weekend.

- Have a "just the two of us" date every Tuesday evening.

- Have a family dinner at least twice a week.

- Have 24 consecutive hours every weekend with no planned activities with anyone except each other and our kids. During that time, turn off our mobile phones and computers. And theirs.

- Each week, ask Liam, Jean, and Michele whether they have found us attentive—thumbs-up or thumbs-down.

Bella, Jitesh, and Nora and Alexander blended performance and practice measures so they have at least one of each. They've committed to stretch targets, though they would be satisfied just to get close.

You may not be used to being this thorough in your goal setting and pursuit of your ambitions. However, measuring your progress in the right way is vital to harvesting this book's full benefit and maximizing your Return on Ambition. Be assured that as you practice and increase your level of awareness, you will require less and less time and energy to continue to track your progress in this way in the future.

ELEMENT 3: FRENEMY WATCHLIST

The third element in your Immediate Priority, the Frenemy Watchlist, is a critical step for improving your Return on Ambition. Your Frenemies can help you move forward, just as they helped you get where you are today. However, they might manifest in ways that hamper your progress and mess up your aspiration.

Watch out for the one Frenemy you think will make the biggest difference between your success and failure. Putting that Frenemy on your watchlist is enough to make a difference. That helps you to plug into two distinctively different forms of self-awareness: how the targeted Frenemy affected you in the past, and what it might still be prone to doing any minute.

Acknowledging old patterns creates "conceptual self-awareness." You now understand new things about your past, how you "show up" in life, and what drives your behaviors. There is a pattern in some of your thoughts and behaviors that is now visible to you. Being aware of how a Frenemy played you in the past, however, does not guarantee that you'll notice when it starts playing you again.

The other kind of awareness you need is "embodied self-awareness."[4] You cannot strengthen that just by reading a book—you need to take action, to observe yourself, and to sense what is happening in the moment. You will feel bodily sensations and emotional outbursts when you are in situations that don't suit your instincts and where you go against your behavioral habits or normal thought patterns. Your subconscious tries to warn you through an intensified heartbeat, a tightening in the gut, or other bodily sensations. Anger, disgust, or anxiety tend to unfold with that. With embodied self-awareness, you'll pay attention to these tensions and notice how your Frenemies are about to creep up on you in real time. That allows you to pause and make alert, conscious choices about whether you want them in play or not.

Your Frenemy will still surprise you, though you are more conceptually aware. In fact, you may be more surprised because you thought you knew by now how to master this Frenemy.

We illustrated the *Competitiveness* Frenemy earlier in this book with Careem co-founder Magnus Olsson, who noticed how insistent he could get to win an argument. It's one thing to gain the insight that you might be too intense in some meetings, and a completely different thing to notice in real time that you're becoming increasingly tense during a collegial discussion that is slowly, but steadily, heating up. This calls for being aware of your actions and heeding the saying "Life can only be understood backward; but it must be lived forward."[5]

Olsson received feedback and reflected on it. That helped him increase his conceptual self-awareness, but he still had to work on his embodied self-awareness and instinctive reactions in the moment. Essentially, the difference rests in whether you notice when conditions are emerging for a Frenemy to intervene. Unless you are aware that the Frenemy is about to manage you, you cannot make the conscious choice to do something about it right now, in the moment. Your Frenemy Watchlist will help you to think about which Frenemy to watch for so you can avoid running out of fuel or being derailed.

There are three main ways your Frenemies can show up and slow you down:[6]

- An old Frenemy tries to push you against your new intentions.

- Two Frenemies try to help you in conflicting ways, making you feel torn about whether to follow one or neither of them.

- You depend on a Frenemy that suddenly refuses to help you.

Typically, an old Frenemy shows up and is overly active. You may be in the process of moving ahead when the Frenemy shows up loudly and in the least friendly fashion. *Competitiveness* could start barking—just as Olsson described it in discussions where he wasn't winning. You could be a considerate, collaborative colleague and then, suddenly, push your full weight into winning a discussion with a teammate just for the sake of winning—and just when you thought you had tamed that old Frenemy. It takes only an inattentive moment for it to create a lot of noise and damage.

The second way is that you may experience a situation where several Frenemies are competing. You may be having a collision of overactive Frenemies, jockeying to disrupt each other. Imagine *Desire* hustling to make things better while *Flexibility* is pushing to be more sensitive to everyone's opinions. Especially during times of change, you may be prone to feeling torn between competing demands. Your Frenemies are not helping you out of that mess but are only making it bigger.

Finally, the Frenemy could fail to show up. While you could usually depend on, say, *Boldness*, it could temporarily go on strike, leaving you unable to move forward. Instead of feeling intense, as when a Frenemy would be noisy, you can feel low energy. That can lead to a feeling of exhaustion or melancholy. You used to have a strong sense of what is right and wrong, but you are suddenly insecure, and your dear old Frenemy refuses to give you that usual push.

Any of these three scenarios could apply to you, just as any of the seven Frenemies could threaten your Immediate Priority. The watchlist exercise draws on your conceptual self-awareness and stimulates your embodied self-awareness by asking you to imagine how your Frenemies could disturb you. That's the essence of it, but after you put a Frenemy on your watchlist, go one step further. Ask what would make that Frenemy reappear or disappear.

The more you acknowledge the motives of the Frenemy on your watchlist, the better your odds of catching it and redirecting it before its friendly side lets you down or the enemy in it goes against you. Something could be going on in that Frenemy's realm that you aren't yet seeing. What could make *Boldness* go on strike or impel *Competitiveness* to respond harshly to a colleague for no constructive reason?

When you consider what makes a disturbing Frenemy act out, you are ultimately asking yourself what you are subconsciously perceiving as a threat. Your Immediate Priority and your good old Frenemy are not in alignment. The tension between the two is neither rational nor trivial. Discovering the true source of your dilemma usually involves delving into your Frenemy's deep-rooted motivations.

For example, you can be passionately committed to going on a diet, and your Frenemy *Flexibility* can help you get off to a good start. After the first few weeks of progress, *Flexibility* might, however, help you to bond with your family and enjoy the good food that comes along with their way of showing care. The diet is your aspiration while *Flexibility* wants you to adapt to show your appreciation and be appreciated. *Flexibility* is a part of you, and now you suddenly don't want to follow along. The two of you used to go together, but now there is friction.

As you embrace your Immediate Priority, ask yourself which Frenemy it conflicts with the most. Take the time to shine a light on your core beliefs. Pushing yourself to explore what's really going on with your Frenemies will enable you to identify which beliefs do not serve you, and help you pursue your new aspirations more consciously.

Let's see how our friends are digging out their hidden assumptions and using them to tame their dominant Frenemies:

Bella gets excited as she makes her Frenemy Watchlist because she knows the tension between hope and fear is central to her objective to remain purposeful and optimistic in her art and her life. Considering each Frenemy's typical behaviors and her underlying mindset, she takes a walk out in the midnight-blue city before returning to her pen and paper. She jots this down:

Desire—This Frenemy wants to lash out when it feels that I'm neglecting my work. It is concerned that I should've achieved a lot more by now, and it's never satisfied. I worry that I keep chasing new, perceptively better things, rather than seeing each piece of art clearly for what it really is. Desire doesn't trust me to be good enough, so it is afraid I will fail.

The idea of fear and the motives of Frenemies are still a bit

continued

alien to Jitesh, so he needs to think. Given his objective to lead two team members to improve, he wonders which Frenemy is most likely to derail him. After a long silence, he types the name of that Frenemy and its main motive into a note on his phone:

Independence—I have a tendency to do things by myself, and I know this Frenemy can hit me the moment I have my first setback with Sarah or Mateo. This Frenemy would see their lack of progress as proof that I can't trust them, and that they are slowing me down, so I should just do the work myself. I need to watch out for this mindset and have patience, because I know that I can achieve more with their help, even though it may take time to get them set up in the beginning.

Nora and Alexander almost regret agreeing to use the tools together. Alexander has been teasing Nora by calling her "More More" after reading about the *Desire* Frenemy in Part 2. He continues even though she is now hitting back by calling him "my bulldozer," referring to his susceptibility to excess *Perseverance*.

They know they have these Frenemies, but they have to find time for a deeper conversation to dig out which Frenemy is the biggest enemy of their new, joint objective to specify their work hours so they have more family time. They identify the following:

Flexibility—It pushes us to accommodate all the requests from every aspect in our lives, even though the requests might not be important or could wait or be resolved by others.

Nora and Alexander had to acknowledge that while other Frenemies might also be in play, they had to pay the most heed to the one that seemed to be their biggest, most immediate obstacle.

Like Bella, Jitesh, and Nora and Alexander, you will identify the Frenemy that has the biggest potential to get in the way of your Immediate Priority. Then, pay continuous attention to the Frenemy on your watchlist so that you lower the risk of being triggered.

ELEMENT 4: A TIME FRAME OF ONE TO THREE MONTHS

The final element of the Immediate Priority is to settle on a timeline that is between one and three months. Three months is short enough to force you to act, and one month is long enough to allow you to make a difference in the area you identify. Selecting a timeline is another way to create a healthy stretch. You are better off setting too little time than too much. If you do your best, but don't quite make your deadline, you can always define a new related Immediate Priority.

The most effective people select the aspect of their work with the highest potential and use it to move faster than other people.[7] Instead of defining a wide area of improvement that demands plenty of time, they slice and dice their identified potential and make progress with a sequence of smaller stabs.

Nailing down your timeline has the practical aspect of making you think through your calendar. Time is the ultimate currency you invest in your ambitions, so make sure your scheduling works. Is an upcoming event driving your Immediate Priority? If so, structure your timing to accommodate it. If your time is scarce, consider prioritizing your other activities. Is a holiday coming up? Perhaps use the start of it as a deadline so you can go on your break with a clear conscience.

Studying your calendar is a crucial reality check, but time-deprived people, paradoxically, often can't find the time to do it until something forces them to focus—whether that's a badly timed flu or a commitment to set an Immediate Priority. Achieving a high Return on Ambition requires continuous awareness of time as part of your overview, prioritization, and fine-tuning.

Let's see how our friends are doing with their schedules:

Bella sets a timeline of one month for her Immediate Priority. Being so self-disciplined and measuring her actions this way still feels experimental to her. Since she's doing it as a test, she chooses

continued

the shortest possible timeline. After she takes her final notes, she closes her rolltop desk and heads out.

Jitesh goes for the full three months. His HR partner advises him not to expect quick miracles and to take the time to internalize his new way of working with his colleagues. He considers how his workout coach gets him to build his physical strength and realizes he can use that as a model for gradual, persistent improvement—with an occasional tough bench press.

As Bella did, Nora and Alexander set a one-month time frame. They want a test period to make sure they haven't overengineered their measurements. They agree to evaluate after a month and to discuss whether and how to adjust. Their commitment to change is indisputable, but with three kids and full-time jobs and all the things that can go wrong in a busy house, they are aware that they'll need the good aspects of *Flexibility* on their side so they aren't blown away by every household demand.

While they're talking, they want to spend a little more time defining their measurements, but Jean needs help with geometry, Michele has to have an ironed white shirt for tomorrow's school play, and Liam won't eat.

OVER TO YOU—YOUR SECOND SELF-COACHING SESSION

The ball is now in your court again! Your second one-hour coaching session is coming. As in the previous session, let your thoughts and feelings flow. For context, look again at your Philosophy of Ambition and the scores from your Chapter 3 self-assessments.

Spice up your thinking by asking selected colleagues, family members, or friends where they think you're doing particularly well and where they see the largest potential for you to improve your well-being, growth, or achievement. Check your recent performance evaluations, old assessment reports, or other structured feedback to see what you can use before you start your second hour of self-coaching.

TOOL 2: IMMEDIATE PRIORITY

WHY

Your Immediate Priority helps you identify and specify your short-term focus area for improving your Return on Ambition. This is the frame against which you should evaluate your current efforts.

WHEN

Always have a working, ongoing Immediate Priority with a defined horizon of one to three months. Do your best within the committed time and formulate a new Immediate Priority again after that. Your new Immediate Priority can be similar to your old one, if your most significant potential for raising your Return on Ambition is still within the same sphere. Ending one Immediate Priority and starting a new one calls for evaluating yourself, extracting insights from your effort, and using the data to articulate your priority for the next one to three months.

Align your Immediate Priority with your calendar so that an upcoming event, deadline, or holiday marks the end of one Immediate Priority and the beginning of another.

You are ready for your self-coaching session when you have an hour alone with no disturbance or distraction. Bring something to write with and your calendar. You can use your mobile phone in flight mode.

continued

HOW

This self-coaching session has six rounds: (1) explore your immediate potential, (2) frame your objective, (3) define your measures, (4) put one Frenemy on your watchlist, (5) set your timeline, and (6) review your notes from afar and make any final modifications.

ROUND 1: EXPLORE YOUR IMMEDIATE POTENTIAL

In the first round, ask a few questions, one by one, and go back and forth between them. The purpose is to explore where you are now, so ask what makes sense. What seems right? What do you feel? Identify as many possible areas with potential to be your Immediate Priority as you can. Don't write anything down yet. Take your time. It's perfectly fine to spend 10–20 minutes on this first round. Consider these questions:

- Are you keen to live any of the principles in your new Philosophy of Ambition more fully?

- Which of the three factors of achievement, growth, and well-being do you have the strongest urge to strengthen right away?

- Do the next one, two, or three months offer any great opportunities for reaching a higher level in any regard, or are you seeking balance as you move onward?

ROUND 2: FRAME YOUR OBJECTIVE

Now, draft your first notes while going through the following sequence of questions:

HOW

- What Immediate Priority offers you the biggest potential to improve your Return on Ambition over the next one to three months?

- Can you capture this one objective in a single, self-explanatory sentence?

- Are you truly passionate about it? Could you articulate it in a way that would make you feel even more strongly about it?

- Is your sentence aspirational (something you want to create or do) without representing avoidance (something you want to stop creating or doing)? If not, could you make it aspirational?

- Is your objective qualitative (expressed through its character and not simply by a number)? If not, how do you make it both meaningful and qualitative?

ROUND 3: DEFINE YOUR MEASURES

Keep taking notes and start making small sketches, drawing arrows among related points, and doing whatever else helps you solve problems and see a complete picture. Consider the following:

- What are your desired outcomes? Specify performance-oriented measures based on them.

- What actions or new habits will you commit to? Specify related practice-oriented measures.

continued

- What are the two to five measurements that together would provide the best guidance and help you track your progress?

- Is each one aspirational? If not, then consider how to move from avoidance to frame the measurements as something you aspire to create or actively do.

- How can you make each measurement quantitative (tracked by numbers or answered yes or no)?

- What are your targets for each quantitative measure?

- Can you stretch one or more of your performance-oriented measures to challenge old thought patterns about what is possible? If so, set targets where you feel challenged and excited, but not overwhelmed.

- Is it easy to formulate your measures? If so, then try to come up with more until it becomes tricky. You can generate more than five measures now, as long as you prioritize them before concluding your Immediate Priority.

ROUND 4: PUT ONE FRENEMY ON YOUR WATCHLIST

Please prepare yourself for a new and very different round of self-coaching. You should be introspective and look deeper into yourself. Take the time to dig deep as needed. Freely reflect on the questions below before writing down the name of the Frenemy and, at the end, its motive.

HOW

Arrange yourself in a comfortable position and take a couple of deep, slow breaths, centering yourself and preparing yourself for the following questions:

- Imagine that you are not pursuing your new Immediate Priority as intended. How do you see yourself behaving instead, or what aren't you doing as intended? Please think of actual behaviors that you might carry out or not. This isn't a question about thoughts and feelings, but about observable behaviors (actions that you and others can verify objectively). What could you be doing or not doing that could derail your progress?

- When imagining how you might violate your objective, can you connect that behavior to a particular Frenemy disrupting you (*Convention, Boldness, Independence, Competitiveness, Perseverance, Desire, or Flexibility*)?

- Which of the seven Frenemies would disturb you the most and deter you from effectively pursuing your objective?

- What motive would the Frenemy have for acting against your objective? Is this driven by an underlying need or fear? What is this Frenemy trying to protect or accomplish?

When you are done, note the name and motive of a specific Frenemy for your Frenemy Watchlist.

continued

ROUND 5: SET YOUR TIMELINE

This round is practical, so keep your pen ready.

- Start with a quick overview of your calendar for the next three months. Are any pivotal events coming up?

- Do you have any obligations for these events or other responsibilities that your calendar doesn't reflect?

- What is a realistic yet challenging timeline for achieving your objective?

- Is the timeline a stretch for at least one quantitative measure so you feel challenged and excited, but not overwhelmed?

ROUND 6: REVIEW YOUR NOTES FROM AFAR AND MAKE ANY FINAL MODIFICATIONS

You have covered a lot of ground in your one-hour Immediate Priority self-coaching session. Please run through your notes and circle the key points.

- Have you captured what is most essential?
- Could anything be missing and, if so, what?
- Are you passionately committed to your new Immediate Priority in its final form?

WHAT

Define the four elements of your Immediate Priority.

1. A qualitative and aspirational objective:

_____

_____

_____

_____

2. Two to five quantitative and aspirational measures (at least one performance oriented, and one practice oriented) and target values for each (ideally, set a target for at least one performance measure with an 80% chance of success):

_____

_____

_____

_____

_____

3. Frenemy Watchlist (name and motive):

_____

_____

_____

continued

WHAT

4. A time frame of one to three months:

_____

_____

_____

_____

NOTES

What reflections and insights do you have from this self-coaching session beyond the "What" outcome itself? What do you now know about yourself that you didn't know before? How could this help you in the future?

_____

_____

_____

_____

_____

_____

FIFTEEN

Tool 3—Weekly Deliberation

Your Weekly Deliberation helps you consider your intentions for three opportunities over the coming week and the lessons you learn along the way.

ON A RECENT walk with his 12-year-old daughter, Nicolai T asked what she was excited about these days.

Completely serious, Margaux answered, "I'm looking into life hacking."

When he asked what had piqued her interest in life hacking, his daughter described a YouTube video in which a teenage vlogger removed a splinter from her finger by pressing a shot glass against it. Margaux explained with enthusiasm how the hack makes the splinter come out almost by itself.

We hope splinters are not an issue for you, though you are likely interested in other helpful hacks—such as the best hacks for acting on your Immediate Priority in a way that sustainably improves your Return on Ambition over time. We are now moving from Tools 1 and 2—which you use periodically—to Tools 3 and 4, which you apply weekly. This chapter outlines the Weekly Deliberation tool and illustrates its power by looking at how it impacts your brain. As you will see, you can hack the chemical releases in your brain and progress on your Immediate Priority and, by extension, help you improve your Return on Ambition. The self-coaching session at the end of this chapter will help you conduct your first Weekly Deliberation.

The Power of Learning Loops

The Weekly Deliberation tool has four main elements and works as follows:

- Identify three opportunities in the coming week for progressing with your Immediate Priority.

- For each one, formulate an intention about how to use it to move ahead.

- When an opportunity materializes, do what needs to be done and observe what plays out.

- After the opportunity, reflect on your lessons learned.

That is, Intend, Do, Observe, and Reflect.[1]

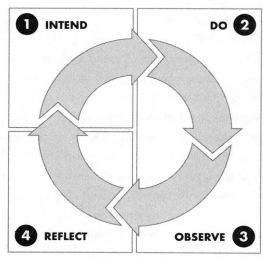

Identify at least three opportunities—they could be events, tasks, or time spent on your own—that can help you progress with your Immediate Priority in the coming week. For each of them, formulate an intention. The intention should be a desired outcome, or what you want to do better or differently, or what you want to learn.

Finally, and not before, reflect on the extent to which you fulfilled your intentions, and whether there were any extraordinary circumstances that made it easier or more difficult for you to pursue them. You should think about where your attention was directed, what you want to continue to do, and what you want to do better or differently in the future.

Act on your intention while doing and observing what is happening at the moment, what effects your actions have, and how the situation unfolds. There is no space for self-evaluation—neither appraisal nor judgment. Just do and observe, do and observe, do and observe...

Figure 15.1—The Weekly Deliberation Loop

This loop is incredibly powerful for developing yourself. For each opportunity, formulate a brief intention about how to handle it better or differently than before. That sharpens you and accelerates the speed and precision with which you change your way of thinking and acting.

The modern world would not be the same without pioneering variations of the Intend-Do-Observe-Reflect loop. As an example, the loop was a major force in establishing the current wealth of an entire nation. Japan's manufacturing industry went from being driven by cheap labor to—within a few decades—challenging industrialists all over the world on innovation and performance.

The human suffering and material losses were massive in 1945 when the United States dropped nuclear bombs on Hiroshima and Nagasaki. The 124th emperor of Japan, Hirohito, surrendered when the United States, along with Britain, China, and the Soviet Union, continued to exert massive military pressure against Japan.

Japan's economy was in ruins together with its national pride. Almost nothing in Japan worked, or it did so poorly. The nation had significant problems, including a dire need to improve its manufacturing base. Somewhat coincidentally, an American engineer ended up teaching statistical quality control to Japanese engineers and, after a while, also to managers. His name was W. Edwards Deming, and his work with the Japanese helped give birth to total quality management—or TQM. It also helped Japan make its leap forward.

TQM was a major inspiration for the Lean approach, which the Toyoda family instilled nearly religiously at their famous car factories. The heart of TQM is the so-called Deming's Cycle: Plan, Do, Check, and Act. Four short words on a string, repeated over and over. A range of similar concepts has seen the light of day in engineering, consulting, software development, and psychology.

In fact, Deming got his idea from an earlier pioneer in statistical quality control, who in turn borrowed it from a centuries-old scientific method with a loop resembling Intend-Do-Observe-Reflect, which constitutes your Weekly Deliberation.

The Loop in Action

Timing is vital to realizing the magic in the Intend-Do-Observe-Reflect loop. You could define a goal at the beginning of a three-month self-development effort during which you act and observe, and then reflect after the three months. That means you'd complete a single Intend-Do-Observe-Reflect loop in three months.

Or you could do multiple loops each month. Imagine that before starting each new week during the three months, you identify three opportunities that support your overall goal. Then you carry out three Intend-Do-Observe-Reflect loops per week for about twelve weeks, equaling thirty-six cycles in three months. That allows you systematically to think more deeply, gain more insights, and keep building on the lessons you've already learned.

This has great benefits but there is no gain without pain. You must slow down more frequently when it comes time to reflect. Unless you establish a routine for slow thinking right away, it's unlikely to last long. Make your Weekly Deliberation a small ritual before you start your weekend, or as you head into the workweek. Use it to wrap your head around what lies ahead. Some people relax better and enjoy their weekend more when they do their Weekly Deliberation beforehand. Then they can make their arrangements for the coming week so they don't need to worry about it. Others find it more natural to conduct their Weekly Deliberation at the end of the weekend or on Monday morning.

Let's run through each of the four steps in the loop to give you a feel for them before you use the self-coaching instructions at the end of the chapter to guide you through your first Weekly Deliberation.

Intend is the first step. Once a week, sit down, contemplate your three largest opportunities to progress with your Immediate Priority, and write down your intention for each one. Doing the Intend part will take you around 15 minutes. Aim for a fixed time every week, even if you might have to shift your time slot for some weeks. What counts is quickly getting into a routine of sitting down to think so you throw your energy into the reflection itself.

It's crucial that you create excitement with each intention. Your Weekly Deliberation should be a world apart from a traditional dull and lengthy to-do list. You should zoom in on each of your three opportunities to make progress in the coming week. Contemplate the possible, notice the nuances of what you could do, and give yourself a sound challenge. When you do so, you are turning a situation, which otherwise could have passed almost unnoticed in life, into the equivalent of a computer game where you have just reached a new level and now are excited about reaching your personal best.

Your effort should, like computer games, become what psychologists call intrinsically motivating. "Intrinsic motivation" means that doing the activity carries the reward in itself. You don't need to promise yourself a treat if you succeed. You are, instead, drawn toward the activity and enjoy doing what you do for its own sake. That contrasts with "extrinsic motivation," for which an external prize—ranging from a sweet treat to Singapore's five C's—is the incentive for acting. Both types of motivations are important for ambitious people. Yet you get access to more energy and can utilize your full potential better when you construct an activity so that it becomes intrinsically motivating.

Your creativity is the only limit on this opportunity to move ahead with your Immediate Priority. The opportunities you choose to deliberate about can be an event involving other people, a task for which you set aside time to accomplish on your own, or any kind of practice session or rehearsal. State each intention in a sentence or a short paragraph. You can use a few mental tricks to infuse your statements with positive energy.[2]

1. Envision your future after you fully attain your Immediate Priority, and contrast this picture with the way you'd normally approach the kind of opportunity you've identified as important.

2. Focus on what an attractive outcome looks like.

3. Consider how your Frenemies could advance your goal or deter it. Which one will you call on as a strength? Can you prepare in a way that reduces the risk of a Frenemy interruption?

4. Formulate your intention for each opportunity, making it intrinsically motivating to carry it out. Ask what you will do better or different.

Hint: Step up your game by writing a short note. This is important because your reflections will get sharper when you synthesize your thoughts, articulate the resulting aspiration, and go through the physical act of writing them down.

When Bella looks ahead during her first Weekly Deliberation, she identifies the submission of an art project that is due on Friday for one of her professors as the single, paramount opportunity for progressing with her Immediate Priority in the coming week. She has been working on a concept—or rather a range of potential installation concepts—for a while, but she isn't convinced any of them will be useful. Her normal way of working would be to keep making sketches and to go more and more in depth with those that feel best, while still creating additional drawings as ideas come to her.

Such a process is intense and isolating, since Bella works alone. Recently, she has doubted whether her process is taking her toward becoming her best. In the spirit of her recent reflections about ambition, she lets herself experiment with this assignment.

She feels daring as she forms the notes outlining her three opportunities and her intentions for each one:

- Monday: I will reflect on what's possible with the concept and encapsulate those possibilities in one overarching message.

- Tuesday: I will make three sketches from scratch, all wildly different from one another.

- Wednesday and Thursday: I will conduct a marathon session to complete the installation concept based on the sketch that most appeals to me at breakfast on Wednesday.

Bella has never worked like this before, in such a tight time frame. She's not comfortable, but she's curious about how her new artistic process will work out. It's scary to leave only two days to complete the concept with the illustrations and texts she needs to explain the installation and its significance to her professor. In reality, Bella seldom spends enough time actually finishing her submissions since she keeps working on new sketches that she scraps in a quest for better work.

Jitesh doesn't need much courage to select his three opportunities, since he's already thought about them so much, but he pushes himself to formulate bold intentions for each one. He finally works out the schedule in his head while swimming laps. He now just needs to write it down:

- Monday 10:00–10:30 a.m.: During my first weekly session with Sarah, I will help her take ownership for one task, which we will specify and prioritize for this week. I should give Sarah feedback on her thoroughness and quality of her thoughts, but I also must be honest and say that I want her to be accountable and to reach out to me about any problems before she has to make excuses for not meeting the deadline.

- Monday 11:00–11:30 a.m.: In my first weekly session with Mateo, I will work with him to clarify what should go into his monthly status report to finance. I should tell Mateo how much I appreciate that he is always on time, but that he must work harder to double-check the report to make sure all the data is up to date and consistent.

- Friday 1:00–2:00 p.m.: I will invite Sarah and Mateo for a nice lunch at the café around the corner and hold our first exchange of weekly two-way feedback. I will devote enough time to observe both of them and their work between now and then so I can be specific about what they did well and what is important for them to do even better next week. I will listen to their feedback without becoming defensive.

continued

Nora and Alexander sit down for breakfast Monday morning and realize that they have not yet done their Weekly Deliberation. As usual, the weekend got away from them. It doesn't take them long to identify three important opportunities to live up to their Immediate Priority in the upcoming week:

- Monday afternoon: Nora and her team must agree on the outline of their big, pending client report so they can submit everything finalized before the weekend.

- Tuesday evening: Alexander will arrange a date for Nora, just as he did when they first met each other and fell in love. He won't plan anything fancy, but his goal is that they can forget time and just talk about whatever comes to mind.

- Sunday: This week they resolve finally to take their kids on that much-discussed picnic in the forest, where they will make sure everything is nicely planned (not like their last hurried foray—remember cutlery this time!) so that they can both be fully present with each other and with Jean, Michele, and Liam.

As they make their plans, Alexander realizes that re-creating date night with Nora and participating in planning family dinners and excursions are really helping to relieve his sense of loneliness. The rush of their family life continues, but now he is becoming more enmeshed in it instead of watching it fly by.

Do and **Observe** are the next two steps that happen when the time arrives to act on your opportunity. They might sound straightforward, but people's normal attention level ignores a strong current of valuable insights that they could easily tap into to gain more momentum. Your *Competitiveness* Frenemy might spot a sideshow and try to join it, though it has nothing to do with your intention. *Boldness* might seduce you to move forward so fast that you don't notice nuances unfolding in your relationships. *Flexibility* might undermine your intentions and lead you to go dashing after any surprise. Each of your old Frenemies could make you miss out.

To keep them in place, focus on what really counts in the moment: actions that help you fulfill your intention. Concentrate so you're occupied only with what you intend to do, what is going on, and no more. Doing and observing should flow together and become like one. Your attention should oscillate seamlessly between them. This is like meditating while fully awake and engaged in an activity. For you, there is nothing else in the moment.

For example, while giving a speech, inwardly "observe" yourself for a moment: how you're engaging your audience, how you're standing, and what you're saying. Keep watching yourself. Do, observe, do, observe, do, observe. This takes practice. Doing something with deep concentration is one matter, but it is quite another thing to observe yourself intensely while you are doing it. And yet it's very different to move seamlessly between the two so you do and observe almost simultaneously and become one with your activity.

When you are in the middle of doing and observing, keep the temptation of evaluating and judging yourself at bay. Otherwise, your Frenemies will jump in. *Desire* always believes you could do much better. *Convention* fears for your social standing if you deviate from the etiquette expected of somebody like you. *Independence* likes pushing you to move ahead alone with whatever you have in mind and ignore what's going on around you. As helpful as these and other Frenemies might be otherwise, you don't want to distract yourself with their inner dialogues while you are acting on an intention, observing your actions, and trying to do your best.

You can't keep them from showing up, but you are responsible for not letting them hang around once you notice them. Your Frenemies' favorite topics include how others judge you: "Did I sound smart?" "Should I have said that differently?" "What are people thinking of me?" That's not relevant now. What matters is your intention and how you progress toward it by doing and observing.

The Do and Observe steps are similar to watching a movie at the theatre, rather than streaming it at home. You must watch the entire movie in one sitting and extract everything you can while it is playing. You can't pause or scroll back along the way. You are forced to be fully present. While you're doing and observing, connect the dots between what has just happened and what is about to happen. It's too soon to start debating with yourself or others whether or not you like the show. If you get distracted, then you won't capture what's going on.

To become better at doing and observing, reserve a moment in advance to detach and revisit your intention before you start. At least for a while, think of your intention, no matter how humble, as the most critical drive in the universe. Consider whatever you are about to do as if you're going to make a speech to a thousand people. Most speakers would take that rather seriously. You would probably go to the venue in advance to see whether everything is ready, what the stage is like, and how you turn the microphone on and off. You would remind yourself to switch off your phone and run through your speech mentally one more time. You could benefit from taking a couple of deep breaths before entering the stage and moving toward the microphone. A good start gets you far, but a rush can make you rash.

Reflect is the step that concludes the loop. Once you are finished doing and observing an activity, consider the big picture of what happened and evaluate how you contributed, what lessons you learned, and where you might benefit from acting differently in the future. The sooner you do this after the event, the better. A rule of thumb is to spend five minutes reflecting within 45 minutes after ending the activity.

Your recollection of actual details is much sharper in that time frame, enabling more precise learning. If, for some reason, you can't take a moment to think so soon after an event, do it later even though the contours of causes and effects may not remain as clear in your memory.

Ask yourself four especially helpful questions:

1. *How did I live up to my intention, and what facts support my perception?* Go back and revisit your intention and the degree to which you fulfilled it. You might have done everything you can to reach the desired outcome without fulfilling it, or you might have fulfilled it with much less effort than you expected.

2. *What did I pay attention to during the event or task?* Self-feedback depends solely on your observations. You cannot capture everything that happened during your intentional doing. You become more conscious about the limitations of your perspective when asking yourself about what you paid particular attention to. That reduces the risk of making false assumptions and gives you food for thought on how to observe yourself and your impact in the future.

3. *Were there any extraordinary circumstances that made it easier or more difficult for me to pursue my intention? (In other words: How was I lucky or unlucky?)* This question picks up on any outside circumstances—or just simple, plain luck. When you get unexpected help, realize that you can't count on that happening again.

4. *What should I keep doing or do differently in the future?* This question makes you clarify what you will keep doing and where you should enhance your game. This is important, whether you did everything perfectly or not. You can improve and grow just as well after failures as after successes. Please notice that the fourth question is positive by nature. It's not about what you didn't do well enough, but about what you did well and can grow to do even better.

Following up after your Intend, Do, and Observe steps, the Reflect step is an excellent source of self-feedback. The stated intention narrows your focus. You know what outstanding looks like. Your concentrated doing and observing generated facts. The quality of feedback you give yourself in the Reflect step can be as valuable as information that anybody else could give you. You need others to point at your blind spots, but you can see a lot that they cannot see when you put your spotlight on an event or task with a clear intention in mind. Never undervalue self-feedback—especially when it's part of an Intend-Do-Observe-Reflect loop.

Bella, Jitesh, and Nora and Alexander are also learning some help-ful lessons as they follow the Intend-Do-Observe-Reflect loop.

Bella realized on Wednesday morning that she felt much stronger and more confident than usual about choosing the right sketch as the conceptual basis for her installation. Its message was crystal clear to her already on Monday, and she playfully explored a couple of its possible manifestations on Tuesday. Her work was speaking to her more meaningfully, and Bella didn't ask—as she would have before—which of her ideas her professor would appreciate. Her usual impulse would be to scrap her work and keep trying new things, driven by self-doubt and a desire for perfection. However, this time she went with her intuition. Bella doubted that she had been just lucky. She promised herself not to underestimate what it would take to apply the same trust in her heartfelt choices in the future.

Jitesh could see how much it meant to Sarah and Mateo that he had invited them out for a nice lunch on Friday. The feed-back session was also beneficial. Sarah said Jitesh was much easier to work with than before, but asked him to think ahead more at the beginning of next week, since he tended to get so many ideas during the week that she found it difficult to take charge of implementation. Jitesh saw that he was going to need to spend more time alone with Mateo. In the past few days, Jitesh had dis-covered that Mateo had not updated his old assumptions about variable costs, which had caused a lot of last-moment stress. What appeared to be bad luck was something Jitesh knew could happen again with Mateo. He resisted the urge to take over and do the work himself, intent on continuing to coach Mateo. "More reps, more reps," he told himself.

Nora and Alexander had a lovely trip to the forest with their three children on Sunday. Their picnic was picturesque, everything was delicious, and the kids truly enjoyed themselves. However, Nora was forced to bring her phone because her client had sent her a stream of text messages starting late Friday after receiving her report. The forest had poor network coverage (as Alexander had feared), so her attempts to reply on time were challenging. While her family previously wouldn't have noticed such multitasking between work and their activities, now Nora felt the tension. She promised herself and her family to submit future reports on Thursdays, instead of Fridays, so she would have a workday to engage with clients about possible questions.

Hacking Your Brain

Before we move to the third self-coaching session, let us illustrate the importance of setting deliberate intentions, monitoring and reflecting on your progress, and learning from it, by looking at the workings of your brain.

Intentions help you put your creative energies in motion. Your thoughts incubate when you formulate an intention well in advance. Intentions make your subconscious mind work in the background and reduce the unpredictability of your Frenemies.

The human body is the most complex known organism in the universe. You have almost 100 billion neurons in your brain—and that's without counting the neurons in your heart and gut. There is an awful lot that science cannot explain yet and probably never will. Just a simple thought can cause a plentitude of chain reactions in your head and the rest of your body.

The way dopamine is released and its impact are among the well-researched aspects of your brain. Dopamine motivates you to take focused action by stimulating you up to and during an action, and while you're reaching a challenging outcome. It boosts your mental energy and expands your short-term memory. When you are wrong about puzzles like Chapter 14's Kahneman-type math riddle about the assistant's salary, the reason is usually an overflow of information in your short-term memory. Thinking too fast is an instinctive, subconscious reaction to the disorientation associated with such an overflow.

Your dopamine level influences how far you will get with each Intend-Do-Observe-Reflect loop. This is self-enforcing. Using the loop stimulates your dopamine level, which encourages you to engage in your effort. The attitude you have as you approach each loop—believe it or not—actually affects your dopamine level. If you had taken a moment to contemplate and establish an intention to do your absolute best when you realized we were about to give you a tricky puzzle, then that would have increased your odds of resolving it. This performance-enhancing boost happens without drugs. It is a purely thought-based life hack that demands an explanation. Your dopamine level increases the moment you form an expectation about a reward-giving event. That's why you should construct your intention so that the Do step becomes intrinsically motivating. The effort itself is rewarding, forming a positive expectation, irrespective of what you might get out of your effort extrinsically.

Your dopamine level normalizes again after you have formed an expectation and get closer to the event. If you have a high probability of success, levels will remain low until you get the reward. At that moment, your dopamine expands again, depending on how positively surprised you are. However, a disappointment gives you relatively less dopamine.

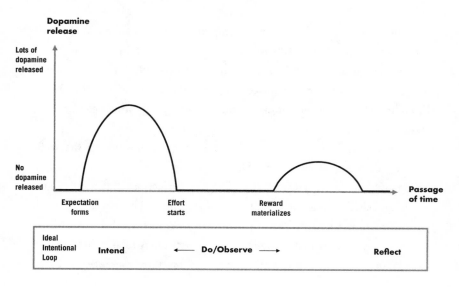

Figure 15.2 Dopamine releases associated with known rewards (100% chance of reward)[3]

Figure 15.2 shows the dopamine curve and how it evolves from when you form an expectation of a reward to when you receive it, for the case when you are 100% certain that you will get the reward. Your dopamine level is higher when you're forming expectations about a reward than doing the actual work to win it. This means that, all other factors being equal, you'll have a more motivated mind in the Intend step than in the Do step. Typically, the dopamine boost from getting the reward itself is moderate compared to the boost of expectation. In other words, paradoxically, the expectation is more stimulating than getting the reward, and how much you appreciate the reward once you win it depends on how well it surpasses your expectations (rather than its actual size).

The picture changes if you are uncertain about whether you will get the reward. The same peaks occur with expectations and reward, but the flat lowland between expectation and payoff—the area marking your effort to get the reward—is different. If getting a reward is uncertain, your brain releases more dopamine during the effort. The bigger the uncertainty is, the higher the intensity. The sweet spot lies somewhere around a 50% probability of success. This effect is reduced when the reward's probability becomes higher or lower.

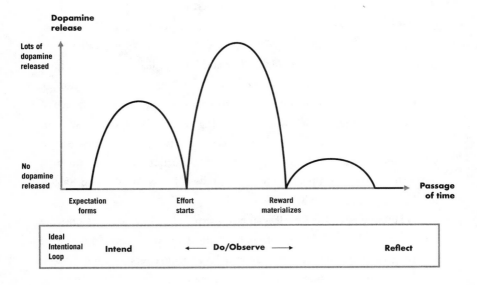

Figure 15.3—Dopamine release associated with a 50% chance of reward[4]

This is what happens when you get an idea for a post on social media and consider getting a like as a reward. Uncertainty about whether it will be a hit or not makes you even more stimulated when formulating your post and deciding which emoticons to insert. The classic yellow smiley face probably won't generate much excitement. Maybe you can find an emoticon few people have seen before that will draw attention like a magnet. Or will it? Maybe people won't like it.

You finish your text, select a few emoticons, press Share, and wait. For the next minutes and hours, it is tempting to check over and over whether you are getting likes and how they are accumulating. Social media is so addictive for this very reason, and the engineers who design the user experience know this better than anyone else. There is an intentional reason why your postings on Instagram, Twitter, TikTok, Facebook, LinkedIn, and Medium are so compelling.

With the Intend-Do-Observe-Reflect loop, you now can hack your dopamine releases for your own purpose: progressing on your Immediate Priority and, thereby, improving your Return on Ambition. Making an intrinsically motivating intention stimulates dopamine—even more so when you stretch yourself to do better, as stretching creates uncertainty and, therefore, injects more dopamine into your effort.

We recommend that you stretch yourself in each deliberate loop so your chance of succeeding is 50%–85%. The objective of each loop is to progress and learn. You can get farther and be less discouraged by allowing yourself higher odds than the 50% that maximizes your dopamine release. A recent study of cognitive learning shows that an 85% chance of success is the sweet spot for optimal learning for certain types of tasks—in this case answering questions on a screen with two possible answers, of which one is right and the other is wrong.[5] Anecdotal evidence furthermore shows that a probability roughly midway between 50% and 85% is ideal for elite athletes when they practice.

When you stretch yourself, you also learn more about what is possible for you to do than you knew before. Obviously, you don't consciously learn anything by repeating the same approach. That just sets up a new habit. Habits are incredibly powerful and the ultimate form of learning when the purpose is to put another aspect of your life on autopilot. A Weekly Deliberation has the exact opposite effect: You take the steering wheel and move outside your zone of comfort.

Leaving your comfort zone is a popular but often misunderstood metaphor. There is no purpose in seeking discomfort for its own sake; however, the steepest improvement in performance happens beyond the edge of your current competence and beyond the effort that immediately feels comfortable.[6]

During your Weekly Deliberation, you can use your discomfort to guide you toward excellent learning opportunities. If you feel uncomfortable thinking about a meeting or a task in the coming week, that feeling might indicate that it's at the edge of what you have currently mastered. The fact that you may want to avoid thinking of it—or that you feel your energy drain when you do—is an invitation to try to explore ways to do it better or differently.

Be mindful that reaching too far outside your competency and comfort can lead to anxiety and unproductive negative stress. This is where the concept of conducting safe-to-fail experiments is helpful.[7] You can stretch far beyond your comfort area without necessarily risking all that much. Have this potential in mind when you select opportunities to use the Intend-Do-Observe-Reflect loop. Your Weekly Deliberations are ultimately about learning, since that is what helps you perform better as your own asset. Cascades of safe-to-fail experiments can take you a long way compared to failure-safe intentions or big risky gambles.

The phenomenon of neuroplasticity makes the Intend-Do-Observe-Reflect life hack even more self-enhancing. Neuroplasticity is the way your brain can slowly change physically based on how you think and behave. Your brain makes you think and act, but your thoughts and behaviors also shape your brain itself over time. This discovery radically changed how scientists perceive adult human beings. The common perception once was that a person's character is fixed at around age seven, while the mind is fully developed and matured in the early twenties. Instead, we now know that you can evolve mentally throughout your life. You can literally *change* your brain.

To harness the benefits of this plasticity, identify opportunities to achieve and learn frequently. Complement your Weekly Deliberations with a reflection before every new day, or at least each workday, where you can identify opportunities to progress or learn and not limit yourself to only thinking about your Immediate Priority.

A Caveat about Hacking Your Brain

We have just introduced an incredibly powerful tool for you to apply so you can get more in tune with yourself and accelerate your performance and development. You will consequently also consume much more energy. We have seen this with people who start to apply the Weekly Deliberation tool regularly—and it is in line with our personal experiences.

If, like most ambitious people, you have a tendency to try to do too much, it's especially important to pay attention to your energy consumption. You might even be tempted to start using Weekly Deliberations more often or beyond the scope of your Immediate Priority. That's possible, but when you increase your concentration during various activities related to achievement, growth, or well-being, you put yourself at a much larger risk of running out of fuel more quickly.

Take proper breaks after completing a deliberate, focused activity and before starting a new one. It's an accomplishment to concentrate fully for 15 minutes, even when you have arranged to avoid interruptions. Few people can work intensely for more than about 90 minutes straight.[8]

Manage your total number of weekly work hours carefully, too. A study from Stanford University shows that working more than 50–55 hours per week, which is common among ambitious people, is associated with a significant fall in productivity.[9] In Chapter 3, we mentioned other dire consequences that an ambitious lifestyle can have on your well-being.

Recovery is an inseparable aspect of the capacity to perform, so also use your weekly reflections to check on how congested your calendar and to-do list are already. Your activities aren't all equally important or urgent, so ask if you really need to do some lower priority activity. Trying to do too much is a pure enemy of your success and fulfillment. Overscheduling limits you even more when you want to preserve the bandwidth to become increasingly focused on your real priorities.

Giving yourself time to let your thoughts flow enables you to pursue your real purposes more effectively. Only when you experience something with no intention except simply to experience it can you truly absorb it and give yourself a chance to see the people and the world around you as they truly are on their own terms. That has an immense value in and of itself.

OVER TO YOU–YOUR THIRD SELF-COACHING SESSION

This chapter outlined the third of the four tools in the toolbox, called the Weekly Deliberation. Applying the four elements in the tool can greatly increase your ability to progress on your Immediate Priority. Its power comes from the structure it enforces, coupled with its focus on reflection and continuous learning.

This next self-coaching session, centered around your three best upcoming opportunities to progress on your Immediate Priority, should take no more than half an hour. It is not a one-off. Keep doing it every week. As you get into a rhythm, you won't need more than 15 minutes a week.

TOOL 3: WEEKLY DELIBERATION

WHY	Use your Weekly Deliberation and related Intend-Do-Observe-Reflect loops to identify and use three opportunities in the coming week to progress as much as possible on your Immediate Priority and learn.
WHEN	This is a recurrent weekly event. Ideally, do it at the same time every week. That makes it easier to remember and helps you maintain momentum. Identify your three most solid opportunities in the coming week to progress with your Immediate Priority and then formulate an intention for each one.

continued

HOW

Find space and time to sit down comfortably for an uninterrupted half hour and have your calendar and note-taking mechanism ready. The first time, reserve half an hour, but in the future, once you are experienced, a quarter of an hour will be adequate.

While checking your calendar, insert a recurrent time slot of 15 minutes at the end of the workweek or just before the beginning of the next. Even though you might occasionally have conflicting appointments, this serves as a timely reminder to look a week ahead. Nothing is lost by sometimes doing this contemplation a little earlier or later. The critical element is that you do it every week. It's a bit like music. The rhythm, and not the melody, makes people dance.

1. Clear your mind and start familiarizing yourself with this approach. Thereafter, capture your notes at the end of this self-coaching guide:

    • Envision where your Immediate Priority will take you and then compare it with where you are currently. It is worthwhile to occupy yourself with that for a few minutes.

    • Identify the three most significant opportunities during the coming week to progress with your Immediate Priority or to enable yourself to succeed with it.

Progress can imply creating outstanding outcomes or learning lessons that enable better outcomes in the future. Conducting plenty of safe-to-fail experiments is an effective way to accomplish both simultaneously.

HOW

Glance at your calendar and to-do list to identify and prioritize opportunities. An opportunity can be an event, meeting, presentation, game, or practice session. It can also be a task involving completing an effort prior to a deadline, dealing with smaller pieces of work, or preparing mentally for an engagement. One of your three opportunities could even be to relax before an important event that is, itself, one of your opportunities. Your individual opportunities could take less than an hour of your week or fill an entire day.

2. Write down your intention for each opportunity by thinking about the following questions:

   • What does a great outcome look like?

   • What will you do better or different than before, or what would you like to learn?

   • Are you stretching yourself to the extent that you—conceptually speaking—have a 50%–85% chance of succeeding fully? (If a lot is at stake, then you can choose to play it safer.)

It's implicit that you should challenge yourself more in your Intend-Do-Observe-Reflect loops than with your Immediate Priority overall. The thrice-weekly opportunities offer a relatively safe place for experimentation, while you should do what you can to succeed with every new Immediate Priority for the one to three months that it lasts.

continued

3. Run through your calendar again, now that you have intensified your coming week with three newly articulated intentions, and check that these three intentions don't create unnecessary time congestion in combination with current commitments that are neither as important nor as urgent. If that is the case, prioritize your time to give yourself enough space to focus on what really counts and to get your rest. We encourage you to put a calendar reminder before each of the three intentions to re-ground yourself in the upcoming intention.

That's all for now—and this was just the first time. You will be able to select and formulate the intentions of your Weekly Deliberations more quickly next time. As you get more accustomed to this way of thinking, never become sloppy about contemplating the difference between "where your Immediate Priority will take you" and "where you are currently" (Point 1). This might seem repetitious, but it sets you up for thinking more aspirationally about how to get the most out of your opportunities.

During the coming week, with each intention, Do, Observe, and Reflect as you take on your three opportunities. Note lessons learned right away, after each occasion, and certainly no later than your next Weekly Deliberation. When possible, do your reflection immediately after finishing the task or event. Within the 45 minutes after the event, your adrenaline level will still be heightened and your recollections will be much clearer. However, reflecting after a longer delay is better than not reflecting at all. Writing your post-reflections

HOW

will further sharpen your contemplation and memory, just as it helped you to write down your intentions in the first place.

In the Reflect step, ask these questions:

- How do I sense that I lived up to my intention, and what facts support that conclusion?

- What did I pay attention to during the event or task?

- How was I lucky or unlucky?

- What should I particularly keep doing or do differently in the future?

Ask the same questions every time, but avoid repeating the same answers. If that happens, try to be more creative when picking opportunities and formulating intentions for them in the Intend step. Also make more of an effort to capture valuable insights when contemplating in the Reflect step.

WHAT

Intention 1 (with post-reflection to follow):

_____

_____

_____

_____

continued

WHAT

Intention 2 (with post-reflection to follow):

_____

_____

_____

_____

Intention 3 (with post-reflection to follow):

_____

_____

_____

_____

NOTES

_____

_____

_____

_____

_____

_____

SIXTEEN

Tool 4—Frenemy Radar

Your Frenemy Radar is an evolving map of where and when your Frenemies cause sensations and friction.

THE FIRST THREE tools help you clarify what you want and move toward it. You can put all you've read so far and your entire focus into that. You will move forward faster, but you will undoubtedly be met with surprises and setbacks. How can you become more aware of setbacks just before they occur or manage them better if they end up happening anyway?

We highlighted the importance of developing both your conceptual and embodied self-awareness back in Chapter 14. This book has so far purposely stimulated your conceptual self-awareness. Meanwhile, life and its moments nurture embodied self-awareness, not books. Your Frenemies will continue to creep up on you or let you down, even though you may be getting better at acknowledging their past patterns. This chapter outlines the fourth and final tool, the Frenemy Radar, which helps you hone your embodied self-awareness and use your senses to spot when a Frenemy is about to make a mess for you.

It starts with a crash course on thoughts and feelings and their underlying triggers, since a clearer understanding of these elements can help fine-tune your Frenemy Radar. We then outline the tool in detail; similar to Tool 3, the Frenemy Radar should be used on an ongoing basis. Following this, we review how your relationship with your Frenemies typically evolves as you grow and develop. Finally, the self-coaching guide at the end of the chapter will help you practice using your Frenemy Radar.

Getting a Grip on Your Thoughts and Feelings

Look deeply into the eyes of your loved one as if they held the entire universe. Leave aside yourself and your wishes, desires, needs, and fears. Just indulge yourself in those eyes and the generous soul behind them . . .

Or hold a child's tiny hand and listen to their energetic voice explaining a story. It might be difficult to follow, but it radiates curiosity and appetite for the wide world that you as an adult mostly take for granted . . .

Or experience yourself laughing with your whole body without being able to stop, even when it starts hurting in your stomach, which is funny in itself and makes the whole matter hilariously worse . . .

Or listen to your all-time favorite piece of music, which you haven't heard for a while so the nuances that you are intimately familiar with can surprise you anew with their evocative beauty . . .

Or—if you enjoy wine—take a sip of a great Médoc red wine from Bordeaux and taste its full-bodied boldness and the harmonious complexity . . .

Or—if you are a football (soccer) fan—watch Lionel Messi defy gravity and fly across the playing field toward the disoriented opponents' goal . . .

The aesthetics are mesmerizing whether your favorite team scores, whether anybody is impressed by the expensiveness of the wine, and whether you are completely alone with your favorite music. The laughing matter might not even be that funny after all. Nonetheless, these events evoked strong emotions and gave you powerful experiences to relish in all of life's richness.

Your emotions and feelings are central to how you experience your life.[1] With deep respect for that, we will show you how to use your feelings as an instrument. The Frenemy Radar helps you learn the way your sensations and feelings reveal what you subconsciously aspire for or are trying to avoid. Metaphorically speaking, your feelings give you hints regarding when your Frenemies are about to cloud your thinking and make you act against your conscious intentions.

The Frenemy Radar helps you use your feelings and senses over time to shift your mindsets and behaviors sustainably and maintain a higher Return on Ambition. That doesn't mean you must give anything up. On the contrary, you will become more aware of what is happening inside and around you. This should also enable you to enjoy more nuances of your experiences even when you are not using your feelings as an instrument but just embracing an experience for its own sake.

To help you make sense of these bold claims, let us ask you a seemingly basic question.

Do your feelings shape your thoughts, or do your thoughts shape your feelings?

This question is fundamental regarding how you perceive yourself and the world around you. Does feeling dictate your thoughts? Or are you, with your thoughts, the creator of your own emotions? The causality can go either way, but many people believe that it's a one-way thing.

You experience every moment of life through feelings and thoughts. The question is, which one comes before the other? When we ask groups of leaders this question, it sparks debate that is passionate and intellectual at the same time.

Many say it starts with feelings. You might think this is obvious, but it's actually not the right answer. It would also be wrong to say that thoughts always precede feelings. The correct answer is that a two-way road connects your feelings and your thoughts.

Feelings tend to come before thoughts when you indulge in your loved one's eyes, get carried away by innocent childish curiosity, or passionately watch football (soccer). Take the agitated debate between fans of opposing football teams about whether there should be a penalty kick or not. Strong feelings shaped by which team you prefer dictate your view. The arguments can be intense, even though the matter ultimately is objective and out of your hands, anyway.

Thoughts can also influence feelings. The life hack in the previous chapter helps you shape your mental state about a certain event or task and, thereby, shape your feelings. Your thinking affects your emotions. That's why clinicians use cognitive psychology as an alternative to medicine to treat non-severe depression. Negative thought patterns can cause and deepen negative feelings, but you can counter them with a more positive thought pattern and a greater awareness of when and where depressive thoughts and feelings originate. Your thinking influences how you perceive what's going on around you, for better or worse.

Feelings can be associated with events or your ongoing inner dialogue with yourself. You also can spark them with beliefs you harbor—your mental baggage so to speak. Everyone is attached to some old perceptions and past experiences and detached from others. Your implicit assumptions guide these patterns. Hopes and fears furthermore play an important subconscious role. Larger forces shape them, like what went well—or didn't—so far in your life, the environment in which you grew up, and, eventually, all the way back through the evolution of the human species.

As a human, you are hardwired to avoid danger and to mate. Such mechanisms helped ensure that your ancestors passed on their genes and avoided de-selection. When gratification is within your reach or threats sneak up on you, your instincts can push you faster than you can act deliberately. That's nature.

Then there's nurture. For an everyday example of how it works, consider how a particularly fantastic or awful experience in a specific place lingers there. It shapes whether you ever want to be there again or not. You could have met your loved one at a particular café or had a bad meeting in a certain office. In your mind, this place will keep a tinge of its past intensity.

Like everyone else, you project your hopes or fears on the world around you, instead of seeing it as it truly is. People tend to have aspirations and dreams that reflect many of their hopes without noticing how much their fears—which eventually are the flip sides of their hopes—are driving them. Subconscious fears strongly influence the choices that we make in life and how we interact with others every day. Let's illustrate this with three deeper examples out of the infinite number of possible scenarios that could affect an ambitious person.[2]

Perhaps you grew up in a family with great expectations for you, and you received more attention and affection when you did well in school or on extracurricular activities. *Convention* became your ticket to winning appreciation, so you started to identify yourself with the path you were on. You felt like yourself when things were progressing, but any risk of failure fundamentally threatened your identity. If you are your success, then failure means you don't exist.[3] Failure puts your entire existence at stake. This can make you willing to do anything to avoid failing—such as falling prey to *Flexibility*, modifying how you present yourself and obscuring your real identity.

Perhaps, instead, you were raised in a broken family with parents or guardians who put their needs before yours—intentionally or out of necessity—and repeatedly broke promises to you. *Boldness* could have helped you step up and spurred you to feel comfortable challenging authority figures from a young age, because you had so little trust in them. You also could have developed a strong degree of *Independence*, giving you the ability to take the lead in your life and using words or physical strength to counterattack anyone who appears to be trying to block your way or challenge your judgment.

Or say you grew up in a highly active family, as the second youngest of five children. Your parents are loving and caring but treat you as much as part of a collective as they treat you as an individual. You are one of the "kids" and far from always called by your name. While being a well-functioning element of the greater whole, you get caught up in daydreams and start looking out in real life for places in which you might fit better. *Desire* becomes your friend together with the idea that there is something better awaiting you out there. When you get into difficult situations, that anticipation gives you the hope of an attractive alternative. Meanwhile, nothing is ever really as good as it could be, so you can easily become restless and seek adventure.

You might have experienced something entirely different, but it doesn't change the point: These stories are typical for ambitious people. The thought patterns, behavioral habits, and personal characteristics they instill can become so interwoven in your personality that you can never become conscious of all of them. Patterns, habits, and traits are layered deep in your subconscious, so ingrained in your thoughts and behaviors that you apply them automatically. But the Frenemy Radar will now help you to become more aware of these patterns to prevent yourself from reacting blindly. It will help you choose consciously whether to allow your Frenemies to manage you or ensure that you manage them.

Supervising Your Frenemies

We brought the seven Frenemies to life to make it easier for you to recognize common mindsets and habits among ambitious people and in your own life. The Frenemies are as follows:

1. Convention

2. Boldness

3. Independence

4. Competitiveness

5. Perseverance

6. Desire

7. Flexibility

Your hopes and fears are the energy that fuels your Frenemies or makes them run out of gas, to good or bad effect. You hope to succeed, but you fear failing and not being in a position to achieve your ambitions.

That explains how the Frenemy Radar works. When you are experiencing a strong upward or downward change in your energy, whether ignited by the near fulfillment of hope or anything linked to a fear, it signals that something is going on inside you, perhaps in your subconscious. In these moments your Frenemies are most likely to throw you offtrack. Even though you are conceptually aware of your Frenemies, the blur of circumstances and your mental baggage and sense-making can conspire to set you off on the wrong foot in a second. The Frenemy Radar enhances your embodied self-awareness and enables you to spot the movements of your Frenemies and make more conscious choices about whether to obey them or not.

You need to feed your Frenemy Radar with data for it to work. When you experience a strong positive or negative change in energy, note it. Wait three hours or up to a day for your emotions to clear. Intense emotions ruin your ability to think clearly. You can be immensely joyful or angry, feel disgust or delight, and be really frightened or totally drained of energy. You might feel normal in a few hours, or you may need a good night's sleep, but don't wait more than 24 hours. When you are ready, reflect on which Frenemy was in play and what motivated it to disrupt you.

Run a simple four-step sequence: Sense, Adapt, Note, and Explore. That's all. The steps are fairly simple in themselves but—as anything worthwhile in life—they require practice.

The first step is **Sense**, and it calls for noticing any shift in your bodily experience or feelings, like sudden strong heartbeats or rising anger. The more you pick up, the better, and yet you need to apply the Frenemy Radar only on the most significant sensations that you experience.

The next step is **Adapt**, which you start doing by taking a few slow, deep breaths. Fill your lungs with air while inhaling, ideally through the nose, before exhaling, preferably through the mouth, initiating a rhythm. This works like pressing a pause button and can help you curb the peak of your sensation. It helps to notice in real time what is happening where in your body. A Frenemy—and in reality, your nervous system—is trying to send you a message and will be less intense when you acknowledge it. The opposite can be the case if you actively try to ignore or suppress the sensation.

In most situations, this should take no more than 10 seconds to soothe your strongest instincts. After your brief break for breathing, choose what to do. If you tend to overreact, then doing nothing can reduce the risk of doing something in the heat of the moment that you will regret later. If your default, instead, is to procrastinate, it might make sense to act, as opposed to doing nothing. The better you get to know yourself, the easier it will become for you to avoid repeating your old mistakes.

Make a **Note** as soon after the incident as possible. The faster you record your reactions, the more precisely you can describe what happened in your body and what you felt. It's also critical to mention when, where, and with whom it happens. The details are valuable, since your Frenemy Radar uses your accumulated data to pick up similar signals in the future to help you avoid surprises and to reduce the risk of outcomes you will later regret.

Finally, dig below the surface and **Explore** which Frenemy was at play and why. This is almost impossible to do in the moment, but waiting from three to twenty-four hours will help you gain some distance from the incident so you can think more rationally about what actually happened and what might have caused the results. This requires introspection. Try to reconnect with the situation and the bodily sensations and emotions that you had. Use this to pinpoint which Frenemy was present and the motivations behind it. Furthermore, reconnecting with the feeling that you experienced but didn't embrace at the time can have a healing effect in itself.

You expand on your conceptual self-awareness by getting a more nuanced picture of your triggers and underlying hopes and fears. That helps you sense similar patterns earlier on in the future and, thereby, enhances your embodied self-awareness.

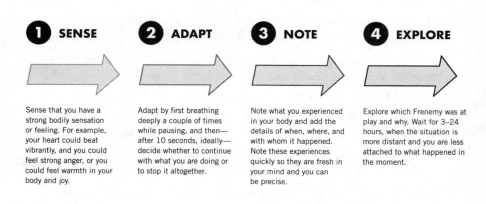

① SENSE

Sense that you have a strong bodily sensation or feeling. For example, your heart could beat vibrantly, and you could feel strong anger, or you could feel warmth in your body and joy.

② ADAPT

Adapt by first breathing deeply a couple of times while pausing, and then—after 10 seconds, ideally—decide whether to continue with what you are doing or to stop it altogether.

③ NOTE

Note what you experienced in your body and add the details of when, where, and with whom it happened. Note these experiences quickly so they are fresh in your mind and you can be precise.

④ EXPLORE

Explore which Frenemy was at play and why. Wait for 3–24 hours, when the situation is more distant and you are less attached to what happened in the moment.

Figure 16.1—The Frenemy Radar Sequence

The Sense-Adapt-Note-Explore sequence is a different sequence than the Intend-Do-Observe-Reflect loop from your Weekly Deliberation.

Your weekly Intend-Do-Observe-Reflect loops should proceed with a steady rhythm, but the Sense-Adapt-Note-Explore sequence is a tool that you should carry along during your waking hours. This is comparable to airplane radar, which constantly scans its surroundings during flights and enables the pilot to adjust course. Technicians regularly upgrade and tune radars to ensure their ability to pick up signals from other flights. If an irregularity occurs, the pilot reviews what happened to discover the root cause and prevent a similar incident from occurring in the future.

The Sense-Adapt-Note-Explore sequence makes you more aware of yourself and more in tune with whatever you do in the future. The more aware you are of the conditions, feelings, and thoughts that cause your sensations, the better you can supervise your Frenemies. You need to determine, no matter whether they are helpful or not, how to act in ways that best serve your interests.

Ideally, each week you should record your three biggest sensations. You never know whether your reaction a moment from now will end up in this week's Top 3. But you will get a much better notion of what sensations are strongest as you begin using the Frenemy Radar regularly. You may find that some weeks you'll record more than three sensations.

That's a major difference between the Weekly Deliberation and the Frenemy Radar. You use the Sense-Adapt-Note-Explore sequence of the Frenemy Radar when something happens out of the blue, and it prepares you for unpredictable situations in the future. On the other hand, you use the Weekly Deliberation and its Intend-Do-Observe-Reflect cycle to plan ahead so you can benefit from upcoming events and tasks.

Sensing When and How Your Frenemies Are at Play

The Frenemy Radar operates on feelings. Everyone has feelings, but people's relationships to them differ. It is quite common that ambitious people are less intimate with their emotions and bodily sensations than others. Ambition implies that you are paying attention to reaching a different, future state, which means that you might not be as present in every moment. For example, people who pushed themselves to do well in the school system can be more at ease in their heads than in the rest of their bodies. Likewise, top athletes learn how to ignore pain and other distracting sensations.

You must be extra careful detecting your sensations to get your radar to work. You'll want to limit the extent to which you fall into three pitfalls, as most people do.

- **PITFALL 1: SUPPRESSING YOUR FEELINGS.** You have met with aversion against expressing most feelings on your way through life. Parents, teachers, sports coaches, or bosses have encouraged you to cheer up, not take things too hard, man (or woman) up, or not be so sensitive. Without noticing it, you've built a solid armor against many of your true feelings or disassociated from them.[4] This impedes your access to those feelings—even when they try to tell you something.

  If you are accustomed to suppressing your feelings, you must make an extra effort to listen to your body. Notice your feelings, which is different from unconditionally embracing them. If you find yourself feeling a strong emotion when you take action on something, use the Sense-Adapt-Note-Explore sequence.

- **PITFALL 2: MIXING UP THOUGHTS AND FEELINGS.** The confusing cocktail of thoughts and emotions has several ingredients. Feelings blur your ability to think logically. Your emotions guide your notion of what is right and wrong quicker than you can contemplate rationally. Your thoughts regarding past feelings are also blurry. When you try to recall feelings, you get only a few highlights but no indication of the intensity of various emotions. Your experienced and remembered feelings are not the same.[5] Otherwise, fewer people would voluntarily work themselves to the bone or endure as many hangovers as they do.

- **PITFALL 3: BELIEVING YOUR SURROUNDINGS CAUSE YOUR FEELINGS.** There may be some people, situations, or even songs that simply make you irritated, frustrated, or angry. In reality, it's *you* who have these feelings, and your hopes and fears spark them. You might notice that other people and various circumstances annoy you more when you are tired, hungry, or stressed. One reason for this is that you have less energy; another is that you ascribe your feeling to what happens around you. It's easier to say, "He makes me so . . ." than it is to tune into your own emotions and say, "I feel so . . . when . . ."

Your feelings are what they are. The Frenemy Radar can help you familiarize yourself with them as they evolve and blend. It's as if your world will get stronger colors, sharper flavors, and clearer nuances little by little when you make a conscious effort. These are benefits beyond building your embodied self-awareness and becoming better able to steer your Frenemies.

How Your Relationship to Your Frenemies Changes as You Develop

When you work against your Frenemies, it feels unnatural because they are so ingrained in how you learned to make sense of yourself and of the world. However, as you grow continually as an adult, you can relate to your Frenemies more deliberately and with increasing awareness and master them. Let's step back in time and observe how these shifts typically occur throughout life, to illustrate what you can expect as you continue to grow your awareness.

Your Frenemies first appeared around age seven. Here, kids leave the magical stage child psychologists call "preoperational" and enter the "concrete operational" phase, where they orient themselves based on time, space, and quantity.[6] At this stage, you now begin to comprehend the difference between the plastic toy airplane in your little hand and the Boeing 747 jumbo jet in the air, or between your little pink dollhouse and a real house.

This newly acquired realism enhances children's ability to strategize for themselves. That's when you begin to think, "Let me do this" or "Oh, no, that's not good, so let me do that instead." Around this time, you might have found out that earning top grades in school and imitation-silver trophies in sports made Mommy and Daddy proud of you. It might have seemed that they loved you and appreciated you more when you kept the stream of good news flowing. Or you might have learned the value of changing your behavior and attitudes to fit into the family, school, and different groups of friends. "Wow! That works. Let me do it again."

At this exact time, you were forming the initial seeds of your future Frenemies. For instance, *Convention* could have been helpful in gaining approval as your parents established the hope that you would live up to their highest expectations, perhaps generating your fear of failing. If you started befriending *Convention* as a child, by now you have repeated its strategies so often that you have internalized them in your thought patterns, habits, and personality. Separating from *Convention* now feels difficult because it was so important in forming your early sense-making.

Neuroplasticity works faster in children than in adults. Your repetitive strategies shaped how you walked and talked, how you entered a room and oriented yourself, and how you timed and toned your conversations with friends, classmates, teachers, fellow athletes, trainers, and—later on—colleagues and maybe a significant other. You became so attached to *Convention* that you didn't notice when it acted as your enemy even when you would have benefitted from breaking free of it.

You are likely to have picked up new Frenemies when school became more serious, you tried out for your first sports team, or you applied to your first-choice college. If *Boldness*, *Independence*, *Competitiveness*, *Perseverance*, or *Flexibility* were not already your Frenemies, then some of them probably became so then. Alternatively, a couple of them could have entered your life when you started your first corporate job and needed to shine in a big, complex organization. The more you have paid attention to your progress in life, the more likely it is that *Desire* became your Frenemy. Most ambitious people closely befriend several Frenemies between the time that they leave the magical age around seven years until they are well into their professional careers. It happens so smoothly that often you don't notice the power that your Frenemies have gained over you.

Here's a case history that illustrates just how influential Frenemies can be in our lives. We have merged a couple of similar client stories to create "Adam."

Nicolai T was coaching Adam, a relatively newly appointed chief executive officer for an admired organization. He wanted to become a more effective leader. Adam's background is an impressive mix of an Ivy League education and working for blue-chip employers. He's always worked hard to succeed.

During their first coaching session, Nicolai T and Adam talked about

Adam's struggles with his team of direct reports. Adam knew that leaders ideally engage their staff members in figuring out the best way forward and determining how to get underway. He had started a collaborative strategy process and invited his immediate team to participate as equals. However, after a few disoriented meetings, Adam was completely disappointed and disillusioned. And his board had asked to see his new strategy as soon as he had it ready.

Adam wanted to answer the board promptly and properly, instead of going through the team process and sharing his team members' so-far vague ideas. He told his team he would cut the process short and present his suggestions to them for joint discussion. For him, this implied doing all the real strategy work himself.

Earlier in their conversation, Adam had shared with Nicolai T that he didn't guide himself according to any greater aspiration for his life. He was a competitive person and wanted to be the best. So Nicolai T asked Adam what he would have risked if he had given the team more space. "I never want to waste time!" Adam responded testily. Next, Nicolai T asked Adam what made him so busy if he wasn't following a defined direction and didn't have a clear destination. That question caused Adam to stop and think.

In this snapshot of a longer conversation, Adam broke his silence by saying, "But I have been like this since I was a small boy. My elder sister was the best in her class, and that made my father so proud. I became afraid he would not love me, and I decided to do better than her." There was nothing traumatic about Adam's childhood, and he is a completely healthy person both mentally and physically. His relationship with his family—including his father and sister—is sound. Nicolai T did not ask about his early life. Adam brought it up himself and realized during their conversation that his old fear had translated back then into the assumption that he had to be the best to be loved. Adam had a flash of insight about himself, as he realized that a lifelong pattern was repeating itself yet again—and now counterproductively.

Adam's whole interaction with his team was indisputably associated with a fear of failure. His *Competitiveness* Frenemy was becoming deeply uncomfortable with the situation and refused to join in giving the board a strategy draft that was not state of the art. Adam was full of anger when he stopped the collaborative effort with his team, and he had felt appalled at what he perceived as his subordinates' lack of seriousness. He believed they were the problem, and he needed to fight against their inadequacy. Furthermore, the team experience had triggered his *Independence* Frenemy, which had convinced him that he would be stronger if he worked alone, rather than as part of a team.

Adam knew intellectually that cutting off his team was not a good leadership practice. *Competitiveness* and *Independence* had been his best friends for so long, but now they had become enemies to his effectiveness as a CEO. A small disturbance—such as his leadership team's inability to think as quickly and constructively as he did—had threatened his self-belief. Their perceived slowness had implied a risk for Adam of not being the best anymore. That triggered his subconscious fear of losing out—and, more deeply, of not being loved—and it made him angry, so he acted abruptly.

During the coaching session, Adam became more conceptually self-aware of how his *Competitiveness* and *Independence* Frenemies have been managing him. The session was an eye-opener that helped him comprehend how far reaching this pattern has been and continued to be in his life. He committed to observing how *Competitiveness* made him react instinctively over the next few weeks. By applying the Frenemy Radar this way, Adam prepared himself to manage his main Frenemy better in the future, instead of letting it manage him. The Frenemy Radar helped him expand his embodied self-awareness, build on the foundation of his newly extended conceptual self-awareness, and notice how new variations of his old pattern unfolded. Little by little, his Frenemy Radar enabled him to make conscious choices in real time about when *Competitiveness* helps him and when he should curb it.

Your Frenemies are inside you. To an extent, you must acknowledge that you are your own Frenemies. Unless you are mindful, you cannot make the conscious choices and take the intentional actions that will set you apart from them when they are not serving you. This is a critical step toward succeeding with your Immediate Priority and ultimately increasing your Return on Ambition.

By Monday evening, Bella had jotted down her first note about a sensation. She had reserved the entire day to create a mission statement for her new installation. The first couple of hours were intoxicating. Bella felt unrestrained in a way that she had rarely experienced since she played as a kid. She was imagining with every inch of her mind and exploring ideas and sensing what they could be like manifested in her art. As the morning turned into afternoon, she felt like she had sucked most of the oxygen out of her renewed freedom, and it started becoming a vacuum.

But that emptiness might just have been hunger. She went to her local café, got some lunch, and fell into talking with some friends who passed by. That invited guilt about having not worked hard enough. Back in her apartment, the big sheet of paper in front of her appeared whiter than the purest snow as she stared into it, struggling to articulate the message of her installation concept— the idea that had been so tantalizingly close that morning.

And then it happened. The telephone rang. Bella had forgotten to turn it off, as she had promised herself to do. Her mother was on the other end asking motherly questions about her well-being and her ongoing assignment faster than Bella could think of reasonable answers. Bella experienced the equivalent of an electric shock, feeling as if her hair were standing up in all directions! She got furious with her caring mother—and angry at herself for not being further along than she was. She was frustrated with her experiment about working differently. She ended up shouting nervously and unconvincingly at her mother that she needed to take another call. Bella almost forgot to record her radar sensations and wrote down "Monday, 4:53 p.m., at my desk when Mom called: Furious anger! Heartbeats and hair raising" before she left to take a walk and decompress.

And, as so often before, the idea came to her while tramping through the city: "Consumption consuming the consumers." Wow! A message like this started a whole avalanche of ideas that

continued

could help her continue on her new piece. Bella almost forgot to reflect on what had happened.

Late in the evening, she realized that breaking her old habits had teased her *Desire* Frenemy, which started barking loudly when her mother called. It was extremely unfair. Her parents were her greatest emotional and financial support. Her mother had called to make sure Bella was okay, since she hadn't called her parents in more than a week. That call prompted her to take the walk, where she met her idea. Later that night, Bella called her mother to thank her and settle the confusion. She made a handwritten note for the Frenemy Radar and wrote a reflection about how well she had been able to carry out her intention for the day after all. She also noted that she hadn't managed to sense the Frenemy emerging and, therefore, wasn't able to slow down and adapt her behavior in the moment, but she promised herself to be more vigilant about that in the future.

Jitesh's biggest sensation during the first week was less dramatic. Thursday at noon he had asked Mateo for a draft of his report, since the deadline was noon the next day. When he skimmed through Mateo's numbers, interpretations, and conclusions, Jitesh felt as if he had been struck in the solar plexus—like a sudden pain in the stomach. Mateo was still using old cost assumptions, even though Jitesh had told him to update his numbers.

Jitesh's energy was punched out of him as he absorbed this hit. For a couple of minutes, he was completely silent as he breathed slowly and began to recover. Then Jitesh's autopilot switched on by itself, and he started looking for the recent cost analysis so he could begin updating the assumptions himself. Jitesh was well into this task when the Frenemy Radar popped up in his mind. He paused and realized that he was reverting to his old ways. He made a note: "Thursday, 1:00 p.m., in the office with Mateo's draft open on the computer: Total lack of trust. Appalled. Like a knockout. Caught myself in the moment—good."

Making the note woke Jitesh out of his robotic effort to clean up after Mateo. He opened Microsoft Outlook on the screen and sent Mateo a calendar invitation for a two-hour slot first thing the next morning with the subject "Can we update the cost assumptions together?" An acceptance email ticked in shortly after from Mateo.

The next morning, after a good workout in the gym, Jitesh sat down for breakfast and thought about his reaction before his early meeting with Mateo. Jitesh realized that his *Independence* Frenemy had gone into overdrive the moment one of his selected subordinates failed to live up to his expectations. Jitesh had struggled a bit getting his head around the Frenemy Watchlist when defining his Immediate Priority. But now, he had been bang on the money. He had actually foreseen what was going to happen, and it had happened anyway. He decided to take the Frenemy Radar more seriously.

Alexander's radar registered his strongest sensation on Tuesday afternoon during a conference call with his boss, Sergey, and the CEO of their company's competitor, who, together with his investment banker, invited Sergey's and Alexander's company to make a bid to acquire the CEO's company. Alexander got nearly ecstatic, as if he had swallowed several glasses of champagne in an instant. He had argued for merging the two companies for a long time, and now it was about to become a reality. His name was all over this deal. He didn't acknowledge the importance of pausing, taking a couple of deep breaths, and choosing what to do when getting the strong emotional sensation. He felt a need to act fast. He would cancel everything in his calendar for the next couple of months and more or less move into the office to get the deal sealed and start integrating the companies.

continued

Sergey was as calm as if nothing had happened. He had joined the company as CEO only a few months prior and was new to the industry. After the call, Alexander argued passionately to Sergey about moving forward quickly with the deal. Sergey's view was in stark contrast to Alexander's. He thought the rival company's leaders wanted to sell only because of their financial troubles. A year or two ago, they would never have dreamed of selling and would have insisted on being the acquirer in any deal.

Without much emotion, Sergey concluded, "Let's go for a beautiful deal! We'll get that only by wanting it—but not too much." He might not have known the industry well technically, but his background included several successful mergers and acquisitions. Sergey's game plan was that Alexander should make himself available over the coming days to meet alternative investment bankers who could advise them on the transaction. In the end, Sergey looked Alexander in the eyes and said, "Calm down, Alexander. It's less exciting than buying your first home—however small that might have been. Promise me to get a good night's sleep. I need you at your best, and there is no place for tiredness at this stage."

Nora laughed when Alexander told her the story that evening during their first Tuesday date, which Sergey had unknowingly saved. Without his decision to move deliberately, Alexander would have still been in the office crunching numbers for the deal. "Oh, my bulldozer," she said, laughing. Alexander had booked a table at the best Turkish restaurant in the neighborhood. Its lack of a liquor license helped guarantee that he could keep their Tuesday date and still be fresh the next morning. He and Nora had a lovely evening. Their conversation included the Frenemy Radar and how Alexander realized that *Perseverance* had made him overly excited and tunnel-visioned. He realized he had not taken slow, deep breaths and adapted accordingly. This deal could be his claim to fame, and yet—with this insight—he was much more convinced that Sergey's approach was right, and his respect for his boss grew.

Meanwhile, Nora told Alexander happily that it looked like she would beat him on points for keeping most of her work inside the time windows as they had agreed upon as part of their Immediate Priority. Alexander responded, "Well, I will stay cool like Sergey and not miss too much time with you and the kids."

"Sounds good," she said. "Start with family dinner tomorrow night."

OVER TO YOU—YOUR FOURTH SELF-COACHING SESSION

This is your last self-coaching session. Half an hour should be enough. This will prepare you to pick up more sensations on your Frenemy Radar in the future so that you are always alert to the forces supporting or pushing you. By then, this kind of reflection will take you only a few minutes each time.

TOOL 4: FRENEMY RADAR

WHY	The Sense-Adapt-Note-Explore sequence will help you make better and more conscious choices in the future based on the insights that you accumulate about your thought patterns, behavioral habits, and personal traits. Over time, you will improve your Frenemy Radar's ability to spot in advance when your Frenemies are about to work against you. You'll also become better at focusing on your current Immediate Priority and keeping your Return on Ambition high.

continued

Try to identify sensations that you are experiencing in relation to your Immediate Priority and that have a very high or very low magnitude of positive or negative energy so they are likely to end up in the Top 3 list of your sensations in the current week. They might have to do with an intention that you formulated as part of your Weekly Deliberation, or they could be completely independent of it as long as they are relevant to your Immediate Priority for the coming one to three months. Initially, you may doubt whether the sensation you are experiencing in the moment will end up in this week's Top 3. Make a note of it anyway to avoid having this experience fade from your recollection. It is okay if you end up looking into a few more than three sensations during a week, since that will give you extra practice.

After a while, you will have a more natural sense of whether a sensation that triggers your Frenemy Radar is likely to make it to this week's Top 3. You'll make a note to yourself when you have a likely Top 3 sensation. Then wait three to twenty-four hours after the incident so you can think with a clearer head again. This reflection does not need to take more than a few concentrated minutes. Some people prefer to have a moment of contemplation just before every new workday, and that is an excellent occasion to reflect on yesterday's sensations.

After a few weeks, go through your old notes and answers. It can be quite amazing to see how your awareness increases and how the way that you experience your feelings has slowly started to change.

HOW

As in the previous self-coaching, there is space to capture your notes at the end of this guide.

Since you apply the Frenemy Radar in the moment, this self-coaching session must cheat a little and go back in time. Please start by thinking of what sensations you have experienced within the last week. Pick three of these sensations for your first self-coaching session.

You can use this script for working regularly with your Frenemy Radar:

ROUND 1: SENSE, ADAPT, AND NOTE

After sensing and adapting, make a note about the sensation that you are experiencing:

When, where, and with whom does the sensation happen, and what kind of feeling and body state do you experience?

The questions contain all five W's, except "why," which is difficult to answer during a sensation due to the emotional blur.

ROUND 2: EXPLORE (AFTER WAITING 3–24 HOURS)

Focusing on yourself and the specific situation, answer these four questions:

- What Frenemy was strongest in play?

- What motive did the Frenemy have for reacting so strongly?

- What limitations could this pattern cause for me?

- What mindset would serve me better in the future?

continued

HOW

Write down the essence of each answer and take a moment to reconnect with the experience to increase your Frenemy Radar's chances of picking up similar signals in the future. That will help you to be more in charge of your own path by making you better at steering free of your Frenemies when they are not being helpful.

WHAT

Note 1 *(Sensation: when, where, with whom, and what)*:

_____

_____

_____

_____

Exploration 1 *(What Frenemy and motives were present? What limitations could the pattern cause? What more constructive mindset could you use?)*

_____

_____

_____

_____

WHAT

Note 2 *(Sensation: when, where, with whom, and what)*:

_____

_____

_____

_____

Exploration 2 *(What Frenemy and motives were present? What limitations could the pattern cause? What more constructive mindset could you use?)*

_____

_____

_____

_____

Note 3 *(Sensation: when, where, with whom, and what)*:

_____

_____

_____

_____

continued

WHAT

Exploration 3 *(What Frenemy and motives were present? What limitations could the pattern cause? What more constructive mindset could you use?)*

_____

_____

_____

_____

NOTES

What reflections and insights are emerging from this self-coaching session beyond the outcome in the "What" box above? What do you know about yourself now that you didn't know before? How could this help you in the future? Does one Frenemy reappear several times, and is there a pattern in that?

_____

_____

_____

_____

SEVENTEEN

The Toolbox in Action

More reps, more reps, more reps!

NOW THAT YOU have gone through the four self-coaching sessions, you have a strong starting point for putting the toolbox into practice. As with any new habit or task, it can seem daunting to get started. However, taking the first steps is more than half the battle, and we strongly encourage you to learn by doing and, when in doubt, have a bias for action.

For one final time, we turn now to Bella, Jitesh, and Nora and Alexander to see how they fared as they took the entire toolbox along and used it in their lives.

You have seen how Bella used each of the four tools for the first time. She defined her Immediate Priority on Sunday, September 20, with the objective "I will approach opportunities with openness, courage, and optimism in my art and life." During the following month, she created four pieces of art that lived up to her criteria of being hopeful and "possibilistic." Bella made it a morning habit to identify which particular fear she wanted to defeat that day. She enjoys her little morning routine, which gives her confidence.

Tuesday, October 20, is a special day. Bella set the timeline

continued

for her first Immediate Priority at one month. She's impressed and proud of how much she's been able to shake herself up and accomplish. She loves the visible results. She has done her best work ever within the last month. Her concepts and sketches now have an audacity she's never before achieved. This level of success seems a bit surreal, especially since she's been so disciplined about pushing herself out of her comfort zone and challenging her old conventions. No fewer than three of her professors have spontaneously, on different occasions, expressed how impressed and excited they are with her recent growth.

Her daily fear-defeating declarations started fairly pragmatically with not giving in to "the fear of reflecting instead of creating," and have since turned more varied. A few days ago, she set out to defeat "the fear of just using plain normal words in front of the academy's discerning hipsters."

Bella wrote most of her Weekly Deliberation intentions and reflections, as well as other notes regarding the Frenemy Radar, on loose scraps of paper she piled into the corner of her antique rolltop desk. She's kept this Tuesday morning, October 20, free to review them and mentally live everything through once again.

She finds it a bit scary to realize how naïve she was just a few weeks ago. That worry battles against her new pride but doesn't conquer it. After all, her writing reflects rapid personal development, which is a strong starting point. Realizing that she's a success has eased her sense of isolation and softened her heart.

As Bella glances through the rest of her notes, she wonders how she can build similar momentum on her next Immediate Priority and what on earth it should be. Maybe she'll call her mother and brainstorm.

Bella is spending less than an hour per week contemplating how she can pursue her creative vision and live more fully. While she was first sitting with her copy of this book in her hands and reading, she was concerned about the one-hour weekly demand on her time. Today, Bella would not want to be without either the art creations that her new discipline has helped foster, or the valuable life lessons and profound joy that they keep motivating. That accumulated hour is undoubtedly a minor fee to pay in the form of attention to achieve all this in return. And it has saved her from many worries and a lot of stress, which otherwise would have stolen more of her time.

Her Weekly Deliberations have become a routine. She writes them in her calendar every Friday from 4:45 p.m. to 5:00 p.m. This ritual now ends her regular workweek. Likewise, activating her Frenemy Radar is now a habit. It comes to her mind whenever she feels an uproar in her body. She generally pays more attention to the nature of her sensations and weighs each of them for whether it might be in the running for this week's Top 3.

Bella bought a small red notebook, which she carries in her everyday bag. Keeping track of all the loose scraps of paper in the corner of her desk had become too confusing. Now, she picks up the notebook when she's thinking a week ahead each Friday and scribbles down her intentions. After every related event or task, she captures her insights on how things went and what she learned. She makes Frenemy Radar notes in the same chronology when she feels a sensation. She leaves some empty space under each record of an event so she can come back to it some hours later and write down whatever revelations have come to her regarding which Frenemy tried to get the better of her and its underlying motives. Bella has even started experimenting with using the Frenemy Radar more broadly, and not only in areas related to her Immediate Priority.

Her new routine and habits run silently in the background of her daily life. When thinking about her new discipline, Bella realizes that everything that lives has a rhythm. Since she wants to change the consciousness of humankind, she also needs a rhythm for that. No orchestra is bigger than this question. Bella promises herself to take one Immediate Priority at a time without much

continued

forethought about what will come next, and yet she is already curious about how her worldview will have changed down the line when she reconsiders her Philosophy of Ambition.

Jitesh gave himself a three-month time frame for his Immediate Priority of helping Sarah and Mateo grow significantly more productive and reliable. He initially struggled with his *Independence* Frenemy, which kept creeping up on him every time he felt Sarah or Mateo were falling short. Jitesh caught himself a few times jumping in and beginning to fix things, and he had to learn quickly how to get out of autopilot!

He got into the habit of discussing his progress with his workout coach, and the consistency of their discussions and reflections helped him stay on track. He realized that honing his embodied self-awareness—his ability to sense when his Frenemy was creeping up on him in real time and then adjust his behavior—required effort and consistency, similar to building physical stamina in the gym.

"More reps, more reps, more reps" became his new mantra at work, when his *Independence* Frenemy made an appearance. Jitesh had no doubt that his increased self-awareness and ability to choose more deliberate responses were helping him become a more effective leader and a better person.

And Mateo had based this week's projections on the newest numbers without being reminded. He even showed some signs of beginning to think more about what the numbers mean. Jitesh knew that Mateo would never have developed these competencies if Jitesh had yielded to *Independence* like he used to.

Nora and Alexander had their ups and downs in terms of keeping their work within designated hours and spending enough quality time with each other and their children. Their life continued to be fast-paced, so taking the time each week for reflection and discussion was challenging. However, their one-month time frame for their Immediate Priority helped, since it gave them short-term goals to focus on. They liked having the ability to continuously adjust their Immediate Priorities every four to six weeks.

Six months after they had first discussed their Philosophy of Ambition, and four Immediate Priorities later, Nora and Alexander sat down once again to reflect more fully on their progress. Life remained busy, and it was challenging to consciously notice the positive changes they had made during their hectic daily sprints, but it was abundantly clear that they had come a long way in six months.

They realized, smiling at each other, that they were working fewer hours but getting as much done professionally as before, while they had rekindled their spark as a couple. They were also getting thumbs-up from their children almost every week, an outcome that meant the world to them. Armed with the knowledge of their Frenemies, in command of their toolbox, and able to lean on each other for support, they felt full of energy and confident that they could conquer anything.

CONCLUSION

The Journey Ahead

Increased awareness and focus expand your ability to make conscious choices and, through this, to increase your Return on Ambition.

YOU HAVE COVERED a lot of ground by now—17 chapters to be precise. However, the framework of the book can be simplified to 3 main questions, and 3+7+4 components.

Part 1 helped you answer the first key question of the book: What is your Return on Ambition? We introduced the core concept of Return on Ambition, which is made up of three factors:

RETURN ON AMBITION = ACHIEVEMENT + GROWTH + WELL-BEING

We thereafter laid out the Return on Ambition Assessment, which provides a quantitative score across each of the three dimensions. We encourage you to redo the assessment regularly and plot your scores over time in order to see the evolution and broader trends in your returns.

Part 2 focused on the second main question of the book: What gets in the way of your Return on Ambition? We introduced the seven Frenemies and showed how each one can both help and hinder you in your ambitions:

 CONVENTION: The ability to follow a well-trodden path and attain success as judged by society . . . or to get stuck in expectation and routine.

 BOLDNESS: The ability to move quickly and throw yourself into new, challenging situations . . . or to miscalculate what is required to attain your ambitions.

 INDEPENDENCE: The ability to get things done by yourself, without help . . . or to fail to include others when needed.

 COMPETITIVENESS: The ability to outcompete others and be the best . . . or to try to win at all costs.

 PERSEVERANCE: The ability to go the extra mile and complete challenging tasks, even when you're overloaded . . . or to exhaust yourself frequently and burn out.

 DESIRE: The ability to push constantly against the limits of possibility and break new boundaries . . . or to chase success for the sake of it.

 FLEXIBILITY: The ability to adapt adroitly to different people and situations . . . or to get constantly swayed by others.

Part 3 helped you answer the third key question of the book: How do you increase your Return on Ambition? We laid out four practical tools and provided space for self-coaching so you can begin to use them in practice:

 PHILOSOPHY OF AMBITION: Your guiding principles for the future, which you can evolve as you continue to learn.

 IMMEDIATE PRIORITY: Your focus for the next one to three months, including a note on what Frenemy to look out for.

 WEEKLY DELIBERATION: Your intentions for three opportunities over the coming week and the lessons you learn along the way.

 FRENEMY RADAR: Your evolving map of where and when your Frenemies cause sensations and friction, and how to handle them.

No single big-bang trick will make you sustainably more successful and fulfilled in life. The concepts and toolbox that we have given form a comprehensive and ongoing approach that will allow you to raise your Return on Ambition over time by increasing your awareness and focus, and expanding your ability to make deliberate choices in life.

It's now up to you to get that done! Now that you know more, it is on you to take responsibility and use your newfound awareness for good. We wrote this book with the intention that the fuel of ambition should propel us all forward in a more collaborative, loving, and peaceful manner. At an aggregate level, we believe this can contribute to changing the future of humanity for the better. Thank you for being a part of this journey.

Acknowledgments

Return on Ambition is its own little world made up of a plentitude of elements. While occasionally we felt like the book was almost writing itself, we never doubted that there would be no book without the many people who have shared their brilliance and enthusiasm.

To everyone who was a part of this journey—thank you from the bottom of our hearts. We will always be grateful to you for your ideas, feedback, support, and encouragement.

We were fortunate to be inspired by and engage in conversations with numerous masters in various aspects of human potential. A huge thank-you to Bob Anderson, Claudio Feser, Jennifer Garvey Berger, Lynn Stewart, Michael Rennie, Mihaly Csikszentmihalyi, Stefan Falk, and Zafer Achi. We could not have written this book without your wisdom and your generous sharing of it.

Ahmad Wehbi, Ayoub Semaan, Barry J. Cummings, Kayvan Kian, Laura Joan Salm, Peter Secher Jensen, and Sabrina Mahieddine gave invaluable feedback on the original synopsis and draft manuscripts. Thank you for taking the time to read, discuss, and provide your thoughts to improve the book.

A special thank-you goes also to psychologist Tomasz Brzdak for gathering and reviewing academic research on ambitions; medical doctor Kirsten Engel for formulating the red flag test in Chapter 3; and neuroscientist Jennifer May for reviewing the sections on the brain in Chapter 15. You have made the book more precise and sharper than it would otherwise have been.

We conducted numerous formal interviews for the book: A big thank-you to Anish Shah, Ashkan Pouya, Axel Hedfors, Bing Chen, Fred Swaniker, Khalid Alkhudair, Magnus Olsson, Pia Mancini, Saeid Esmaeilzadeh, and

Sanford Biggers. Your personal stories and openness helped to bring our concepts to life and are a valuable addition to the book.

Thank you to those who responded to our survey. You provided us with aggregate-level insights and illuminated the breadth and diversity of the ambitions people have.

In addition to the many individuals mentioned above, we've had hundreds of conversations with friends, colleagues, and clients about the book, who each provided keen observations and insights. The list of individuals is extensive, but we can at the very least mention their respective organizations: Aberkyn, Cultivating Leadership, Danish Management Society (VL), Deliberate Development, Growth Edge Network, Institute of Directors, International Coach Federation, Majid Al Futtaim Holding's Leadership Institute, McKinsey & Company, Mobius Executive Leadership, Potential Project, The Leadership Circle, and World Economic Forum.

Before even reaching the publishing stage, the manuscript went through a thorough review and detailed editing to sharpen our ideas and stories. A huge thank-you to Erica Rauzin, who engaged with us over many months and many iterations and pushed our thinking on numerous fronts. Your invaluable experience in the field of editing and publishing helped us extensively, and we are grateful that our paths crossed!

Pil Tesdorf and Peter Hager have been fantastic partners in shaping the graphics and creating the icons and charts, respectively. Your originality made a big difference! Furthermore, a big thank-you to Alberto Pizzoli and Mala Banerjee for your creative ideas, which helped lead us to the final cover design that we have today. Thank you also to Charlotte Kendrick for your meticulous review and thoughtful approach as you copyedited the manuscript.

No one is a serious author without a website—big thanks to Brett Santillan for helping us get there! We are also grateful for the ideas and support from Louiza Hacene and Jessica Palmer, as we ventured into the world of digital marketing and sought to find out what really works in practice. And a special thank-you to Birgith Roosipuu, who has helped us craft and share our key messages as we continue to build a global audience and community of practice beyond the pages of the book.

Last but certainly not least, we would like to thank the wonderful Greenleaf Book Group and Fast Company Press team.

Elizabeth Brown, for the substantive editing and your ability to really streamline the book. Jeffrey Curry, for further enhancing the language and accuracy of the text. Stephanie Bouchard, for your keen eye for detail during the proofreading stage. Chase Quarterman, for your creativity, skillfulness, and patience during the cover and interior design process—we had many ideas and desires, and you helped bring them all together superbly! Jen Glynn, for skillfully keeping everything on track and coordinated. Sally Garland, for your editing oversight and thought leadership in making the book truly come to life. Daniel Sandoval, for the early engagement and for shaping our collaboration efforts. Olivia McCoy and Chelsea Richards, for developing a comprehensive and innovate marketing strategy. O'Licia Parker-Smith, for your support across digital media. Kristine Peyre-Ferry, for ensuring that customers can find *Return on Ambition* in the right place at the right time (no easy task!). Julie Murray, for the logistics coordination and enablement.

We also went to express our gratitude individually.

Nicolai Chen Nielsen—
Thank you, Mama, Baba, and Natasja for your feedback on multiple versions of the book and your continuous encouragement.

And to Samira—you not only helped me find time, space, and energy to embark on and complete this project, but you also provided valuable feedback on the manuscript and were the brainchild behind many of our interviews and creative ideas. Merci, Azizam.

Nicolai Tillisch—
Ida, Margaux, and Axel, you are all amazing! Thank you for your love and support and for forgiving me—I hope by now, at least—for spending

much more time on the book than I expected. Ida, our conversations and your feedback helped me get my head around the book. Your trust in me makes me do more than I imagine possible.

References

Introduction

1. Stillman, Jessica. "Is Too Much Ambition Making You Miserable?" *Inc.*, April 17, 2013: https://www.inc.com/jessica-stillman/is-too-much-ambition-making-you-miserable.html

2. Our experience is based on workshops on the topic of ambition with hundreds of professional, in-depth interviews, comprehensive research, and a survey of more than 175 working professionals globally covering academia and education, music and arts, entrepreneurship, industry and trade, professional services, journalism and media, life sciences, public service, social sector and NGO, and technology. In our survey, 95% of respondents considered themselves to be ambitious or highly ambitious.

3. The book's use of adult development theory is primarily inspired by Harvard professor Robert Kegan's research, the assessment expert Bob Anderson, and the leadership coach Jennifer Garvey Berger.

4. Return on Ambition survey.

Chapter 1

1. Return on Ambition survey.

Chapter 2

1. Extract taken from Project Gutenberg's *Alice's Adventures in Wonderland*, https://www.gutenberg.org/files/11/11-h/11-h.htm

2. McFadden, Cynthia, Whitman, Jake, and McGee, Courtney. "New Zealand's prime minister is unmarried, pregnant and going on maternity leave." NBC News, April 17, 2018: https://www.nbcnews.com/news/world/new-zealand-s-prime-minister-unmarried-pregnant-going-maternity-leave-n866441; and Cooke, Henry. "Jacinda Ardern's long road to power." *Stuff*, October 20, 2017: https://www.stuff.co.nz/national/politics/98010212/jacinda-arderns-long-road-to-power

3. Skapinker, Michael. "Lunch with the FT." *Financial Times*, December 16, 2016: https://www.ft.com/content/c1b27bae-c1fd-11e6-81c2-f57d90f6741a

4. Delahaye, Julie. "Exclusive: Jamie Oliver opens up about family life and juggling his career." *Hello!*, April 26, 2019: https://www.hellomagazine.com/cuisine/2019042672443/jamie-oliver-talks-family-life-juggling-career/

5. "Rihanna." Roc Nation: https://rocnation.com/rihanna/

6. Rihanna (website): http://www.rihannanow.com/

7. Leswing, Kif. "Why Tim Cooks Spends the First Hour of Every Day Reading Emails from Apple Users." Inc.com: https://www.inc.com/business-insider/tim-cook-wakes-up-at-4-to-read-emails-from-apple-users.html

8. "A Day in Oprah's Life." *Parade*, December 22, 2010: https://parade.com/50135/parade/a-day-in-oprah-life/

9. Schilling, Mary Kaye. "Get Busy: Pharrell's Productivity Secrets." *Fast Company*, November 18, 2013: https://www.fastcompany.com/3021377/pharrell-get-busy

Chapter 3

1. Personal conversation with Michael Rennie.

2. Sadaffe Abid's TEDxINSEAD speech "Why the Current Leadership Model Will Fail" elaborates on her experience and gives the context in which she publicly shared it: https://www.youtube.com/watch?v=usSdTPHGpMc

3. Blanchette, D.M., Ramocki, S.P., O'del, J.N., and Casey, M.S. "Aerobic exercise and cognitive creativity: Immediate and residual effects." *Creativity Research Journal* Vol. 17, Nos. 2&3 (2005): 257–264.

4. Williamson, A.M. and Feyer, A.M. "Moderate sleep deprivation produces impairments in cognitive and motor performance equivalent to legally prescribed levels of alcohol intoxication." *Occupational and Environmental Medicine* Vol. 57, No. 10 (2000): 649–655.

5. "Blood Alcohol Content Drink Driving Limits by Country." RUPissed: http://www.rupissed.com/blood_alcohol_limits.html

6. Van Dam, N. and van der Helm, E. "The organizational cost of insufficient sleep." *McKinsey Quarterly*, February 2016.

7. The neuroimmunologist Dr. Nicholas Hall has worked with top athletes within tennis.

8. From author conversation with executive coach Stefan Falk, who worked with Hall.

9. Ibid.

10. Kegan, R. and Lahey, L.L. *An Everyone Culture: Becoming a Deliberately Developmental Organization.* Boston: Harvard Business Review Press, 2016.

11. Ericsson, K.A. "Deliberate practice and the acquisition and maintenance of expert performance in medicine and related domains." *Academic Medicine* Vol. 79, No. 10 (2003).

12. The terms "deliberate practice" and "arrested development" both originate from Swedish psychologist K. Anders Ericsson.

13. Singer R., Hausenblas, H., and Janelle, C. (Eds). *Handbook for Sport Psychology.* New York: Wiley, 2001.

14. Csikszentmihalyi, Mihaly. *Finding Flow: The Psychology of Engagement with Everyday Life.* New York: Basic Books, 1998, and conversations with the author.

15. Kahneman, Daniel. *Thinking, Fast and Slow.* New York: Farrar, Straus and Giroux, 2011.

16. Well-established and validated scales for depression, anxiety, and psychological distress serve as inspiration for the six statements.

17. For research on ambition, stress, anxiety, depression, and burnout: Hornung, C.A. "Status inconsistency, achievement motivation, and psychological stress." *Social Science Research* Vol. 9, No. 4 (1980): 362–380; Kivimaki, M., Kalimo, R., and Julkunen, J. "Components of Type A behavior pattern and occupational stressor-strain relationship: Testing different models in a sample of industrial managers." *Behavioral Medicine* Vol. 22, No. 2 (1996): 67–76; Wang, K.T., Slaney, R.B., and Rice, K.G. "Perfectionism in Chinese university students from Taiwan: A study of psychological well-being and achievement motivation." *Personality and Individual Differences* Vol. 42 (2007): 1279–1290; Löve, J., Hagberg, M., and Delive, L. "Balancing extensive ambition and a context overflowing with opportunities and demands: A grounded theory on stress and recovery among highly educated working young women entering male-dominated occupational areas." *Qualitative Studies on Health and Well-Being* Vol. 6, No. 3 (2011); Bachkirova, T. "The role of the self and identification

with an organisation as factors influencing work-related stress: Implications for helping." *Counselling Psychology Quarterly* Vol. 25, No. 1 (2012): 49–62; Békés, V., Dunkley, D.M., Taylor, G., Zuroff, D.C., Lewkowski, M., Foley, J.E., Myhr, G., and Westreich, R. "Chronic stress and attenuated improvement in depression over 1 year: The moderating role of perfectionism." *Behavior Therapy* Vol. 46, No. 4 (2015): 478–492; and Katza, D.A., Greenberg, M.T., Jennings, P.A., and Cousino Klein, L. "Associations between the awakening responses of salivary-amylase and cortisol with self-report indicators of health and well-being among educators." *Teaching and Teacher Education* Vol. 54 (2016): 98–106.

18. For research on ambition and workaholism: Burke, R.J., Matthiesen, S.B., and Pallesen, S. "Personality correlates of workaholism." *Personality and Individual Differences* Vol. 40 (2006): 1223–1233; Mazzetti, G., Schaufeli, W.B., and Guglielmi, D. "Are workaholics born or made? Relations of workaholism with person characteristics and overwork climate." *International Journal of Stress Management* Vol. 21, No. 3 (2014): 227–254.

19. For research on ambition and various mild forms of mania: Lozano, B.E. and Johnson, S.L. "Can personality traits predict increases in manic and depressive symptoms?" *Journal of Affective Disorders* Vol. 6 (2001): 103–111; Fulford, D., Johnson, S.L., and Carver C.S. "Commonalities and differences in characteristics of persons at risk for narcissism and mania." *Journal of Research in Personality* Vol. 4 (2008): 1427–1438; Johnson, S.L., Freeman, M.A., and Staudenmeier, P.J. "Mania risk, overconfidence and ambition." *Journal of Social and Clinical Psychology* Vol. 34, No. 7 (2015): 611–621. For research on ambition-related health issues: Howard, J.H., Cunningham, D.A., and Rechnitzer, P.A. "Health patterns associated with type A behavior: A managerial population." *Journal of Human Stress* Vol. 2, No. 1 (1976): 24–32.

Chapter 4

1. "Freedom." Genius: https://genius.com/Beyonce-freedom-lyrics

2. Baldwin, Alan. "Swimming: Blume Wins Denmark's First Swim Gold Since 1948." Reuters, August 13, 2016: https://www.reuters.com/article/us-olympics-rio-swimming-w-50mfree/swimming-blume-wins-denmarks-first-swim-gold-since-1948-idUSKCN10P018

3. "Strangest Moments: Snowboarder Lindsey Jacobellis Learns a Valuable Lesson." YouTube Olympic Channel: https://www.youtube.com/watch?v=agDfxdpHY3M

Chapter 5

1. Shah quotes from author interview with Anish Shah.

2. Official website of Danica Patrick: http://www.danicapatrick.com/danica; and Schawbel, Dan. "Danica Patrick's 5 secrets to living a successful and happy life." *CNBC*, January 11, 2018: https://www.cnbc.com/2018/01/11/nascar-driver-danica-patricks-secrets-of-a-successful-happy-life.html

3. Gell, Aaron. "Danica Patrick Spent Years Preparing to Retire—by Laying the Groundwork for a New Career" *Entrepreneur*, June 27, 2018: https://www.entrepreneur.com/article/315298

4. Ibid.

5. "Glassdoor reveals the highest rated CEOs for 2014." Glassdoor: https://www.glassdoor.com/about-us/glassdoor-reveals-highest-rated-ceos-2014/

6. "Jeff Weiner." *Super Soul Sunday. OWN*, September 2016: https://www.aol.com/video/view/linkedin-ceo-jeff-weiner-on-meeting-his-wife-that-was-a-complete-game-changer/57d9f5071c689950401d9254/

7. Shah quotes from author interview with Anish Shah.

8. Goodman, Doug. "Patrick: 'Roscoe will always be home for me.'" *Rockford Register Star*, May 23, 2008: http://www.rrstar.com/x2118745430/Patrick-Roscoe-will-always-be-home-for-me

9. Csikszentmihalyi, Mihaly. *Finding Flow: The Psychology of Engagement with Everyday Life.* Basic Books, 1998.

10. Kirschenbaum, S., Ordman, A.M., Tomarken, A.J., et al. "Effects of differential self-monitoring and level of mastery on sports performance: Brain power bowling." *Cognitive Therapy and Research* Vol. 6 (1982): 335–341.

11. Return on Ambition survey.

12. Shah quotes from author interview with Anish Shah.

13. Caldwell, Dave. "That Might Not Be the End of Danica Patrick, Race-Car Driver." *Forbes*, May 28, 2018: https://www.forbes.com/sites/davecaldwell/2018/05/28/we-might-not-have-seen-the-last-of-danica-patrick-race-car-driver/#3d98545484fe

14. Gell, Aaron. "Danica Patrick Spent Years Preparing to Retire—by Laying the Groundwork for a New Career" *Entrepreneur*, June 27, 2018: https://www.entrepreneur.com/article/315298

15. Schwantes, Marcel. "LinkedIn's CEO Just Gave Some Brilliant Life Advice. Here It Is in 1 Sentence." *Inc.*, September 30, 2017: https://www.inc.com/marcel-schwantes/linkedins-ceo-just-gave-some-brilliant-life-advice-here-it-is-in-1-sentence.html

Chapter 6

1. "Danger Zone." Genius: https://genius.com/Kenny-loggins-danger-zone-lyrics

2. Swaniker quotes from author interview with Fred Swaniker.

3. Fred Swaniker. TED: https://www.ted.com/profiles/9423/fellow

4. Fred Swaniker. World Economic Forum: https://www.weforum.org/people/fred-swaniker

5. "The Top 10 Youngest Power Men in Africa." *Forbes*, September 13, 2011: https://www.forbes.com/pictures/54f4e71fda47a54de8245cdf/the-10-youngest-power-men/#7da28253fed8

6. Swaniker quotes from author interview with Fred Swaniker.

7. Segall, Laurie. "Mark Zuckerberg's growing up moment." *CNN*, April 9, 2018: https://money.cnn.com/2018/04/09/technology/mark-zuckerberg-congressional-testimony-preparation/index.html; and Segall, Laurie. "Mark Zuckerberg in his own words: The CNN interview." CNN, March 21, 2018: https://money.cnn.com/2018/03/21/technology/mark-zuckerberg-cnn-interview-transcript/index.html

8. Hedfors quotes from author interview with Axel Hedfors.

9. Swaniker quotes from author interview with Fred Swaniker.

10. Ibid.

11. Hedfors quotes from author interview with Axel Hedfors.

12. Moore, Don A. and Schatz, Derek. "The three faces of overconfidence." *Social and Personality Psychology Compass* Vol. 11, No. 8, August 2017: https://onlinelibrary.wiley.com/doi/abs/10.1111/spc3.12331

13. Lichtenstein, S., Fischhoff, B., and Phillips, L.D. "Calibration of probabilities: The state of the art to 1980." In *Judgment Under Uncertainty: Heuristics and Biases*, edited by D. Kahneman, P. Slovic, and A. Tversky, 306–334. New York: Cambridge University Press, 1982.

14. Kruger, J. and Dunning, D. "Unskilled and Unaware of It: How Difficulties in Recognizing One's Own Incompetence Lead to Inflated Self-Assessments." *Journal of Personality and Social Psychology* Vol. 77, No. 6, January 2000: 1121–34: https://www.researchgate.net/publication/12688660_Unskilled_and_Unaware_of_It_How_Difficulties_in_Recognizing_One's_Own_Incompetence_Lead_to_Inflated_Self-Assessments

15. Robertson, Ian. *The Winner Effect*. London: Bloomsbury, 2012.

16. Swaniker quotes from author interview with Fred Swaniker.

17. Ibid.

18. Fessler, Leah. "'You're no genius': Her father's shutdowns made Angela Duckworth a world expert on grit." *Quartz*, March 26, 2018: https://qz.com/work/1233940/angela-duckworth-explains-grit-is-the-key-to-success-and-self-confidence/

19. McLeod, Saul. "The Zone of Proximal Development and Scaffolding." *SimplyPsychology*: https://www.simplypsychology.org/Zone-of-Proximal-Development.html

20. Hedfors quotes from author interview with Axel Hedfors.

21. Kenmare, Jack. "Cristiano Ronaldo Trains In The Gym At 2 am After Champions League Away Games." *SPORTbible*, August 24, 2018: https://www.sportbible.com/football/news-reactions-legends-take-a-bow-cristiano-ronaldo-trains-in-the-gym-at-2am-after-champions-league-away-20180824

22. Ibid.

23. Jabbar, Nasir. "Douglas Costa Confirms Cristiano Ronaldo Is An Absolute Machine." *SPORTbible*, August 7, 2018: https://www.sportbible.com/football/news-douglas-costa-confirms-cristiano-ronaldo-is-an-absolute-machine-20180807

24. Fessler, Leah. "'You're no genius': Her father's shutdowns made Angela Duckworth a world expert on grit." *Quartz*, March 26, 2018: https://qz.com/work/1233940/angela-duckworth-explains-grit-is-the-key-to-success-and-self-confidence/

25. Ibid.

26. Swaniker quotes from author interview with Fred Swaniker.

Chapter 7

1. McMahon, Daniel. "Tour de France, world's biggest annual sporting event, is an amazing race and breathtaking logistical feat." *Business Insider*, June 29, 2016: http://uk.businessinsider.com/tour-de-france-2016-numbers-2016-6?r=US&IR=T/#-1

2. Pouya and Esmaeilzadeh quotes from author interview with Ashkan Pouya and Saeid Esmaeilzadeh.

3. Biggers quotes from author interview with Sanford Biggers.

4. Ibid.

5. Ibid.

6. Ibid.

7. Pouya and Esmaeilzadeh quotes from author interview with Ashkan Pouya and Saeid Esmaeilzadeh.

8. Biggers quotes from author interview with Sanford Biggers.

9. Ibid.

10. Pouya and Esmaeilzadeh quotes from author interview with Ashkan Pouya and Saeid Esmaeilzadeh.

11. Biggers quotes from author interview with Sanford Biggers.

Chapter 8

1. "Calciopoli." Wikipedia: https://en.wikipedia.org/wiki/2006_Italian_football_scandal; and Warren, Dan. "Italian football's tangled web." *BBC Sport*, July 14, 2006: http://news.bbc.co.uk/sport2/hi/football/europe/4989484.stm

2. Author interview with Magnus Olsson.

3. Olsson quotes from author interview with Magnus Olsson.

4. Li quotes from Li, Na. *My Life*. London: Penguin Books, 2012.

5. Feloni, Richard. "Billionaire Peter Thiel Explains Why He Would Tell His Younger Self To Be Less Competitive." *Business Insider*, February 10, 2014: https://www.businessinsider.fr/us/peter-thiel-on-success-2014-10/

6. Peter Thiel's commencement address at Hamilton College on May 22, 2016: https://www.youtube.com/watch?time_continue=46&v=id4ywg5oemc

7. Highfield, Roger. "Relative wealth 'makes you happier.'" *The Telegraph*, November 22, 2007: http://www.telegraph.co.uk/news/science/science-news/3315638/Relative-wealth-makes-you-happier.html; University of Bonn, "Money motivates – especially when your colleague gets less," (press release): https://www.uni-bonn.de/Press-releases/101_2007; and Fliessbach, K., Weber, B., Trautner, P., Dohmen, T., Sunde, U., Elger, C.E., and Falk, A. "Social Comparison Affects Reward-Related Brain Activity in the Human Ventral Striatum." *Science*, November 23, 2007.

8. Baer, Drake. "Here's the advice billionaire investor Peter Thiel wishes he could've given his younger self." *Business Insider*, February 4, 2015: https://www.businessinsider.com/peter-thiel-advice-to-younger-self-2015-2

9. Li quotes from Li, Na. *My Life*. London: Penguin Books, 2012.

10. Baer, Drake. "Here's the advice billionaire investor Peter Thiel wishes he could've given his younger self." *Business Insider,* February 4, 2015: https://www.businessinsider.com/peter-thiel-advice-to-younger-self-2015-2

11. Burleigh, T.J. and Meegan, D.V. "Keeping up with the Joneses affects perceptions of distributive justice." *Social Justice Research* Vol. 26, No. 2 (2013): 120–131.

12. Garcia, S. and Tor, A. "Rankings, standards, and competition: Task vs. scale comparisons." *Organizational Behavior and Human Decision Processes* Vol. 102, Issue 1, January 2007: 95–108: https://www.sciencedirect.com/science/article/pii/S0749597806001129?via%3Dihub; and Garcia, S.M., Tor, A., and Gonzalez, R. "Ranks and Rivals: A Theory of Competition." *Personality and Social Psychology Bulletin* Vol. 32, No. 7: 970–982: http://journals.sagepub.com/doi/10.1177/0146167206287640

13. Deffler, S., Leary, M., and Hoyle, R. "Knowing what you know: Intellectual humility and judgments of recognition memory." *Personality and Individual Differences* Vol. 96, July 2016: 255–259: https://www.sciencedirect.com/science/article/pii/S0191886916301489

14. Kibeom, L. and Ashton, M. "Getting mad and getting even: Agreeableness and Honesty-Humility as predictors of revenge intentions." *Personality and Individual Differences* Vol. 52, Issue 5, April 2012: 596–600: https://www.sciencedirect.com/science/article/pii/S019188691100571X

15. Olsson quotes from author interview with Magnus Olsson.

16. Li quotes from Li, Na. *My Life.* London: Penguin Books, 2012.

17. Clifford, Catherine. "Why billionaire Peter Thiel suggests being less competitive could give you an edge." CNBC, March 31, 2017: https://www.cnbc.com/2017/03/30/peter-thiel-suggests-being-less-competitive-could-give-you-an-edge.html

Chapter 9

1. Leibs, Scott. "Arianna Huffington: What Lying in a Pool of Blood Taught Me." *Inc.*, June 2014: https://www.inc.com/magazine/201406/scott-leibs/arianna-huffington-new-book-thrive-sleep-advocate.html; Stillman, Jessica. "3 Small Changes to Help You Not Just Survive But Thrive." *Inc.*, April 14, 2014: https://www.inc.com/jessica-stillman/3-small-changes-to-help-you-survive-and-thrive.html; and Authors@Wharton (podcast series). "Arianna Huffington on How to 'Thrive.'" Wharton School of the University of Pennsylvania, April 11, 2014: http://knowledge.wharton.upenn.edu/article/third-metric-success-arianna-huffington/

2. "World's Billionaires List: The Richest in 2020." *Forbes*: https://www.forbes.com/billionaires/list/#version:realtime

3. Gelles, D., Stewart, J., Silver-Greenberg, J., and Kelly, K. "Elon Musk Details 'Excruciating' Personal Toll of Tesla Turmoil." *The New York Times*, August 16, 2018: https://www.nytimes.com/2018/08/16/business/elon-musk-interview-tesla.html

4. Ibid.

5. Stephenson, Marissa. "Amelia Boone Is Stronger Than Ever." *Runner's World*, June 19, 2018: https://www.runnersworld.com/runners-stories/a20652405/amelia-boone-is-stronger-than-ever/

6. "2016: A Year of Healing." Amelia Boone (blog), December 28, 2016: http://www.ameliabooneracing.com/blog/rehab/2016-a-year-of-healing/#more-529; and Murphy, Jen. "A Tough Mudder Learns to Listen to Her Pain." *The Wall Street Journal*, December 10, 2016: https://www.wsj.com/articles/a-tough-mudder-learns-to-listen-to-her-pain-1481371204

7. Stephenson, Marissa. "Amelia Boone Is Stronger Than Ever." *Runner's World*, June 19, 2018: https://www.runnersworld.com/runners-stories/a20652405/amelia-boone-is-stronger-than-ever/

8. Coren, Michael. "The days and nights of Elon Musk: How he spends his time at work and play." *Quartz*, June 8, 2017: https://qz.com/1000370/the-days-and-nights-of-elon-musk-how-he-spends-his-time-at-work-and-play/

9. Stephenson, Marissa. "Amelia Boone Is Stronger Than Ever." *Runner's World*, June 19, 2018: https://www.runnersworld.com/runners-stories/a20652405/amelia-boone-is-stronger-than-ever/

10. "On Being Broken, Rehab and Recovery." Amelia Boone (blog), December 22, 2014: http://www.ameliabooneracing.com/blog/uncategorized/on-being-broken-rehab-and-recovery/

11. Leibs, Scott. "Arianna Huffington: What Lying in a Pool of Blood Taught Me." *Inc.*, June 2014: https://www.inc.com/magazine/201406/scott-leibs/arianna-huffington-new-book-thrive-sleep-advocate.html

12. Clifford, Catherine. "Here's Elon Musk's morning routine—and his top productivity tip." CNBC, June 21, 2017: https://www.cnbc.com/2017/06/20/elon-musks-morning-routine-and-top-productivity-tip.html

13. Stephenson, Marissa. "Amelia Boone Is Stronger Than Ever." *Runner's World*, June 19, 2018: https://www.runnersworld.com/runners-stories/a20652405/amelia-boone-is-stronger-than-ever/

14. Huffington, Arianna. "An Open Letter to Elon Musk." Thrive Global, August 17, 2018. https://thriveglobal.com/stories/open-letter-elon-musk/

15. Coren, Michael. "The days and nights of Elon Musk: How he spends his time at work and play." *Quartz*, June 8, 2017: https://qz.com/1000370/the-days-and-nights-of-elon-musk-how-he-spends-his-time-at-work-and-play/

16. Authors@Wharton (podcast series). "Arianna Huffington on How to 'Thrive.'" Wharton School of the University of Pennsylvania, April 11, 2014: http://knowledge.wharton.upenn.edu/article/third-metric-success-arianna-huffington/

Chapter 10

1. Khalid Alkhudair. World Economic Forum: https://www.weforum.org/agenda/authors/khalid-alkhudair/

2. Author interview with Khalid Alkhudair.

3. Alkhudair quotes from author interview with Khalid Alkhudair.

4. Author interview with Pia Mancini.

5. "Pia Mancini." Wikipedia: https://en.wikipedia.org/wiki/Pia_Mancini

6. Mancini quotes from author interview with Pia Mancini.

7. Ibid.

8. Alkhudair quotes from author interview with Khalid Alkhudair.

9. Mancini quotes from author interview with Pia Mancini.

10. Alkhudair quotes from author interview with Khalid Alkhudair.

11. Ibid.

12. Mancini quotes from author interview with Pia Mancini.

Chapter 11

1. https://www.youtube.com/watch?v=950lAeiJ1zI

2. Ibid.

3. Author interview with Bing Chen.

4. Chen quotes from author interview with Bing Chen.

5. "Chimamanda Ngozi Adichie." Wikipedia: https://en.wikipedia.org/wiki/Chimamanda_Ngozi_Adichie

6. Ngozi Adichie, Chimamanda. "The danger of a single story." TED: https://www.ted.com/talks/chimamanda_adichie_the_danger_of_a_single_story/transcript?referrer=playlist-the_most_popular_talks_of_all#t-57210

7. Chen quotes from author interview with Bing Chen.

8. Ngozi Adichie, Chimamanda. "The danger of a single story." TED: https://www.ted.com/talks/chimamanda_adichie_the_danger_of_a_single_story/transcript?referrer=playlist-the_most_popular_talks_of_all#t-57210

9. Chen quotes from author interview with Bing Chen.

10. Shunatona, Brooke. "How Being 'Real' on Instagram Helped Yoga Girl Gain Almost 2 Million Followers." *Cosmopolitan*, March 8, 2016: https://www.cosmopolitan.com/style-beauty/beauty/interviews/a54420/yoga-girl-and-philosophy-interview/; and Prinzivalli, Leah. "The internet's biggest yogi just slammed social media in the best rant ever." *sheknows*, July 1, 2016: https://www.sheknows.com/health-and-wellness/articles/1125515/yogi-just-slammed-social-media

11. Ibid.

12. Brathen, Rachel. "I look at this social media world and don't fucking know what's going on." Instagram post, July 1, 2016: https://www.instagram.com/p/BHU2MKmBf6r/?utm_source=ig_embed

13. Chen quotes from author interview with Bing Chen.

14. Ibid.

15. Ngozi Adichie, Chimamanda. "Groundbreaker Honoree speech for the 2015 Girls Write Now Awards." YouTube video: https://www.youtube.com/watch?v=3uNcvtjT8Pk

Chapter 13

1. The notion of a "Big Hairy Audacious Goal" comes from Collins, Jim and Porras, Jerry. *Built to Last*. New York: HarperBusiness, 1994.

2. Brickman, P., Coates, D., and Janoff-Bulman, R. "Lottery Winners and Accident Victims: Is Happiness Relative?" *Journal of Personality and Social Psychology* Vol. 36, No. 8 (1978): 917–927.

3. "Our History." Kleiner Perkins: https://www.kleinerperkins.com/our-history/

4. Rao, Leena. "Kleiner Perkins On the Past, Present and Future." *TechCrunch*, October 13, 2012: https://techcrunch.com/2012/10/13/kleiner-perkins-on-the-past-present-and-future/

5. Wigglesworth, Robin. "Jack Bogle, Index Fund Pioneer, 1929–2019." *Financial Times*, January 16, 2019: https://www.ft.com/content/91054b00-19dd-11e9-9e64-d150b3105d21

6. "Fast facts about Vanguard." Vanguard: https://about.vanguard.com/who-we-are/fast-facts/

7. Levy, Rachael and Copeland, Rob. "Ray Dalio Is Still Driving His $160 Billion Hedge-Fund Machine." *The Wall Street Journal*, January 31, 2020: https://www.wsj.com/articles/ray-dalio-is-still-driving-his-160-billion-hedge-fund-machine-11580504150

8. The story is partly inspired by Foroohar, Rana. "Vivienne Ming: 'The Professional Class Is about to Be Blindsided by AI.'" *Financial Times*, July 27, 2018: https://www.ft.com/content/3aac2330-8f38-11e8-b639-7680cedcc421; Ming, Vivienne. "TEDxBerkeley: Making a Better Person." YouTube: https://www.youtube.com/watch?v=5-aIq4cRlss; and Ming, Vivienne. "The Future of Human Potential." SingularityU South Africa Summit, October 24, 2017. YouTube: https://www.youtube.com/watch?v=d4fxmSdrchs

Chapter 14

1. For an overview of accelerating trends in today's world, see
    for example Friedman, Thomas. *Thank You for Being Late: An
    Optimist's Guide to Thriving in the Age of Accelerations*. New York:
    Picador, 2016.

2. Kegan, Bob and Lahey, Lisa. *Immunity to Change*. Boston: Harvard
    Business Review Press, 2009.

3. The method is molded by others' research and practices, and our
    own. We feel an obligation to mention four especially important
    sources of inspiration: Bob Anderson (coaching methods related
    to Reactive and Creative mindsets); David Burn (the cognitive
    psychology approach that he popularized in *Feeling Good*, New
    York: HarperCollins, 1980); Stefan Falk (application of Objective
    Key Results, or OKRs, in coaching); Bob Kegan's stages of
    adult development and, together with Lisa Lahey, the method
    described in *Immunity to Change*, Boston: Harvard Business
    Review Press, 2009.

4. The terminology of "conceptual self-awareness" and "embodied
    self-awareness" comes from Alan Fogel's book *The Psychophysiology
    of Self-Awareness*, New York: W.W. Norton, 2009.

5. This is a quote by the philosopher Søren Kierkegaard.

6. The three constellations are all inspired by scenarios for the
    transition from the Socialized to the Self-Authored Mind from
    Robert Kegan's *In Over Our Heads*, Cambridge, Massachusetts:
    Harvard University Press, 1994. (Kegan does not apply the notion
    of Frenemies.)

7. We are in particular referring to research, studies, and practices by
    K. Anders Ericsson and Timothy Gallwey.

Chapter 15

1. The application of the Intend-Do-Observe-Reflect loop is inspired by the research behind and user trials of the My Daily Goals software solution.

2. Partly inspired by Gollwitzer, P. and Oettingen, G. "Strategies of setting and implementing goals: Mental contrasting and implementation intentions." In *Social Psychological Foundations of Clinic Psychology*, edited by J.E. Maddux and J.P. Tangney, 114–134. New York: Guilford Press, 2010.

3. The illustration is inspired by and modified from: Sapolsky, Robert M. *Behave*. New York: Penguin, 2018.

4. Ibid.

5. Wilson, R., Shenhav, A., Straccia, M., and Cohen, J. "The Eighty Five Percent Rule for optimal learning." *Nature Communications* Vol. 10 (2019): https://www.nature.com/articles/s41467-019-12552-4#citeas

6. The insight builds on research by K. Anders Ericsson, among others, reflected in his book with Robert Pool, *Peak: Secrets from the Science of Expertise*, New York: Eamon Dolan/Houghton Mifflin Harcourt, 2016.

7. See Snowden, David J. and Boone, Mary E. "A Leader's Framework for Decision Making." *Harvard Business Review*, November 2007: https://hbr.org/2007/11/a-leaders-framework-for-decision-making

8. See Newport, Cal. *Deep Work: Rules for Focused Success in a Distracted World*. New York: Grand Central Publishing/Hachette Book Group, 2016.

9. Sullivan, Bob. "Memo to work martyrs: Long hours make you less productive." CNBC, January 26, 2015: https://www.cnbc.com/2015/01/26/working-more-than-50-hours-makes-you-less-productive.html

Chapter 16

1. We use the words 'feelings' and 'emotions' interchangeably in the text.

2. The three examples follow Enneagram type 3, 7, and 8 inspired by how they are explained in Riso, Don R. and Hudson, Russ, *The Wisdom of the Enneagram*, New York: Bantam, 1999; and described in Kaplan, Bob, Drath, Wilfred, and Kofodimos, Joan R., *Beyond Ambition: How Driven Managers Can Lead Better and Live Better*, San Francisco: Jossey-Bass, 1991. It should be mentioned that type 3, 7, and 8 also relate to five out of the six other Enneagram types, for which they are associated with disintegration or integration.

3. This formulation is inspired by Bob Anderson, author of *Mastering Leadership*, New York: Wiley, 2015, and *Scaling Leadership*, New York: Wiley, 2019.

4. Blake, Amanda. *Your Body Is Your Brain: Leverage Your Somatic Intelligence to Find Purpose, Build Resilience, Deepen Relationships and Lead More Powerfully*. Trokay Press, 2018.

5. Kahneman, Daniel. *Thinking, Fast and Slow*. New York: Farrar, Straus and Giroux, 2011.

6. Piaget, Jean and Inhelder, Bärbel. *The Psychology of the Child*. New York: Basic Books, 1969.

Index

About the Authors

NICOLAI CHEN NIELSEN is an associate partner at McKinsey & Company, where he advises clients on leadership development, culture change, and agile transformations. He is the co-author of the book *Leadership at Scale* and has published several articles on personal development. Nicolai is furthermore an Advisory Board Member for the Supertrends Institute and an Alumni of the World Economic Forum's Global Shapers Community.

Nicolai is passionate about personal development and the lifelong journey towards enlightenment. He is fascinated by the universal truths found in ancient wisdom traditions and seeks to understand them in order to live a more loving and peaceful life. He is currently based in New York with his wife Samira and their two dogs Napoleon and Caesar.

NICOLAI TILLISCH works with ambitious people to help them utilize their potential and make a greater difference. He combines deep insight into human beings with a wide understanding of professional work environments. He is associated with Cultivating Leadership, a global firm specializing in adult development and complexity. Furthermore, he is a co-founder of Deliberate Development, which developed and offers the StepUpYourDay software platform.

Nicolai began his professional career as a management consultant at McKinsey & Company and has since worked as an executive at DDB Worldwide, Hutchison, and Nokia Siemens Networks. He currently lives with his wife, Ida, and their children, Margaux and Axel, in Copenhagen, after previously residing in Dubai, London, and Stockholm.